# ESSAYS IN ZEN BUDDHISM

## (Second Series)

DAISETZ TEITARO SUZUKI, D. LITT.

*Late Professor of Buddhist Philosophy in the Otani University, Kyoto*

WITH TWENTY-FIVE REPRODUCTIONS
OF OLD MASTERS

*Edited by*

CHRISTMAS HUMPHREYS

*President of the Buddhist Society, London*

Samuel Weiser, Inc.

York Beach, Maine

Samuel Weiser, Inc.
Box 612
York Beach, ME 03910

Third printing, 1985

ISBN 0-87728-075-4

Printed and bound in Great Britain by
Anchor Brendon Ltd, Tiptree, Essex

TO

YAKICHI ATAKA

on the occasion of his attaining
the age of sixty-one, as an appreciative offering for his long friend-
ship and his constant wholе-
hearted encouragement in all the
author's literary undertakings,
and with the Pranidhana that
his useful Bodhisattva life may
continue for many years yet to
come to benefit the world in
its spiritual advance towards
universal enlightenment

# CONTENTS

CONTENTS

## ESSAY III

## ESSAY IV

# ILLUSTRATIONS

9

## EDITOR'S FOREWORD

Daisetz Teitaro Suzuki, D.Litt., Professor of Buddhist Philosophy in the Otani University, Kyoto, was born in 1869. He is probably now the greatest living authority on Buddhist philosophy, and is certainly the greatest authority on Zen Buddhism. His major works in English on the subject of Buddhism number a dozen or more, and of his works in Japanese as yet unknown to the West there are at least eighteen. He is, moreover, as a chronological bibliography of books on Zen in English clearly shows, the pioneer teacher of the subject outside Japan, for except for Kaiten Nukariya's *Religion of the Samurai* (Luzac and Co., 1913) nothing was known of Zen as a living experience, save to the readers of *The Eastern Buddhist* (1921–1939), until the publication of *Essays in Zen Buddhism* (First Series) in 1927.

Dr. Suzuki writes with authority. Not only has he studied original works in Sanskrit, Pāli, Chinese and Japanese, but he has an up-to-date knowledge of Western thought in German and French as well as in the English which he speaks and writes so fluently. He is, moreover, more than a scholar; he is a Buddhist. Though not a priest of any Buddhist sect, he is honoured in every temple in Japan, for his knowledge of spiritual things, as all who have sat at his feet bear witness, is direct and profound. When he speaks of the higher stages of consciousness he speaks as a man who dwells therein, and the impression he makes on those who enter the fringes of his mind is that of a man who seeks for the intellectual symbols wherewith to describe a state of awareness which lies indeed 'beyond the intellect'.

To those unable to sit at the feet of the Master his writings must be a substitute. All these, however, were out of print in England by 1940, and all remaining stocks in Japan were destroyed in the fire which consumed three-quarters of Tokyo in 1945. When, therefore, I reached Japan in 1946, I arranged with the author for the Buddhist Society, London—my wife and myself as its nominees—to begin the publication of his Collected Works, reprinting the old favourites, and printing as fast as possible translations of the many new works which the Professor, self-immured in his house at Kyoto, had written during the war.

This undertaking, however, was beyond the powers of the Buddhist Society, and we therefore secured the assistance of Rider and Co., who, backed by the vast resources of the House of Hutchinson, can honour the needs of such a considerable task.

Of Zen itself I need say nothing here, but the increasing sale of books on the subject, such as *The Spirit of Zen* by Alan Watts (Murray), my own *Zen Buddhism* (Heinemann), and the series of original translations of Chinese Zen Scriptures and other works published by the Buddhist Society, prove that the interest of the West is rising rapidly. Zen, however, is a subject extremely easy to misunderstand, and it is therefore important that the words of a recognized expert should come readily to hand.

It is proposed to publish the works of Dr. Suzuki in groups of three, each group to contain, if possible, one of his larger works, a smaller work, and a work as yet unpublished in English. The first three chosen were the First Series of his *Essays in Zen Buddhism*, his valuable *Introduction to Zen Buddhism*, with a translation by Miss Constance Rolfe of Dr. C. G. Jung's long Foreword to the German edition, and a new work which appears under the title of *The Zen Doctrine of No-Mind* (*The Significance of the Sūtra of Hui-nêng* [Wei Lang]). The Sūtra itself is published for the Buddhist Society by Luzac and Co. as *The Sūtra of Wei Lang*.

The second group, of which this is one, also includes

another of the smaller works, *The Manual of Zen Buddhism*, and a completely new work, *Living by Zen*. The choice for later groups will be influenced by popular demand.

CHRISTMAS HUMPHREYS
*President of the Buddhist Society,*
*1950*                                              *London*

# PREFACE TO FIRST EDITION

When the First Series of *Zen Essays* appeared in 1927, the author's intention was to write the Second Series soon after; but in the meantime the study of the *Laṅkāvatāra* as an important text of Zen Buddhism claimed his attention. The result appeared as *Studies in the Laṅkāvatāra Sūtra* (1930), an English translation of the Sanskrit text of the Sūtra itself (1932), and a Sanskrit, Chinese, and Tibetan Index of the Sūtra (1933).

In this Second Series of *Zen Essays*, the chief stress has been placed on the study of 'The Koan Exercise', which at present constitutes almost the alpha and omega of Zen discipline, especially as it is practised in the Rinzai School of the Zen sect. The koan technique is full of pitfalls, but its development was inevitable, and without it Zen might not have survived. My study of the koan exercise as presented in this Series is not a very complete one, but I hope I have given the reader a general idea of what it is. I further hope that the psychologist and the philosopher will take up this study as facts of experience specifically developed in the Far-eastern mind.

'The Secret Message of Bodhidharma', 'The Two Zen Text-books', and 'Passivity in the Buddhist Life' have already appeared in the *Eastern Buddhist*. But each of these articles has undergone a thorough revision, and new materials have been added.

Since the recent discovery of some valuable Zen documents which were kept buried at Tun-huang for more than one thousand years, we have much new light shed on the history of Zen Buddhism in China, especially around the time of Hui-nêng (637–713). In the Fourth Series I intend to write a new history of Chinese Zen as can be gathered up from the documents thus made accessible to us. The Third Series is already prepared, and I hope it will see the light before long.

In this volume I have inserted some *Suiboku* paintings by Japanese and Chinese artists. To those who are used to Western objects of art, some of them may appear to be crazy specimens of oriental work. But we must remember that the Mind knows many avenues to reach and express Reality. Even among Western readers of this book there may be some who can approach these pictures with something of artistic appreciation.

The name of my good friend (*kalyānamitra*), Yakichi Ataka, is to be deeply engraved in the heart of the reader who for whatever purpose happens to peruse this book; for without him it might never have appeared in this form before the world.

As before, the author owes much to his wife, Beatrice Lane Suzuki, who has been good enough to go over the entire MS. and read the proof-sheets.

In this intensely rationalistic age of science and machinery may not a little of the oriental philosophy of life prove to be a kind of gospel of relaxation and at the same time an opening to a world of spiritual irrationalities?

DAISETZ TEITARO SUZUKI

*Kyoto, February 1933*

# SÁKYA COMING OUT OF HIS MOUNTAIN RETREAT

By LIANG-KAI
*(Early XIIIth Century)*

This is a most ambitious subject for an artist. Whoever first tried his brush on it must have been a bold daring spirit but full of confidence in his spiritual power and artistic imagination. For the entire significance of the Buddhist life is derived from this leaving by Sakyamuni of his mountain retreat after the Enlightenment. While Buddhism starts with Enlightenment and ends in Enlightenment, the connecting passage must be paved with love and compassion. When the eye of Prajñā opens for the first time, a man's feeling is that of absolute loneliness, for he has gone over to the other side of Nirvana; but no time is allowed to him to remain in this solitude. The loneliness of transcendental wisdom departs, and an all-embracing love affirms itself, in which the entire universe is revealed with all its pluralities and complexities. Are the eyes of the Enlightened One gazing at the far-off land of perfect freedom where ignorance and misery are entirely subjugated? Or are they looking inward into the realm of transcendental insights, which is revealed to him, shorn of all its external trumperies, i.e., of all its conceptual encasements? That he walks alone, like the king of beasts, among the inanimate objects of nature—rocks, trees, and shrubs—is significant enough to direct the reader's attention to the ideals of the Zen life, which is filled with a certain kind of intellectual atmosphere.

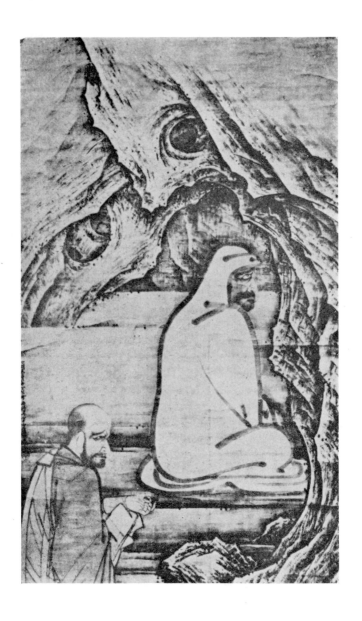

# BODHIDHARMA AND HUI-K'Ê

By SESSHU
(*1420–1506*)

As was noticed in the First Series of *Zen Essays*, pp. 176-7, some historians doubt the historicity of this dramatic incident, that is, Hui-k'ê's cutting off his own arm; for Tao-hsüan who compiled the *Biographies of Eminent Priests* in A.D. 645 ascribes the loss of his arm to the attack of a highwayman. But it is evident that this legend must have been in circulation in the seventh century, i.e., in early T'ang (618–922), perhaps already when Tao-hsüan was engaged in his historical work. For Shên-hui (who died in 760), and Ching-chiao, the author of *Masters and Disciples of the Lanka*, which must have been written sometime in the Kai-yüan era (713–746), refers to the incident as having really taken place.

# THE KOAN EXERCISE

## AS THE MEANS FOR REALIZING
## SATORI OR ATTAINING
## ENLIGHTENMENT

### PART I

#### 1. *An Experience Beyond Knowledge*

In the First Series of my *Zen Essays* (p. 333 *f.*) I have
promised the reader in the Second Series to discuss fully
the subject of 'koan'.[1] In fact, the koan system has effected
a special development in Zen Buddhism, and is a unique
contribution Zen has made to the history of the religious
consciousness. When the importance of the koan is understood, we may say that more than the half of Zen is understood.

The Zen masters, however, may declare that the universe
itself is a great living, threatening koan challenging your
solution, and that when the key to this great koan is
successfully discovered all other koans are minor ones and
solve themselves, and, therefore, that the main thing in the
study of Zen is to know the universe itself and not the problem of koan as set forward by the old masters. On the other
hand, we can say this, that the universal koan is com-
pressed in a nutshell into every one of the 'seventeen
hundred koans', and when it is understood in a most
thoroughgoing way the greatest one will also yield up its
secrets.

In the little index finger of T'ien-lung[2] lies revealed the

---

[1] *Kung-an* in Chinese is pronounced in Japan *kō-an*; literally, it means
'a public document'. It is said that there are 1700 koans to be solved by
the Zen student before he can be called a fully qualified master.

[2] *Essays in Zen Buddhism* (First Series), pp. 35–6 *f.*

mystery of the whole universe, and in the '*Kwatz*' cry of Lin-chi we hear the heavenly harmony of the spheres. However this is, I shall try in the following pages to inquire into the historical significance of the koan in Zen, its office in the realization of satori, its psychological aspect, its relation to the Nembutsu[1] as a form of the Buddhist experience, etc.

That the ultimate aim of Zen discipline is to attain what is known as 'Satori' in Japanese, and 'Sambodhi' or 'abhisamaya' (enlightenment) in Sanskrit, has already been explained in my previous writings. The *Laṅkāvatāra Sūtra* as a Zen text naturally emphasizes the importance of Satori, which is defined here as the *svapratyātmāryajñāna-gatigocara*, that is to say, 'the state of consciousness in which Noble Wisdom realizes its own inner nature'. And this self-realization constitutes the truth of Zen, which is emancipation (*moksha*) and freedom (*vaśavartin*). In order to make clear what is meant by self-realization, let me quote from the *Avataṁsaka Sūtra* :[2]

'Sudhana asked : How does one come to this emancipation face to face? How does one get this realization?

'Sucandra answered : A man comes to this emancipation face to face when his mind is awakened to Prajñāpāramitā[3] and stands in a most intimate relationship to it; for then he attains self-realization in all that he perceives and understands.

'Sudhana : Does one attain self-realization by listening to the talks and discourses on Prajñāpāramitā?

'Sucandra : That is not so. Why? Because Prajñāpāramitā sees intimately into the truth and reality of all things.

---

[1] *Buddhānusmṛiti* in Sanskrit and *nien-fo* in Chinese. It has a technical sense in Japanese Buddhism, and its relation to the koan exercise is discussed in the second part of this article.

[2] The forty-fascicle *Avataṁsaka*: Fas. XXXII. The passages quoted here do not occur in any other *Avataṁsakas*, nor in the Sanskrit *Gaṇḍavyūha*. The forty-fascicle one being a later compilation contains much additional material.

[3] Prajñāpāramitā and Aryajñāna may be considered synonyms.

'Sudhana: Is it not that thinking comes from hearing and that by thinking and reasoning one comes to perceive what Suchness is? And is this not self-realization?

'Sucandra: That is not so. Self-realization never comes from mere listening and thinking. O son of a good family, I will illustrate the matter by analogy. Listen! In a great desert there are no springs or wells; in the spring-time or in the summer when it is warm, a traveller comes from the west going eastward; he meets a man coming from the east and asks him: I am terribly thirsty; pray tell me where I can find a spring and a cool refreshing shade where I may drink, bathe, rest, and get thoroughly revived?

'The man from the east gives the traveller, as desired, all the information in detail, saying: When you go further east the road divides itself into two, right and left. You take the right one, and going steadily further on you will surely come to a fine spring and a refreshing shade. Now, son of a good family, do you think that the thirsty traveller from the west, listening to the talk about the spring and the shady trees, and thinking of going to that place as quickly as possible, can be relieved of thirst and heat and get refreshed?

'Sudhana: No, he cannot; because he is relieved of thirst and heat and gets refreshed only when, as directed by the other, he actually reaches the fountain and drinks of it and bathes in it.

'Sucandra: Son of a good family, even so with the Bodhisattva. By merely listening to it, thinking of it, and intellectually understanding it, you will never come to the realization of any truth. Son of a good family, the desert means birth and death; the man from the west means all sentient beings; the heat means all forms of confusion; thirst is greed and lust; the man from the east who knows the way is the Buddha or the Bodhisattva who, abiding in all-knowledge has penetrated into the true nature of all things and the reality of sameness; to quench the thirst and to be relieved of the heat by drinking of the refreshing fountain means the realization of the truth by oneself.

'Again, son of a good family, I will give you another illustration. Suppose the Tathāgata had stayed among us for another kalpa and used all kinds of contrivance, and, by means of fine rhetoric and apt expressions, had succeeded in convincing people of this world as to the exquisite taste, delicious odour, soft touch, and other virtues of the heavenly nectar; do you think that all the earthly beings who listened to the Buddha's talk and thought of the nectar, could taste its flavour?

'Sudhana: No, indeed; not they.

'Sucandra: Because mere listening and thinking will never make us realize the true nature of Prajñāpāramitā.

'Sudhana: By what apt expressions and skilful illustrations, then, can the Bodhisattva lead all beings to the true understanding of Reality?

'Sucandra: The true nature of Prajñāpāramitā as realized by the Bodhisattva—this is the true definitive principle from which all his expressions issue. When this emancipation is realized he can aptly give expression to it and skilfully illustrate it.'

From this we can distinctively conceive that Prajñāpāramitā which emancipates is something which must be personally experienced by us, and that mere hearing about it, mere learning of it, does not help us to penetrate into the inner nature of Reality itself. Why, one may ask, cannot the truth of self-realization be made graspable by means of knowledge? This is answered in another place in the *Avataṁsaka Sūtra*[1] by Śilpābhijñā to the following effect:

'The truth of self-realization [and Reality itself] are neither one nor two. Because of the power of this self-realization, [Reality] is able universally to benefit others as well as oneself; it is absolutely impartial, with no idea of this and that, like the earth from which all things grow. Reality itself has neither form nor no-form; like space it is beyond knowledge and understanding; it is too subtle to be expressed in words and letters.

'Why? Because it is beyond the realm of letters, words,

[1] The forty-fascicle one, Fas. XXXI. This is also a later addition.

speeches, mere talk, discriminative intellection, inquiring and speculative reflection; and again it is beyond the realm of the understanding which belongs to the ignorant, beyond all evil doings which are in accordance with evil desires. Because it is neither this nor that, it is beyond all mentation; it is formless, without form, transcending the realm of all falsehoods; because it abides in the quietness of no-abode which is the realm of all holy ones.

'O son of a good family, the realm of self-realization where all the wise ones are living is free from materiality, free from purities as well as from defilements, free from grasped and grasping, free from murky confusion; it is most excellently pure and in its nature indestructible; whether the Buddha appears on earth or not, it retains its eternal oneness in the Dharmadhātu. O son of a good family, the Bodhisattva because of this truth has disciplined himself in innumerable forms of austerities, and realizing this Reality within himself has been able to benefit all beings so that they find herein the ultimate abode of safety. O son of a good family, truth of self-realization is validity itself, something unique, reality-limit, the substance of all-knowledge, the inconceivable, non-dualistic Dharmadhātu, and the perfection of emancipation in which all the arts find their complete expression.'

Further down in the forty-fascicle *Avataṁsaka*[1] we read this:

'Sudhana: Where is the abode of all Bodhisattvas?

'Mañjuśrī: In the most excellent ultimate truth they have their abode. This is the truth that knows neither birth nor death, neither loss nor destruction, neither going nor coming; these are all words, and the truth has nothing to do with words; it is far beyond them, it is impossible to be described, it has nothing to do with idle reasoning and philosophical speculation. As it has from the first no words to express itself, it is essentially quiet, realizable only in the inner consciousness of the wise.' . . .

---

[1] Fas. XXXVIII. This is again missing in the other *Avataṁsakas* and in the *Gaṇḍavyūha*.

The distinction between mere learning or mere philoso-
phizing and self-realization, between what is taught and
teachable in words and what altogether transcends one's
verbal expressions as it is to be innerly experienced—this
distinction which is fundamental has been strongly insisted upon by the Buddha; and all his followers have never
forgotten to emphasize this distinction so that the state of
self-realization which they desired would never be lost
sight of. They have, therefore, been taught to be always
intensely vigilant over themselves as if their heads were on
fire, or as if a poisonous arrow had deeply penetrated into
their flesh. They have been urged strongly to endure what is
unendurable, to practise what is the most difficult to practise in the life of an ascetic, in order that they may thus
finally come to the realization of the highest truth which
liberates them from the bondage of existence.

The importance of self-realization in the Buddhist life
has thus been recognized by all the faithful followers of the
Buddha, regardless of their doctrinal differentiations,
Hīnayāna and Mahāyāna. However inexplicable and inexpressible the truth of self-realization is, all the teachings
of Buddhism have centred around it, and Zen, as inheriting
all that is innerly realizable in Buddhism, has faithfully
transmitted its tradition by upholding satori against
ritualism and erudition and all forms of mere philoso-
phizing. If not for this fact, what is the use of the Buddha's
appearing on earth? What is the meaning of all the discipline, of all the moral and spiritual exercises?

The following sermon by Szŭ-hsin Wu-hsin of Huang-
lung (1044–1115)[1] gives vent to what is going on in the
heart of every genuine student of Zen:

'O Brethren, to be born as a human being is a rare event,
and so is the opportunity to listen to discourses on Buddhism. If you fail to achieve emancipation in this life, when
do you again expect to achieve it? While still alive, be
therefore assiduous in practising Dhyāna. The practice

---

[1] Quoted from the *Zen-kwan Saku-shin* (*ch'an-kuan t'sê-chin*). More about
this interesting book later on.

consists in abandonments. "The abandonment of what?" you may ask. Abandon your four elements (*bhūta*), abandon your five aggregates (*skandha*), abandon all the workings of your relative consciousness (*karmavijñāna*), which you have been cherishing since eternity; retire within your inner being and see into the reason of it. As your self-reflection grows deeper and deeper, the moment will surely come upon you when the spiritual flower will suddenly burst into bloom, illuminating the entire universe. The experience is incommunicable, though you yourselves know perfectly well what it is.

'This is the moment when you can transform this great earth into solid gold, and the great rivers into an ocean of milk. What a satisfaction this is then to your daily life! Being so, do not waste your time with words and phrases, or by searching for the truth of Zen in books; for the truth is not to be found there. Even if you memorize the whole Tripitaka as well as all the ancient classics, they are mere idle words which are of no use whatever to you at the moment of your death.'

## 2. *The Significance of Satori in Zen*

Satori is thus the whole of Zen. Zen starts with it and ends with it. When there is no satori, there is no Zen. 'Satori is the measure of Zen', as is announced by a master. Satori is not a state of mere quietude, it is not tranquillization, it is an inner experience which has a noetic quality; there must be a certain awakening from the relative field of consciousness, a certain turning-away from the ordinary form of experience which characterizes our everyday life. The technical Mahāyāna term for it is *parāvṛitti*,[1] 'turning-back' or 'turning-over' at the basis of consciousness. By this the entirety of one's mental construction goes through a complete change. It is wonderful that a satori insight is capable of causing such a reconstruction in one's spiritual

---

[1] *Studies in the Laṅkāvatāra Sūtra*, p. 184 *et passim*.

outlook. But the annals of Zen testify to this. The awakening of Prajñāpāramitā, which is another name for satori, therefore, is the *sine qua non* of Zen.

There are some masters, however, who say that satori is something artificially set up; Zen has really nothing to do with such an excrescent growth as would injure its natural wholesomeness; just to sit quietly—that is enough, the Buddha is here in this doing-nothing-ness; those who make so much fuss about satori are not real followers of Bodhidharma. Such anti-satori masters would further declare that the ultimate truth of Zen consists in holding on to the Unconscious; that if anything marked with conscious strivings comes in, this surely mars the fuller expression of the Unconscious itself; and therefore that the ultimate truth must not be interfered or trifled with; this is the position taken up by some Zen advocates against the upholders of satori. As they oppose satori, they are inevitably also against the koan exercise.

Early in the twelfth century this anti-satori and anti-koan movement in China grew quite strong among Zen followers of the time, and the following is a letter written by Tai-hui[1] to his disciple Lü Chi-i,[2] warning him against those who deny the noetic experience of satori or self-realization:

'Lately there is an evil tendency growing up among certain followers of Zen who regard disease as cure. As they never had a satori in their lives, they consider it as a sort of superstructure, a means of enticement, as something altogether secondary in Zen, which belongs to its periphery and not to its centre. As such teachers have never experienced a satori, they refuse to believe in those who have actually gone through the experience. What they aim at is to realize mere emptiness where there is no life, no noetic

[1] Daiye in Japanese, 1089–1163. He was one of the most outstanding characters Zen Buddhism ever produced in the Chinese soil. He most strongly opposed the teaching and practice of quietism, and was never tired of upholding the importance of satori-awakening in the study of Zen, which he felt to be nothing if not for satori.

[2] The Kōkyō Shoin Edition, T'êng, *VIII, f.* 89a.

quality whatever—that is, a blank nothingness which is regarded by them as something which is eternally beyond the limitations of time.

'In order to reach this state of utter blankness and unfathomability, they consume so many bowls of rice each day and spend their time sitting quietly and stolidly. They think this is what is meant by the attainment of absolute peace. . . . What a pity that they are altogether ignorant of the occasion when there is a sudden outburst [of intuitive knowledge in our minds]!'

The authoritative facts upon which the Zen quietists based their belief are mentioned to be as follows:[1]

'When Śākyamuni was in Magadha he shut himself up in a room and remained silent for three weeks. Is this not an example given by the Buddha in the practice of silence? When thirty-two Bodhisattvas at Vaiśālī discoursed with Vimalakīrti on the teaching of non-duality, the latter finally kept silence and did not utter a word, which elicited an unqualified admiration from Mañjuśrī. Is this not an example given by a great Bodhisattva of the practice of silence? When Subhūti sat in the rock-cave he said not a word, nor was any talk given out by him on Prajñāpāramitā. Is this not an example of silence shown by a great Śrāvaka? Seeing Subhūti thus quietly sitting in the cave, Śakrendra showered heavenly flowers over him and uttered not a word. Is this not an example of silence given by an ordinary mortal? When Bodhidharma came over to this country he sat for nine years at Shao-lin forgetful of all wordy preachings. Is this not an example of silence shown by a patriarch? Whenever Lu-tsu saw a monk coming he turned towards the wall and sat quietly. Is this not an example of silence shown by a Zen master?

'In the face of all these historic examples, how can one pronounce the practice of silent sitting as illegitimate and irrelevant in the study of Zen?'

This is the argument set forward by the advocates of Zen quietism at the time of Tai-hui in China, that is, in

[1] Daiye's discourse delivered at the request of Chien Chi-i.

26

the twelfth century. But Tai-hui declares that mere quiet sitting avails nothing, for it leads nowhere, as no turning-up takes place in one's mind, whereby one comes out into a world of particulars with an outlook different from the one hitherto entertained. Those quietists whose mental horizon does not rise above the level of the so-called absolute silence of unfathomability, grope in the cave of eternal darkness. They fail to open the eye of wisdom. This is where they need the guiding hand of a genuine Zen master.

Tai-hui then proceeds to give cases of satori realized under a wise instructor, pointing out how necessary it is to interview an enlightened one and to turn over once for all the whole silence-mechanism, which is inimical to the growth of the Zen mind. This up-turning of the whole system is here called by Tai-hui after the terminology of a sūtra: 'Entering into the stream and losing one's abode,' where the dualism of motion and rest forever ceases to obtain. He gives four examples:

1. When Shui-lao was trimming the wistaria, he asked his master, Ma-tsu, 'What is the idea of the Patriarch's coming over here from the West?' Ma-tsu replied, 'Come up nearer and I will tell you.' As soon as Shui-lao approached, the master gave him a kick, knocking him right down. This fall, however, all at once opened his mind to a state of satori, for he rose up with a hearty laugh, as if an event, most unexpected and most desired for, had taken place. Asked the master, 'What is the meaning of all this?' Lao exclaimed, 'Innumerable, indeed, are the truths taught by the Buddhas, all of which, even down to their very sources, I now perceive at the tip of one single hair.'

Tai-hui then comments: Lao, who had thus come to self-realization, is no more attached to the silence of Samādhi, and as he is no more attached to it he is at once above assertion and negation, and above the dualism of rest and motion. He no more relies on things outside himself but carrying out the treasure from inside his own mind exclaims, 'I have seen into the source of all truth.' The master recognizes it and does not make further remarks. When Shui-lao was later asked about his Zen understanding, he simply announced, 'Since the kick so heartily given by the master, I have not been able to stop laughing.'

2. Yun-mên asked Tung-shan: 'Whence do you come?' 'From Chia-tu.' 'Where did you pass the summer session?' 'At Pao-tzu, in Hu-nan.' 'When did you come here?' 'August the twenty-fifth.' Yun-mên concluded, 'I release you from thirty blows [though you rightly deserve them].'

On Tung-shan's interview with Mên, Tai-hui comments:

How simple-hearted Tung-shan was! He answered the master straightforwardly, and so it was natural for him to reflect, 'What fault did I commit for which I was to be given thirty blows when I replied as truthfully as I could?' The day following he appeared again before the master and asked, 'Yesterday you were pleased to release me from thirty blows, but I fail to realize my own fault.' Said Yun-mên, 'O you rice-bag, this is the way you wander from the west of the River to the south of the Lake!' This remark all of a sudden opened Tung-shan's eye, and yet he had nothing to communicate, nothing to reason about. He simply bowed, and said: 'After this I shall build my little hut where there is no human habitation; not a grain of rice will be kept in my pantry, not a stalk of vegetable will be growing on my farm; and yet I will abundantly treat all the visitors to my hermitage from all parts of the world; and I will even draw off all the nails and screws [that are holding them to a stake]; I will make them part with their greasy hats and ill-smelling clothes, so that they are thoroughly cleansed of dirt and become worthy monks.' Yun-mên smiled and said, 'What a large mouth you have for a body no larger than a coconut!'

3. Yen, the national teacher of Ku-shan, when he was still a student monk, studied for many years under Hsüeh-fêng. One day, seeing that his student was ready for a mental revolution, the master took hold of him and demanded roughly, 'What is this?' Yen was roused as if from

a deep slumber and at once comprehended what it all meant. He simply lifted his arms and swung them to and fro. Fêng said, 'What does that mean?' 'No meaning whatever, sir,' came quickly from the disciple.

4. One day Kuan-ch'i saw Lin-chi. The latter came down from his straw chair, and without saying a word seized the monk, whereupon Kuan-ch'i said, 'I know, I know.'

After enumerating these four cases Tai-hui concludes that there is after all something in Zen which can neither be imparted to others nor learned from others, and that the trouble with most people is that they are thoroughly dead and do not want to be resuscitated. Tai-hui now talks of his own experience in the following way:

I had been studying Zen for seventeen years, and during that period here and there I had fragmentary satori. I understood a little in the school of Yun-mên, and also a little in the school of Ts'ao-tung, the only trouble being that I had nowhere that decided satori in which I would find myself absolutely cut off from all time and space relations. Later I came to the capital, and staying at the T'ien-ning monastery I listened one day to my teacher's discourse on Yun-mên. He said: 'A monk came to Yun-mên and asked, "Where do all the Buddhas come from?" Yun-mên answered, "The Eastern Mountain walks on water." But I, T'ien-ning, differ from Yun-mên. "Where do all the Buddhas come from?" "A breeze laden with fragrance comes from the south, and the spacious hall begins to be refreshingly cool!"' When my master said this, I felt suddenly as if I were severed from all time and space relations. It was like cutting a skein of tangled thread with one stroke of a sharp knife. I was at the time in a perspiration all over the body.

While I ceased to feel any disturbance in my mind, I found myself to be remaining in a state of sheer serenity. When one day I saw the master in his room, he told me this: 'It is not at all easy for anybody to reach your state of mind; the only regrettable thing is that there is enough death in it but no life whatever. Not to doubt words—this is the great trouble with you. You know this well:

> ' "When thy hands are off the precipice,
>   Conviction comes upon thee all by itself;
>   Let resurrection follow death,
>   And none can now deceive thee."

'Believe me there is really such a thing as is stated here.' The master continued: 'According to my present state of mind, I am perfectly satisfied with myself and the world. All is well with me, and there is nothing of which I have to seek further understanding.'

The master then, putting me in the general dormitory, allowed me to see him three or four times a day like the lay-students of Zen. He just let me hold this, 'To be and not to be—it is like a wistaria leaning on a tree.' Whenever I wanted to speak, he at once shut me up, saying, 'Not so.' This continued for a half year, but I kept on. One day while I together with his lay-disciples was taking supper in the Fang-chang, I found myself so absorbed in the koan that I forgot to use my chopsticks to finish the supper.

The old master said, 'This fellow has only succeeded in mastering Huang-yang wood Zen, which keeps on shrinking all the time.' I then told him by a simile in what position I was. 'My position is that of a dog which stands by a fat-boiling pot: he cannot lick it however badly he wants to, nor can he go away from it though he may wish to quit.' The master said: 'That's just the case with you. [The koan] is really a vajra cage and a seat of thorns to you.'

Another day when I saw the master, I said, 'When you were with Wu-tsu, you asked him about the same koan, and what was his reply?' The master refused to give me his reply. But I insisted: 'When you asked him about it, you were not alone, you were with an assembly. It won't hurt you to tell me about it now.'

The master said: 'I asked him at the time, "To be and

not to be—it is like a wistaria leaning on a tree. What is the meaning of it?" Wu-tsu replied, "You cannot paint it, you cannot sketch it, however much you try." I further said, "What if the tree suddenly breaks down and the wistaria dies?" Wu said, "You are following the words!" '

As soon as I heard my master say this, I understood the whole thing, and said to him, 'O master, I understand.' Hearing me say that, the master remarked, 'Probably you do not.' I asked him to try me, whereupon he gave me some more koans. And every one of them was successfully answered by me. I felt that at last I was at peace with myself, for there was nothing now that obstructed my way.

### 3. Chief Characteristics of Satori

Tai-hui (Daiye) was a great advocate of satori, and one of his favourite sayings was, 'Zen has no words: when you have satori, you have everything.' Hence his strong arguments for it, which came, as has already been shown, from his own experience. Until then, he was quite ready to write a treatise against Zen in which he planned to disclaim everything accredited to Zen by its followers. His interview with his master Yüan-wu, however, rushed all his former determination, making him come out as a most intense advocate of the Zen experience. As I go on with this study of the koan exercise, I shall have many occasions to make further references to Tai-hui. In the meantime I wish to enumerate some of the most salient features of satori, which will later help us understand the role of koan in the whole structure of Zen.

1. *Irrationality.* By this I mean that satori is not a conclusion to be reached by reasoning, and defies all intellectual determination. Those who have experienced it are always at a loss to explain it coherently or logically. When it is explained at all, either in words or gestures, its content more or less undergoes a mutilation. The uninitiated are thus unable to grasp it by what is outwardly visible, while

31

# HUI-NÊNG LISTENING TO THE DIAMOND SUTRA

By Shuai Weng
(*Yüan Dynasty*)

The inscription by Yen-ch'i Kuang-wên (1189–1263) reads:

"The bundle is securely carried on his shoulders,
The homeward way lies before him, nothing thwarting;
    'Awaken the mind without fixing it anywhere'—this is
        perfectly realised;
    And he knows in whose house his kindlings are burning."

Inscribed by *Kuang-wên, Fêng-ch'üan.*

"To awaken the mind without fixing it anywhere"—is the phrase in the *Diamond Sutra* (*Vajracchedika*), listening to which Hui-nêng is said to have realised the truth of Zen.[1] That Hui-nêng was not of aristocratic lineage and that his understanding of Zen was more of the Prajña aspect than of the merely Dhyana aspect, have perhaps exercised greater influence on the direction of the development of Zen in China. For it was since Hui-nêng that Prajña and practicalness came to figure out quite prominently in the history of Zen. The very intimate connection which Zen came to assume with the things of daily life will be illustrated again in the life of Hui-nêng.

[1] *Zen Essays*, First Series, p. 205; *Chuan-téng Lu*, V.

# HUNG-JÊN SEEING OFF HUI-NÊNG

## By Motonobu Kano
### (1476–1559)

Although its historicity is doubted, the incident is recorded in the current edition of the *T'an-ching* ("Platform Sutra") of Hui-nêng, popularly known as the sixth patriarch of Chinese Zen Buddhism. According to it, when Hung-jên, the fifth patriarch, stamped his certification on the spiritual attainment of Hui-nêng, Jên wished to see his favourite disciple quietly and safely leave his monastery. During the night Hui-nêng was taken down as far as the river, where Hung-jên himself rowed the boat to carry Hui-nêng over to the other side. As Hui-nêng then was not yet a regularly ordained monk, he is seen in a layman's dress. The bundle he carries is probably the *kashaya* handed over to him by the master. The upper part of the picture, which is divided off from the lower by means of clouds—which is the artistic device of Japanese painters—represents a portion of the monastery.

This incident is in all likelihood a fiction. (See First Series of my *Zen Essays*, pp. 207–8.) What historical truth we can gather from it is that there was a strong rivalry between Hui-nêng and Shên-hsiu, or, strictly speaking, between the disciples of the two masters.

those who have had the experience discern what is genuine from what is not. The satori experience is thus always characterized by irrationality, inexplicability, and incommunicability.

Listen to Tai-hui once more: 'This matter [i.e. Zen] is like a great mass of fire; when you approach it your face is sure to be scorched. It is again like a sword about to be drawn; when it is once out of the scabbard, someone is sure to lose his life. But if you neither fling away the scabbard nor approach the fire, you are no better than a piece of rock or of wood. Coming to this pass, one has to be quite a resolute character full of spirit.'[1] There is nothing here suggestive of cool reasoning and quiet metaphysical or epistemological analysis, but of a certain desperate will to break through an insurmountable barrier, of the will impelled by some irrational or unconscious power behind it. Therefore, the outcome also defies intellection or conceptualization.

2. *Intuitive insight.* That there is noetic quality in mystic experiences has been pointed out by James in his *Varieties of Religious Experience*, and this applies also to the Zen experience known as satori. Another name for satori is 'ken-sho' (*chien-hsing* in Chinese) meaning 'to see essence or nature', which apparently proves that there is 'seeing' or 'perceiving' in satori. That this seeing is of quite a different quality from what is ordinarily designated as knowledge need not be specifically noticed. Hui-k'ê is reported to have made this statement concerning his satori which was confirmed by Bodhidharma himself: '[As to my satori], it is not a total annihilation; it is knowledge of the most adequate kind; only it cannot be expressed in words.' In this respect Shên-hui was more explicit, for he says that 'the one character *chih* (knowledge) is the source of all mysteries.'[2]

---

[1] Tai-hui's sermon at the request of Li Hsuan-chiao.

[2] *Miao* is a difficult term to translate; it often means 'exquisiteness', 'indefinable subtlety'. In this case *miao* is the mysterious way in which things are presented to this ultimate knowledge. Tsung-mi on *Zen Masters and Disciples.*

Without this noetic quality satori will lose all its pungency, for it is really the reason of satori itself. It is noteworthy that the knowledge contained in satori is concerned with something universal and at the same time with the individual aspect of existence. When a finger is lifted, the lifting means, from the viewpoint of satori, far more than the act of lifting. Some may call it symbolic, but satori does not point to anything beyond itself, being final as it is. Satori is the knowledge of an individual object and also that of Reality which is, if I may say so, at the back of it.

3. *Authoritativeness*. By this I mean that the knowledge realized by satori is final, that no amount of logical argument can refute it. Being direct and personal it is sufficient unto itself. All that logic can do here is to explain it, to interpret it in connection with other kinds of knowledge with which our minds are filled. Satori is thus a form of perception, an inner perception, which takes place in the most interior part of consciousness. Hence the sense of authoritativeness, which means finality. So, it is generally said that Zen is like drinking water, for it is by one's self that one knows whether it is warm or cold. The Zen perception being the last term of experience, it cannot be denied by outsiders who have no such experience.

4. *Affirmation*. What is authoritative and final can never be negative. For negation has no value for our life, it leads us nowhere; it is not a power that urges, nor does it give one a place to rest. Though the satori experience is sometimes expressed in negative terms, it is essentially an affirmative attitude towards all things that exist; it accepts them as they come along regardless of their moral values. Buddhists call this *kshānti*, 'patience', or more properly 'acceptance', that is, acceptance of things in their suprarelative or transcendental aspect where no dualism of whatever sort avails.

Some may say that this is pantheistic. The term, however, has a definite philosophic meaning and I would not see it used in this connection. When so interpreted the Zen experience exposes itself to endless misunderstandings and 'defilements'. Tai-hui says in his letter to Miao-tsung: 'An ancient sage says that the Tao itself does not require special disciplining, only let it not be defiled. I would say: To talk about mind or nature is defiling; to talk about the unfathomable or the mysterious is defiling; to practise meditation or tranquillization is defiling; to direct one's attention to it, to think about it, is defiling; to be writing about it thus on paper with a brush is especially defiling. What then shall we have to do in order to get ourselves oriented, and properly apply ourselves to it? The precious vajra sword is right here and its purpose is to cut off the head. Do not be concerned with human questions of right and wrong. All is Zen just as it is, and right here you are to apply yourself.' Zen is Suchness—a grand affirmation.

5. *Sense of the Beyond.* Terminology may differ in different religions, and in satori there is always what we may call a sense of the Beyond; the experience indeed is my own but I feel it to be rooted elsewhere. The individual shell in which my personality is so solidly encased explodes at the moment of satori. Not, necessarily, that I get unified with a being greater than myself or absorbed in it, but that my individuality, which I found rigidly held together and definitely kept separate from other individual existences, becomes loosened somehow from its tightening grip and melts away into something indescribable, something which is of quite a different order from what I am accustomed to. The feeling that follows is that of a complete release or a complete rest—the feeling that one has arrived finally at the destination. 'Coming home and quietly resting' is the expression generally used by Zen followers. The story of the prodigal son in the *Saddharma-puṇḍarīka* in the *Vajra-samādhi*, and also in the New Testament points to the same feeling one has at the moment of a satori experience.

As far as the psychology of satori is considered, a sense of the Beyond is all we can say about it; to call this the Beyond, the Absolute, or God, or a Person is to go further than the experience itself and to plunge into a theology or metaphysics. Even the 'Beyond' is saying a little too much. When a Zen master says, 'There is not a fragment of a tile above my head, there is not an inch of earth beneath my feet,' the expression seems to be an appropriate one. I have called it elsewhere the Unconscious, though this has a psychological taint.

6. *Impersonal Tone.* Perhaps the most remarkable aspect of the Zen experience is that it has no personal note in it as is observable in Christian mystic experiences. There is no reference whatever in Buddhist satori to such personal and frequently sexual feelings and relationships as are to be gleaned from these terms: flame of love, a wonderful love shed in the heart, embrace, the beloved, bride, bridegroom, spiritual matrimony, Father, God, the Son of God, God's child, etc. We may say that all these terms are interpretations based on a definite system of thought and really have nothing to do with the experience itself. At any rate, alike in India, China, and Japan, satori has remained thoroughly impersonal, or rather highly intellectual.

Is this owing to the peculiar character of Buddhist philosophy? Does the experience itself take its colours from the philosophy or theology? Whatever this is, there is no doubt that in spite of its having some points of similitude to the Christian mystic experience, the Zen experience is singularly devoid of personal or human colourings. Chaopien, a great government officer of the Sung dynasty, was a lay-disciple of Fa-ch'uan of Chiang-shan. One day after his official duties were over, he found himself leisurely sitting in his office, when all of a sudden a clash of thunder burst on his ear, and he realized a state of satori. The poem he then composed depicts one aspect of the Zen experience:

'Devoid of thought, I sat quietly by the desk in my official room,
With my fountain-mind undisturbed, as serene as water;
A sudden clash of thunder, the mind-doors burst open,
And lo, there sitteth the old man in all his homeliness.'

This is perhaps all the personal tone one can find in the Zen experience, and what a distance between 'the old man in his homeliness' and 'God in all his glory', not to say anything about such feelings as 'the heavenly sweetness of Christ's excellent love', etc.! How barren, how unromantic satori is when compared with the Christian mystic experiences!

Not only satori itself is such a prosaic and non-glorious event, but the occasion that inspires it also seems to be unromantic and altogether lacking in super-sensuality. Satori is experienced in connection with any ordinary occurrence in one's daily life. It does not appear to be an extraordinary phenomenon as is recorded in Christian books of mysticism. Someone takes hold of you, or slaps you, or brings you a cup of tea, or makes some most commonplace remark, or recites some passage from a sūtra or from a book of poetry, and when your mind is ripe for its outburst, you come at once to satori. There is no romance of love-making, no voice of the Holy Ghost, no plenitude of Divine Grace, no glorification of any sort. Here is nothing painted in high colours, all is grey and extremely unobtrusive and unattractive.

7. *Feeling of Exaltation.* That this feeling inevitably accompanies satori is due to the fact that it is the breaking-up of the restriction imposed on one as an individual being, and this breaking-up is not a mere negative incident but quite a positive one fraught with signification because it means an infinite expansion of the individual. The general feeling, though we are not always conscious of it, which characterizes all our functions of consciousness, is that of restriction and dependence, because consciousness itself is the outcome of two forces conditioning or restricting each other. Satori, on the contrary, essentially consists in doing away with the opposition of two terms in whatsoever sense —and this opposition is the principle of consciousness as before mentioned, while satori is to realize the Unconscious which goes beyond the opposition.

To be released of this, therefore, must make one feel above all things intensely exalted. A wandering outcast maltreated everywhere not only by others but by himself

finds that he is the possessor of all the wealth and power
that is ever attainable in this world by a mortal being—if
this does not give him a high feeling of self-glorification,
what could? Says a Zen master, 'When you have satori
you are able to reveal a palatial mansion made of precious
stones on a single blade of grass; but when you have no
satori, a palatial mansion itself is concealed behind a simple
blade of grass.'

Another Zen master, evidently alluding to the *Avataṁsaka*, declares: 'O monks, lo and behold! a most auspicious
light is shining with the utmost brilliancy all over the great
chiliocosm, simultaneously revealing all the countries, all
the oceans, all the Sumerus, all the suns and moons, all
the heavens, all the lands—each of which number as many
as hundreds of thousands of kotis. O monks, do you not see
the light?' But the Zen feeling of exaltation is rather a quiet
feeling of self-contentment; it is not at all demonstrative,
when the first glow of it passes away. The Unconscious does
not proclaim itself so boisterously in the Zen consciousness.

8. *Momentariness*. Satori comes upon one abruptly and is
a momentary experience. In fact, if it is not abrupt and
momentary, it is not satori. This abruptness (*tun*) is what
characterizes the Hui-nêng school of Zen ever since its
proclamation late in the seventh century. His opponent
Shên-hsiu was insistent on a gradual unfoldment of Zen
consciousness. Hui-nêng's followers were thus distinguished
as strong upholders of the doctrine of abruptness. This
abrupt experience of satori, then, opens up in one moment
(*ekamuhūrtena*) an altogether new vista, and the whole
existence is appraised from quite a new angle of observation.
Tung-shan's utterance, which was quoted elsewhere, amply
testifies to this fact. Bukkō Kokushi's *Udāna*[1] too is suggestive in this respect.

---

[1] The First Series, pp. 255-7.

4. *Psychological Antecedents of Satori Prior to the
Koan System—Some Practical Examples*

Before proceeding further to see how the koan exercise
came to be recognized as the necessary step towards the
realization of satori in Zen Buddhism, I wish to inquire
into the psychological equipments of those Zen masters
who flourished before the time of the koan. When I speak
of this as something indispensable in the mastery of modern
Zen, it may be asked why it is so and what was done by
the ancient masters prior to the development of the koan.
The koan came in vogue towards the end of the ninth
century—that is, about one hundred and fifty years after
Hui-nêng.

During these years Zen was practised, satori was realized,
and the transmission of the Buddha-mind successfully
went on. No koans were needed for the masters to train
their disciples. How did they come to the Zen realization?
A state of things quite different from what we see in these
modern days must have then prevailed. What are the conditions of the difference? This kind of inquiry is needed
to elucidate the nature of koan, to find out what psychological role it plays in the Zen experience, and finally to see
in what relationship it stands to the Nembutsu, which is the
essence of the Pure Land teaching.

Here I wish to see what are these psychological equipments or antecedents that lead up to satori. As we have
already seen, this state or what may be called Zen consciousness comes on in connection with the most trivial
incidents such as the raising of a finger, uttering a cry,
reciting a phrase, swinging a stick, slapping a face, and so
on. As the outcome is apparently incongruous with the
occasion, we naturally presume some deep-seated psychological antecedents which are thereby abruptly brought
to maturity. What are these antecedents? Let us examine
a few of the classical cases of satori as recorded in the annals
of Zen.

The study of these antecedents is important, for there is no doubt that they determine the nature of the experience, and, from the practical point of view, the Zen masters can thereby give the necessary instructions to their pupils in the understanding of Zen. Among the questions that may be asked here are the following: What are the intellectual factors, if there are any, in the ripening of Zen consciousness? Has the will anything to do with the experience? Is there anything approaching auto-suggestion?

In the following pages I shall try to construct something definite and tangible in the psychological history of satori. This is in a way not an easy task, as there are no autobiographical records of any sort before the koan exercise came into vogue, nor are there any detailed and accurate objective observations on the process of consciousness prior to the outburst of satori. But something constructive may be gathered up even from the vague and fragmentary records left by the Chinese when they are sympathetically analysed.

1. The story of the interview of Hui-k'ê with Bodhidharma, the first patriarch of Zen in China, is somewhat veiled with historical inaccuracies and suffers much from its dramatic treatment, but even with these disadvantages we still have an intelligent account of the interview. For historical accuracy is not always the necessary condition for determining what actually took place. Whatever literary treatment the event receives later on also helps to understand the situation. We may well remember that the imagination often depicts so-called facts psychologically more truthfully than the historian's objective narration.

According to *The Transmission of the Lamp* Hui-k'ê (or Hui-k'o, 487–593)[1] was a liberal-minded, open-hearted sort of person, thoroughly acquainted with Confucian and Taoist literature, but always dissatisfied with their teachings because they appeared to him not quite thoroughgoing. When he heard of Bodhidharma coming from India, he went to Shao-lin Szŭ where the master stayed. He

[1] The First Series, p. 192.

tried to get a chance to talk with him on the subject upon which he wished to be enlightened, but the master was always found sitting silently facing the wall.

Hui-k'ê reflected: 'History gives examples of ancient truth-seekers, who were willing for the sake of enlightenment to have the marrow extracted from their bones, their blood spilled to feed the hungry, to cover the muddy road with their hair, or to throw themselves into the mouth of a hungry tiger. What am I? Am I not also able to give myself up on the altar of truth?'

On the ninth of December of the same year, he stood in the fast-falling snow and did not move until the morning when the snow had reached his knees. Bodhidharma then took pity on him and said, 'You have been standing in the snow for some time, and what is your wish?'

Replied Hui-k'ê, 'I am come to receive your invaluable instruction; pray open the gate of mercy and extend your hand of salvation to this poor suffering mortal.'

Bodhidharma then said: 'The incomparable teaching of the Buddha can be comprehended only after a long and hard discipline and by enduring what is most difficult to endure and by practising what is most difficult to practise. Men of inferior virtue and wisdom who are light-hearted and full of self-conceit are not able even to set their eyes on the truth of Buddhism. All the labour of such men is sure to come to naught.'

Hui-k'ê was deeply moved, and in order to show his sincerity in the desire to be instructed in the teachings of all the Buddhas, he cut off his left arm with the sword he carried and presented it before the quietly meditating Bodhidharma. Thereupon, the master remarked, 'You are not to seek this [truth] through others.'

'My soul is not yet pacified. Pray, Master, pacify it.'

'Bring your soul here and I will have it pacified,' said Bodhidharma.

After a short hesitation, Hui-k'e finally confessed, 'I have sought it for many years and am still unable to take hold of it.'

Here Tai-hui makes the comment: 'Hui-k'ê well understood the situation in which he found himself after studying all the scriptures, and it was good of him that he gave the master a straightforward answer. The "thing", he knew, was not to be sought after with a purpose, or without a purpose; nor was it to be reached by means of words, nor by mere quietude; nor was it to be logically grasped, nor illogically explained. It was nowhere to be encountered nor was it to be inferred from anything; no, not in the five Skandhas, not in the eighteen Dhatus. He did well in answering this way.'

'There! Your soul is pacified once for all,' Bodhidharma confirmed.

This confirmation on the part of the master at once opened Hui-k'ê's eye of satori. Tai-hui again remarks: 'It was like the dragon getting into water, or the tiger leaning against the rock. At that moment, Hui-k'ê saw not the master before him, nor the snow, nor the mind that was reaching out for something, nor the satori itself which took possession of his mind. All vanished away from his consciousness, all was emptiness. So it was said that "Loneliness reigns here, not a figure in the monastery of Shao-lin." But did Hui-k'ê remain in this emptiness? No, he was awakened abruptly to a new life. He threw himself down over the precipice, and lo, he came out fully alive from certain death. And surely he felt then the cold shivering snow piled up in the temple court. As before, his nose rested above his upper lip.'[1]

The characteristic points I wish to notice in the case of Hui-k'ê are: that he was a learned scholar; that he was not satisfied with mere scholarship but wished to grasp something innerly; that he was most earnest in his search for an inmost truth which would give peace and rest to his soul; that he was prepared to sacrifice anything for the purpose; that he devoted some years to the hard task of locating his soul so-called, for evidently he thought in accordance with the traditional view that there was a 'soul' at the centre of

[1] Tai-hui's sermon at the request of Yang-yüan.

43

his being and that when it was grasped he would attain the desired end; that while Hui-k'ê's interview with Bodhidharma is narrated as if it were an event of one day or one evening, it is possible that some days or months of intense mental lucubration took place between it and the master's exhortation; that the statement 'I have not been able to take hold of my soul', was not a plain statement of fact but meant that the whole being of Hui-k'ê was thrown down, that is, he reached here the end of his life as an individual existence conscious all the time of its own individuality; that he was dead unto himself when the master's remark unexpectedly revived him—this can be seen from the remark as above cited, 'Loneliness reigns here, there is not a soul in the monastery of Shao-lin.'

This 'loneliness' is an absolute loneliness in which there is no dualistic contrast of being and non-being. The cry—for it was a cry and not a proposition—that 'there is no soul to be taken hold of', could not be uttered until this state of absolute loneliness was reached. It was also just because of this realization that Hui-k'ê was able to rise from it upon Bodhidharma's remarking, 'Pacified then is your soul!' When we carefully and sympathetically follow the course of events that led up to Hui-k'ê's satori, we naturally have to fill up in the way here proposed the gaps in the record of his life. My point of view will become clearer as we proceed.

2. The case of Hui-nêng (638–713),[1] who is regarded now as the sixth patriarch of Zen in China, presents some contrasts to that of Hui-k'ê so long as Hui-nêng is made out to be an unlearned pedlar. This treatment given to Hui-nêng is in a way interesting as it reveals a certain tendency among followers of Zen who ignore learning and the study of sūtras. In Hui-nêng's case, however, there was a historical background which made him stand against his rival, Shên-hsiu,[2] who was noted for his wide knowledge and

[1] The First Series, p. 205.
[2] Died 706.

44

scholarship. In reality, Hui-nêng was not such an ignoramus as his followers wanted him to appear, for his sermons known as the Platform Sūtra contain many allusions to Buddhist literature. All we can say of him as regards his learning is that he was not so erudite as Shên-hsiu. According to history, his first knowledge of Zen came from the *Vajracchedikā Sūtra*. While he was peddling wood and kindling he overheard one of his patrons reading that sūtra. This inspired him and he decided to study Zen teachings under Hung-jên, the fifth patriarch of Zen. When he saw the master, the latter asked:

'Where do you come from? What do you want here?'

'I am a farmer from Hsin-chou and wish to become a Buddha.'

'So you come from the South,' said the master, 'but the southerners have no Buddha-nature in them; how could you expect to be a Buddha?'

Hui-nêng protested, 'There are southerners and there are northerners, but as to Buddha-nature, no distinction is to be made between them.'

If Hui-nêng had had no preliminary knowledge or experience of Buddhism he could not have answered like that. He worked under Hung-jên in the granary of the monastery as a rice-cleaner and not as a regular monk, and remained there for eight months. One day the fifth patriarch, wishing to decide on his successor, wished to see how much of his teaching was understood by his followers, who numbered above five hundred. The poem composed by Shên-hsiu, the most scholarly of his five hundred disciples, ran as follows:

'This body is the Bodhi-tree,
The soul is like a mirror bright;
Take heed to keep it always clean,
And let not dust collect upon it.'

Hui-nêng was not satisfied with it and composed another which was inscribed beside the learned Shên-hsiu's:

'The Bodhi is not like the tree,
The mirror bright is nowhere shining;
As there is nothing from the beginning,
Where can the dust collect itself?'[1]

So far as we can judge by these poems alone, Hui-nêng's is in full accord with the doctrine of Emptiness as taught in the *Prajñāpāramitā Sūtra*, while Shên-hsiu's, we may say, has not yet quite fully grasped the spirit of Mahāyāna Buddhism. Hui-nêng's mind, thus, from the first developed along the line of thought indicated in the *Vajracchedikā* which he learned even before he came to Hung-jên. But it is evident that he could not have composed the poem without having experienced the truth of Emptiness in himself. The first inspiration he got from the *Vajracchedikā* made him realize the presence of a truth beyond this phenomenal world. He came to Hung-jên, but it required a great deal of trained intuitive power to get into the spirit of the *Prajñāpāramitā*, and even with the genius of Hui-nêng this could not have been accomplished very easily. He must have worked very hard while cleaning rice to have delved so successfully into the secrets of his own mind.

The eight months of menial work were by no means all menial;[2] a great spiritual upheaval was going on in the

---

[1] According to the Tun-huang MS. copy of the *Platform Sūtra*, the third line reads: 'The Buddha-nature is ever pure and undefiled.' This book, compiled by Hui-nêng's disciples, has suffered a somewhat vicissitudinous fate, and the current edition differs very much from such ancient copies as the Tun-huang MS. and the Japanese edition recently recovered at the Kōshōji monastery, Kyoto.

[2] Is it not illuminating to note that Hui-nêng passed his life in a most prosaic and apparently non-religious employment while in the monastery, working up his mind to develop into the state of satori? He did not repeat the name of the Buddha, he did not worship the Buddha according to the prescribed rules of the monastery life, he did not confess his sins and ask for pardon through the grace of God, he did not throw himself down before a Buddha and offer most ardent prayers to be relieved of the eternal bond of transmigration. He simply pounded his rice so that it could be ready for his Brotherhood's consumption. This ultra commonplaceness of Hui-nêng's role in the monastery life is the beginning of the Zen discipline which distinguishes itself remarkably from that of other Buddhist communities.

mind of Hui-nêng. The reading of Shên-hsiu's poem gave him the occasion for giving utterance to his inner vision. Whatever learning, insight, and instruction he had had before were brought finally into maturity and culminated in the poem which was the living expression of his experience. His *Vajracchedikā* thus came to life in his own being. Without actually experiencing the *Prajñāpāramitā*, Hui-nêng could not have made the statement which he did to Ming, one of his pursuers after he left Hung-jên. When Ming wanted to be enlightened, Hui-nêng said, 'Think not of good, think not of evil, but see what at the moment thy own original features are, which thou hadst even before coming into existence.'

The points which I wish to note in the case of Hui-nêng are:

*a.* He was not a very learned man though he was in fact well acquainted with several Mahāyāna sūtras. He was decidedly not one of those scholars who could write recondite and well-informed commentaries on the sūtras and śastras. His main idea was to get into the true meaning of a text.

*b.* The test which first attracted his attention was the *Vajracchedikā*, which was very likely most popular in his day. This sūtra belongs to the *Prajñāpāramitā* group. It is not a philosophical work but contains deep religious truths as they represented themselves to the Indian Mahāyānist genius. They are expressed in such a way as to be almost incomprehensible to ordinary minds, as they often seem contradictory to one another, as far as their logical thoroughness is concerned. Writers of the *Prajñāpāramitā Sūtras* are never tired of warning their readers not to get alarmed with their teachings, which are so full of audacious statements.

*c.* The object of Hui-nêng's coming to Huang-mei-shan was to study Zen and to breathe the spirit of the *Prajñāpāramitā*, and not to turn the rice mill or to chop wood. But there is no doubt that he did a great deal of thinking within himself. Hung-jên must have noticed it and given him occasional instructions privately as well as publicly, for we cannot think that all his five hundred pupils were left to themselves to understand the deep meaning of the *Vajracchedikā*, or the *Laṅkāvatāra*, or any other Zen literature. He must have given them frequent discourses on Zen, during all of which time Hui-nêng's mind was maturing.

*d.* It is probable that Shên-hsiu's poem was the occasion for Hui-nêng to bring out to the surface all that was revolving about in his deep consciousness. He had been seeking for ultimate truth, or to experience in himself the final signification of the *Prajñāpāramitā*. Shên-hsiu's poem, which went against its significance, produced in Hui-nêng's inner mind a contrary effect and opened up a more direct way to the *Prajñāpāramitā*.

*e.* With Hui-nêng, Zen begins to shoot out its own native roots, that is to say, what used to be Indian now turns to be genuinely Chinese. Zen has become acclimatized by Hui-nêng and firmly rooted in Chinese soil. His treatment of Ming and his sermons at Fa-hsing monastery prove his originality.

*f.* What is most original with Hui-nêng and his school, and what distinguishes them from Shên-hsiu, is the emphasis they place upon the abruptness of satori. For this reason the school is known as *Tun-chiao*, meaning 'abrupt teaching', in contradistinction to Shên-hsiu's *Chien-chiao*, which means 'gradual teaching'. The former flourished in the south and the latter in the north, and this geographical distribution caused them to be also known as 'Southern School' (*nan-tsung*) and 'Northern School' (*pe-tsung*). The north tended to value learning and practical discipline, while the south strongly upheld the intuitive functioning of Prajñā, which takes place 'abruptly', that is, immediately without resorting to logical process.

Learning is a slow tedious journey to the goal; and even when it is thought that the goal is reached it does not go beyond conceptualism. There are always two types of mind, intuitive and ratiocinative. The intuitive type, which is generally represented by religious geniuses, is impatient over the conceptualistic tendency of the scholar. Thus naturally the abrupt school of Hui-nêng was at war in its earlier days with the gradual school of Shên-hsiu and later with the quietist movement of some of the Zen masters of the Sung. As the history of Zen proves, the abrupt school represents more truthfully the principle of Zen consciousness which has achieved such a signal development in China and Japan ever since the day of Bodhidharma. It was Hui-nêng who became conscious of this peculiarly Zen principle and did not fail to emphasize it against the sūtra-studying and the quiet-sitting type of Zen followers. In fact, the opposition between these two tendencies has been going on throughout the history of Zen.

3. Tê-shan (780–865), who is noted for his swinging a staff, was also a student of the *Vajracchedikā* before he was converted to Zen. Different from his predecessor, Hui-nêng, he was very learned in the teaching of the sūtra and was extensively read in its commentaries, showing that his knowledge of the *Prajñāpāramitā* was more systematic than was Hui-nêng's. He heard of this Zen teaching in the south, according to which a man could be a Buddha by immediately taking hold of his inmost nature. This he thought could not be the Buddha's own teaching, but the Evil One's, and he decided to go down south. In this respect his mission again differed from that of Hui-nêng. The latter wished to get into the spirit of the *Vajracchedikā* under the guidance of the fifth patriarch, while Tê-shan's idea was to destroy Zen if possible. They were both students of the *Vajracchedikā*, but the sūtra inspired them in a way diametrically opposite. Tê-shan's psychology reminds us of that of St. Paul as he walked under the summer sun along the road to Damascus.

Tê-shan's first objective was Lung-t'an where resided a Zen master called Ch'ung-hsin. On his way to the mountain he stopped at a tea-house where he asked the woman-keeper to give him some refreshments. 'Refreshment' is *tien-hsin* in Chinese, meaning, literally, 'to punctuate the mind'. Instead of setting out the requested refreshments for the tired monk-traveller, the woman asked, 'What are you carrying on your back?'

He replied, 'They are commentaries on the *Vajracchedikā*.'

'They are indeed!' said the woman. 'May I ask you a question? If you can answer it to my satisfaction, you will have your refreshments free; but if you fail, you will have to go somewhere else.'

To this Tê-shan agreed.

The woman-keeper of the tea-house then proposed the following: 'I read in the *Vajracchedikā* that the mind is obtainable neither in the past, nor in the present, nor in the future. If so, which mind do you wish to punctuate?'

This unexpected question from an apparently insignificant country-woman completely upset the knapsackful scholarship of Tê-shan, for all his knowledge of the *Vajracchedikā* together with its various commentaries gave him no inspiration whatever. The poor scholar had to go without his lunch. Not only this, he also had to abandon his bold enterprise to defeat the teachers of Zen; for when he was no match even for the keeper of a roadside tea-house, how could he expect to defeat a professional Zen master? Even before he saw Ch'ung-hsin, master of Lung-t'an, he was certainly made to think more about his self-imposed mission.

When Tê-shan saw Ch'ung-hsin, the master of Lung-t'an, he said, 'I have heard people talk so much of Lung-t'an (dragon's pool), yet as I see it, there is no dragon here, nor any pool.'

Ch'ung-hsin quietly said, 'You are indeed in the midst of Lung-t'an.'

Tê-shan finally decided to stay at Lung-t'an and to study Zen under the guidance of its master. One evening he was sitting outside the room quietly and yet earnestly in search of the truth. Ch'ung-hsin said, 'Why do you not come in?' 'It is dark,' replied Tê-shan. Whereupon Ch'ung-hsin lighted a candle and handed it to Shan. When Shan was about to take it, Hsin blew it out. This suddenly opened his mind to the truth of Zen teaching. Shan bowed respectfully.

'What is the matter with you?' asked the master.

'After this,' Shan asserted, 'whatever propositions the Zen masters may make about Zen, I shall never again cherish a doubt about them.'

The next morning Tê-shan took out all his commentaries on the *Vajracchedikā*, once so valued and considered so indispensable that he had to carry them about with him wherever he went, committed them to the flames and turned them all into ashes.[1]

The case of Tê-shan shows some characteristic points differing much from those of the preceding case. Shan was learned not only in the *Vajracchedikā* but in other departments of Buddhist philosophy such as the Abhidharmakośa and the Yogācāra. But in the beginning he was decidedly against Zen, and the object of his coming out of the Shu district was to annihilate it. This at any rate was the motive that directed the surface current of his consciousness; as to what was going on underneath he was altogether unaware of it. The psychological law of contrariness was undoubtedly in force and was strengthened as against his superficial motive when he encountered a most unexpected opponent in the form of a tea-house keeper. His first talk with Ch'ung-hsin concerning the Dragon's Pool (Lung-t'an) completely crushed the hard crust of Shan's mentality, releasing all the forces deeply hidden in his consciousness. When the candle was suddenly blown out, all that was negated prior to this incident unconditionally reasserted itself. A complete mental cataclysm took place. What had been regarded as most precious was now not worth a straw.

Afterwards, when Shan himself became a master, he used to say to an inquirer, 'Whether you say "yes", you get thirty blows; whether you say "no", you get thirty blows just the same.' A monk asked him, 'Who is the Buddha?' 'He is an old monk of the Western country.' 'What is en-

[1] See also the First Series, pp. 239, 247.

lightenment?' Shan gave the questioner a blow, saying, 'You get out of here; do not scatter dirt around us!' Another monk wished to know something about Zen, but Shan roared, 'I have nothing to give, begone!'

What a contrast this is to all that had been astir in Shan's mind before his arrival at Lung-t'an! It does not require much imagination to see what sort of a mental revolution was going on in Shan's mind after his interview with the woman-keeper of the tea-house, and especially when he was sitting with his master, outwardly quiet but innerly so intensely active as to be oblivious of the approach of the darkness.

4. Lin-chi (died 866) was a disciple of Huang-po, and the founder of the school that bears his name (in Japanese, Rinzai). His Zen experience presents some interesting features which may be considered in a way typically orthodox in those days when the koan system of Zen discipline was not yet in vogue. He had been studying Zen for some years under Huang-po when the head-monk asked, 'How long have you been here?' 'Three years, sir.' 'Have you ever seen the master?' 'No, sir.' 'Why don't you?' 'Because I do not now what question to ask him.' The head-monk then told Lin-chi, 'You go and see the master and ask, "What is the principle of Buddhism?" '

Lin-chi saw the master as he was told and asked, 'What is the principle of Buddhism?' Even before he could finish the question, Huang-po gave him several blows. When the head-monk saw him coming back from the master, he inquired about the result of the interview. Said Lin-chi sorrowfully, 'I asked him and was beaten with many blows.' The monk told him not to be discouraged but to go again to the master. Lin-chi saw Huang-po three times but each time the same treatment was accorded to him, and poor Chi was not any the wiser.

Finally Chi thought it best to see another master and the head-monk agreed. The master directed him to go to Tai-yü. When Lin-chi came to Tai-yü, the latter asked, 'Where do you come from?'

'From Huang-po.'

'What instruction did he give you?'

'I asked him three times about the ultimate principle of Buddhism and each time he gave me several blows without any instruction. I wish you would tell me what fault I committed.'

Tai-yü said, 'No one could be more thoroughly kindhearted than that dotard master, and yet you want to know where you were faulty.'

Thus reprimanded, Lin-chi's eye was opened to the meaning of Huang-po's apparently unkind treatment. He exclaimed, 'After all there is not much in Huang-po's Buddhism!'

Tai-yü at once seized Lin-chi's collar and said: 'A while ago you said you could not understand, and now you declare that there is not much in Huang-po's Buddhism. What do you mean by that?'

Lin-chi without saying a word probed Tai-yü's ribs three times with his fist. Tai-yü loosened his hold on Chi and remarked, 'Your teacher is Huang-po; I am not at all concerned with the whole business.'

Lin-chi returned to Huang-po who asked him, 'How is it that you are back so soon?'

'Because your kindness is much too grandmotherly.'

Huang-po said, 'When I see that fellow Tai-yü, I will give him twenty blows.'

'Don't wait to see him,' said Lin-chi, 'have it now!' So saying he gave the old master a hearty slap.

The old master laughed a hearty laugh.

What attracts our attention in the present case is Lin-chi's silence for three years, not knowing what to ask the master. This appears to me to be full of significance. Did he not come to Huang-po to study Zen Buddhism? If so, what had he been doing before the head-monk advised him to see the master? And why did he not know what to ask him? And finally what made him so thoroughly transformed after seeing Tai-yü? To my mind, Lin-chi's three years under Huang-po were spent in a vain attempt to grasp by thinking it out—the final truth of Zen. He knew full well that Zen was not to be understood by verbal means or by intellectual analysis, but still by thinking he strove for self-realization. He did not know what he was really seeking or where his mental efforts were to be directed. Indeed, if he had known the what and the where, it would have to be said that he was already in possession of something definite, and one who is in possession of something definite is not far from truly understanding Zen.

It was when Lin-chi was in this troubled state of mind, wandering about on his spiritual pilgrimage, that the head-monk from his own experience perceived that the time had come for him to give some timely advice to this worn-out truth-seeker. He gave Lin-chi an index whereby he might successfully reach the goal. When Chi was roughly handled by Huang-po, he was not surprised, nor was he angered; he simply failed to understand what the blows indicated and was grieved. On his way to Tai-yü he must have pondered the subject with all the mental powers at his command. Before he was told to ask the master concerning the ultimate truth of Buddhism, his troubled mind was reaching out for something to lean on; his arms, as it were, were stretched out in every direction to grasp something in the dark. When he was in this desperate situation, a pointer came to him in the form of 'thirty blows', and Tai-yü's remark about 'a kind-hearted dotard master', which finally led him to grasp the object at which all the pointers had been directed. If it had not been for the three years of intense mental application and spiritual turmoil and vain search for the truth, this crisis could never have been reached. So many conflicting ideas, lined with different shades of feelings, had been in *mêlée*, but suddenly their tangled skein was loosened and arranged itself in a new and harmonious order.

## 5. *Factors Determining the Zen Experience*

From the above examples chosen rather at random from the earlier history of Zen in China, I wish to observe the following main facts concerning the Zen experience: (1) There is a preliminary intellectual equipment for the maturing of Zen-consciousness; (2) There is a strong desire to transcend oneself, by which is meant that the true student of Zen must aspire to go beyond all the limitations that are imposed upon him as an individual being; (3) A master's guiding hand is generally found there to open the way for the struggling soul; and (4) A final upheaval takes place from an unknown region, which goes under the name of 'satori'.

1. That the content of the Zen experience is largely intellectual is easily recognizable, and also that it shows a decided non-theistic or pantheistic tendency, if the theological terms, though with a great deal of reservation, are at all applicable here. Bodhidharma's demand: 'Bring your own soul and I will have it pacified'; Hui-nêng's, 'Think not of good, nor of evil, and at that very moment what are your original features?'; Nan-yüeh's, 'When it is said to be a somewhat, one altogether misses the mark'; Ma-tsu's, 'I will tell you what, when you drink up in one draught all the water of the Western Lake'—all these utterances are characteristically non-sentimental, 'non-religious', and, if anything, simply highly enigmatical, and to a certain extent intellectual, though of course not in the technical sense. Compared with such Christian expressions as 'the glory of God', 'love of God', 'the Divine Bride', etc., the Zen experience must be judged as singularly devoid of human emotions. There is in it, on the contrary, something that may be termed cold scientific evidence or matter-of-factness. Thus in the Zen consciousness we can almost say that what corresponds to the Christian ardour for a personal God is lacking.

The Zen followers are not apparently concerned with

'trespasses', 'repentance', 'forgiveness', etc. Their mentality is more of a metaphysical type, but their metaphysics consists not of abstractions, logical acuteness, and hair-splitting analysis, but of practical wisdom and concrete sense-facts. And this is where Chinese Zen specifically differs from Indian Mahāyāna Dhyāna. Hui-nêng is generally considered, as was mentioned before, not to be especially scholarly, but his mind must have been metaphysical enough to have grasped the import of the *Vajracchedikā*, which is brimful of high-sounding metaphysical assertions. When he understood the *Prajñāpāramitā Sūtra*, the highly philosophical truth contained in it was turned into the practical question of 'Your original features even prior to your birth', and then into Ma-tsu's 'drinking up the whole river in one draught', etc.

That Zen masters were invariably students of philosophy in its broadest sense, Buddhist or otherwise, before their attention was directed to Zen, is suggestive. I say here 'Buddhist philosophy' but it is not philosophy in the strict sense of the term, for it is not the result of reasoning; especially such a doctrine as that of Emptiness is not at all the outcome of intellectual reflection, but simply the statement of direct perception in which the mind grasps the true nature of existence without the intermediary of logic. In this way '*sarvadharmānāṁ śūnyatā*' is declared.

Those who study Buddhism only from its 'metaphysical' side forget that this is no more than deep insight, that it is based on experience, and not the product of abstract analysis. Therefore, when a real truth-seeker studies such sūtras as the *Lankāvatāra* or the *Vajracchedikā*, he cannot lightly pass over those assertions which are made here so audaciously and unconditionally; in fact he is dazzled, taken aback, or becomes frightened. But still there is a certain power in them which attracts him in spite of himself. He begins to think about them, he desires to come in direct touch with the truth itself, so that he knows that he has seen the fact with his own eyes. Ordinary books of philosophy do not lead one to this intuition because they are no more than philosophy; whatever truth philosophy teaches is exhausted within itself, and fails to open up a new vista for the student. But in the study of Buddhist sūtras which contain the utterances of the deepest religious minds, one is inwardly drawn into the deeper recesses of consciousness; and finally one becomes convinced that those utterances really touch the ground of Reality.

What one thinks or reads is always qualified by the preposition 'of', or 'about', and does not give us the thing itself. Not mere talk about water, nor the mere sight of a spring, but an actual mouthful of it gives the thirsty complete satisfaction. But a first acquaintance with the sūtras is needed to see the way pointed and know where to look for the thing itself. Without this pointing we may be at a loss how and where to concentrate our efforts. Therefore say the sūtras, 'I am both the director [or leader] and the truth itself.'

We can thus see that the antecedent that leads to the Zen experience is not adoration, obedience, fear, love, faith, penitence, or anything that usually characterizes a good Christian soul; but it is a search for something that will give mental peace and harmony by overruling contradictions and joining tangled threads into one continuous line. Every Zen aspirant feels this constant and intense seeking for mental peace and wholeness. He generally manages to have an intellectual understanding of some sort concerning himself and the world, but this invariably fails to satisfy him thoroughly, and he feels an urge to go on deeper so that the solid ground of Reality is finally reached.

Tê-shan, for example, was content with a conceptual grasp of the doctrine of Emptiness while he was studying the *Prajñāpāramitā*, but when he heard of the southern teaching his peace was disturbed. His apparent motive for going down to the South was to smash the heretical Zen, but he must have felt all the time a hidden sense of uneasiness in his deeper consciousness though he was apparently determined to suppress the feeling by his reasoning. He failed in this, for the thing which he wished to suppress suddenly raised its head, perhaps to his great discomfort, when he was challenged by the woman-keeper of the tea-house. Finally, at Lung-t'an the blowing-out of a lighted candle placed him where he was to be from the very beginning. Consciously, he never had any idea as to this final outcome, for nothing could be planned out in this matter of Zen experience. After this, that is, after the attainment of Zen intuition, the swinging of a staff was thought by him to be the only necessary thing in directing his followers to the experience of Zen.

He never prayed, he never asked for the forgiveness of his sins, he never practised anything that popularly goes under the name of religious deeds;[1] for the bowing to the Buddha,[2] the offering of incense, the reading of the sūtras, and saying the Nembutsu[3]—these were practised just because they had been practised by all the Buddhas, and manifestly for no other reason. This attitude of the Zen master is evidenced by the remarks of Huang-po[4] when he was asked as to the reason of these pious acts.

2. This intense seeking[5] is the driving force of Zen consciousness. 'Ask and it shall be given you; seek and ye shall find; knock and it shall be opened unto you.' This is also the practical instruction leading up to the Zen experience. But as this asking or seeking is altogether subjective and the biographical records of Zen do not give much information in this regard, especially in the earlier periods of Zen history, its importance is to be inferred from various circumstances connected with the experience. The presence and intensity of this seeking or inquiring spirit was

[1] When Chao-chou was asked what constituted the deeds to be properly performed by a monk, he said, 'Be detached from the deeds.'

[2] A monk came to Chao-chou and said, 'I am going as a pilgrim to the South, and what advice would you be good enough to give?' Said the master, 'If you go south, pass quickly away from where the Buddha is, nor do you stay where there is no Buddha.'

[3] A monk asked Ta-kuan of Chin-shan, 'Do you ever practise the *Nembutsu* ("reciting the name of the Buddha")?' The master replied, 'No, I never do.' 'Why do you not?' 'For I am afraid of polluting the mouth.'

[4] For Yao-shan's remark see elsewhere.

[5] This 'seeking' is technically known as *kufū* in Japanese and *kung-fu* in Chinese.

58

visible in Hui-k'ê when he was said to have stood for some time in the snow; so great was his desire to learn the truth of Zen. The biographers of Hui-nêng emphasize his lack of learning, make much of his poem on 'Emptiness', and neglect to depict his inner life during the months he was engaged in cleaning rice. His long and hazardous travelling from the south to the monastery where Hung-jên resided must have been a great undertaking in those days, the more so when we know that he was only a poor farmer's boy. His reading of the *Vajracchedikā*, or his listening to it as recorded in his biography, must have stirred up a very strong desire to know really what it all meant. Otherwise, he would not have dared such a venturesome journey; and thus, while working in the granary his mind must have been in a great state of spiritual excitement, being most intensely engaged in the search for truth.

In the case of Lin-chi, he did not even know what to ask of the master. If he had known, things would have gone probably much easier with him. He knew that there was something wrong with him, for he felt dissatisfied with himself; he was searching for some unknown reality, he knew not what. If he could define it, this meant that he had already come to its solution. His mind was just one great question-mark with no special object; as his mind was, so was the universe; just the mark, and nowhere to affix it, as there was yet nothing definite anywhere.

This groping in the dark must have lasted for some time in a most desperate manner. It was indeed this very state of mind that made him ignorant as to what specific question he might place before his master. He was not in this respect like Hui-nêng who already had a definite proposition to solve, even before he came to Hung-jên; for his problem had been the understanding of the *Vajracchedikā*. Hui-nêng's mind was perhaps the simpler and broader, while Lin-chi like Hui-k'ê was already too intellectually 'tainted', as it were; and all they felt was a general uneasiness of mind, as they knew not how to cut asunder all the entanglements which were made worse by their very learning. When the head-monk told Lin-chi to ask the master about 'the fundamental principle of Buddhism', it was a great help indeed, for now he had something definite to take hold of. His general mental uneasiness was brought to an acute point, especially when he was repulsed with 'thirty blows'. The fruit of his mental seeking was maturing and ready to fall on the ground.

The final shaking—quite a severe one, it must be admitted—was given by Huang-po. Between this shaking and the final fall under Tai-yü, Lin-chi's question-mark pointed to one concrete fact where all his three years of accumulated efforts were most intensely concentrated. Without this concentration he could not have exclaimed, 'There is not much after all in the Buddhism of Huang-po!'

It may not be inopportune to say a few words concerning auto-suggestion with which the Zen experience is often confused. In auto-suggestion there is no intellectual antecedent, nor is there any intense seeking for something, accompanied by an acute feeling of uneasiness. In auto-suggestion a definite proposition is given to the subject, which is accepted by him unquestioningly and whole-heartedly. He has a certain practical result in view, which he desires to produce in himself by accepting the proposition. Everything is here from the first determined, prescribed, and suggested.

In Zen there is an intellectual quest for ultimate truth which the intellect fails to satisfy; the subject is urged to dive deeper under the waves of the empirical consciousness. This diving is beset with difficulties because he does not know how and where to dive. He is at a complete loss as to how to get along, until suddenly he somehow hits a spot that opens up a new field of vision. This mental *impasse*, accompanied by a steady, untiring, and whole-hearted 'knocking', is a most necessary stage leading to the Zen experience. Something of the psychology of auto-suggestion may be working here as far as its mechanical process is concerned, but the entire form into which this psychology is fitted to work is *toto caelo* different from what is ordinarily understood by that term.

The metaphysical quest which was designated as an intellectual antecedent of Zen consciousness opens up a new course in the life of a Zen student. The quest is attended by an intense feeling of uneasiness, or one can say that the feeling is intellectually interpreted as a quest. Whether the quest is emotionally the sense of unrest, or whether the unrest is intellectually a seeking for something definite—in either case the whole being of the individual is bent on finding something upon which he may peacefully rest. The searching mind is vexed to the extreme as its fruitless strivings go on, but when it is brought up to an apex it breaks or it explodes and the whole structure of consciousness assumes an entirely different aspect. This is the Zen experience. The quest, the search, the ripening, and the explosion—thus proceeds the experience.

This seeking or quest is generally done in the form of meditation which is less intellectual (*vipaśyanā*) than concentrative (*dhyāna*). The sitter sits cross-legged after the Indian fashion as directed in the tract called *Tso-ch'an I*, 'How to sit and meditate.'

In this position, which is regarded by Indians and Buddhists generally as being the best bodily position to be assumed by the Yogins, the seeker concentrates all his mental energy in the effort to get out of this mental *impasse* into which he had been led. As the intellect has proved itself unable to achieve this end, the seeker has to call upon another power if he can find one. The intellect knows how to get him into this *cul-de-sac*, but it is singularly unable to get him out of it.

At first the seeker knows of no way of escape, but get out he must by some means, be they good or bad. He has reached the end of the passage and before him there yawns a dark abyss. There is no light to show him a possible way to cross it, nor is he aware of any way of turning back. He is simply compelled to go ahead. The only thing he can do in this crisis is simply to jump, into life or death. Perhaps it means certain death, but living he feels to be no longer possible. He is desperate, and yet something is still holding him back; he cannot quite give himself up to the unknown.

When he reaches this stage of Dhyāna, all abstract reasoning ceases; for thinker and thought no longer stand contrasted. His whole being, if we may say so, is thought itself. Or perhaps it is better to say that his whole being is 'no-thought' (*acitta*). We can no longer describe this state of consciousness in terms of logic or psychology. Here begins a new world of personal experiences, which we may designate 'leaping', or 'throwing oneself down the precipice'. The period of incubation has come to an end.

It is to be distinctly understood that this period of incubation, which intervenes between the metaphysical quest and the Zen experience proper, is not one of passive quietness but of intense strenuousness, in which the entire consciousness is concentrated at one point. Until the entire consciousness really gains this point, it keeps up an arduous fight against all intruding ideas. It may not be conscious of the fighting, but an intense seeking, or a steady looking-down into the abysmal darkness, is no less than that. The one-pointed concentration (*ekāgra*) is realized when the inner mechanism is ripe for the final catastrophe. This takes place, if seen only superficially, by accident, that is, when there is a knocking at the eardrums, or when some words are uttered, or when some unexpected event takes place, that is to say, when a perception of some kind goes on.

We may say that here a perception takes place in its purest and simplest form, where it is not at all tainted by intellectual analysis or conceptual reflection. But an epistemological interpretation of Zen experience does not interest the Zen Yogin, for he is ever intent upon truly understanding the meaning of Buddhist teachings, such as the doctrine of Emptiness or the original purity of the Dharmakāya, and thereby gaining peace of mind.

3. When the intensification of Zen consciousness is going on, the master's guiding hand is found helpful to bring about the final explosion. As in the case of Lin-chi, who did

not even know what question to ask of Huang-po, a student of Zen is frequently at a loss what to do with himself. If he is allowed to go on like this, the mental distraction may end disastrously. Or his experience may fail to attain its final goal, since it is liable to stop short before it reaches the stage of the fullest maturity. As frequently happens, the Yogin remains satisfied with an intermediate stage, which from his ignorance he takes for finality. The master is needed not only for encouraging the student to continue his upward steps but to point out to him where his goal lies.

As to the pointing, it is no pointing as far as its intelligibility is considered. Huang-po gave Lin-chi 'thirty blows', Lung-t'an blew out the candle, and Hui-nêng demanded Ming's original form even before he was born. Logically, all these pointers have no sense, they are beyond rational treatment. We can say that the pointers have no earthly use as they do not give us any clue from which we can start our inference. But inasmuch as Zen has nothing to do with ratiocination, the pointing need not be a pointing in its ordinary sense. A slap on the face, a shaking one by the shoulder, or an utterance will most assuredly do the work of pointing when the Zen consciousness has attained a certain stage of maturity.

The maturing on the one hand, therefore, and the pointing on the other must be timely; if the one is not quite matured, or if the other fails to do the pointing, the desired end may never be experienced. When the chick is ready to come out of the egg-shell, the mother hen knows and pecks at it, and lo, there jumps out a second generation of the chicken family.

We can probably state in this connection that this pointing or guiding, together with the preliminary more or less philosophical equipment of the Zen Yogin, determines the content of his Zen consciousness, and that when it is brought up to a state of full maturity it inevitably breaks out as Zen experience. In this case, the experience itself, if we can have it in its purest and most original form, may be said to be something entirely devoid of colourings of any sort,

# BODHIDHARMA

By JASOKU
(*Died 1483*)

This is a triptych of Bodhidharma, with Lin-chi and Tê-shan. Bodhidharma has been always the most favourite subject of painting or drawing for Zen masters of all ages, with or without any artistic impulse. The object they have in sketching him is not necessarily to delineate the historical personage artistically as the term is generally understood; it is to visualise a figure with brush-strokes, which is symbolically expressive of an intense will-power directed concentratively towards the attainment of a certain spiritual condition. One aspect of the Zen life may be said to consist in disciplining our will-power to the of the Zen life may be said to consist in disciplining our will-power to the highest notch. The will is the essence of personality; to be a person means to have free will; the value of the individual, if anywhere, lies in conation. Zen thus being a religion of the will in one sense has naturally come to have its founder represented in the way he is.

Tê-shan is noted, as we have already seen, for his freely swinging a stick (*pang*). Here he has not yet used it, but apparently he is ready to do so at any moment. His intense looking, as it were, into the vacuity of space and the converging of the energetic lines portend what is about to come.

Lin-chi has already given out his ejaculation, "*kwatü!*", which must have broken to pieces all the outer casings, in which securely and snugly enveloped, we imagine we see final Reality. Notice the strong, short, agitated lines of his garment, which vividly contrast with the calmly flowering ones of Bodhidharma's.

Jasoku, the artist, is said to have studied Zen under Ikkyü, who is a well-known character in the history of Japanese Zen.

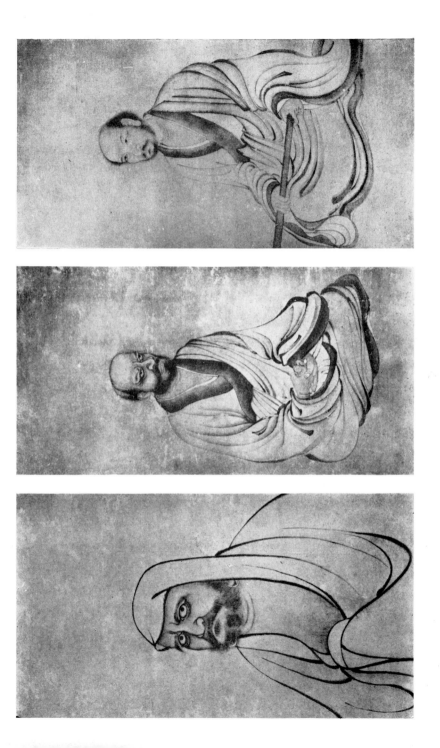

# TWO ZEN FATHERS IN MEDITATION

By SHIH-K'E
(*Xth Century*)

Shih-k'ê is the author of these two remarkable pictures of two Zen fathers who are deeply absorbed in meditation. The work, according to the inscription, was done in A.D. 963. Apart from their artistic significance, we are strongly impressed with the effect, which is wonderfully produced by these few fantastic, sweeping brush-strokes. They appear to have been executed in a most casual manner; but the inner spiritual force which is put forward by them, attempting to give an insight into Reality itself, is felt through the ensemble of those brush-strokes. The tiger itself is feeling the intensity of the thought which possesses the whole being of its master.

As is seen in Jasoku's "Sakya the Ascetic," Zen is an inner gazing into the abyss of being. Zen does not look outward, does not seek for a so-called objective reality, but it desires to reach the ground-floor of Reality, on which each individual has his absolute reason of being. It will be seen that Zen meditation is not "meditation", but an intense seeing into the suchness of things. This is what is known as an "inquiring spirit" among modern Zen masters.

It is interesting to observe that objects of nature, animate and inanimate, take part in Buddhist pictures. The tiger in this picture ceases to be a fierce beast of prey, which is ordinarily by all means to be dreaded and avoided. It comes frequently into the life of a Zen master. Fêng-kan whose picture is reproduced elsewhere is reported to have gone about always on the back of a tiger.

Buddhist or Christian, Taoist or Vedantist. The experience may thus be treated wholly as a psychological event which has nothing to do with philosophy, theology, or any special religious teaching. But the point is whether, if there were no philosophical antecedent or religious aspiration or spiritual unrest, the experience could take place merely as a fact of consciousness.

The psychology, then, cannot be treated independently of philosophy or a definite set of religious teachings. That the Zen experience takes place at all as such, and is formulated finally as a system of Zen intuitions, is principally due to the master's guiding, however enigmatical it may seem; for without it the experience itself is impossible.

This explains why the confirmation of the master is needed regarding the orthodoxy of the Zen experience, and also why the history of Zen places so much stress on the orthodox transmission of it. So we read in the *Platform Sūtra* of Hui-nêng:

'Hsüan-chiao (*d.* A.D. 713)[1] was particularly conversant with the teaching of the T'ien-tai school on tranquillization (*śamatha*) and contemplation (*vipaśyanā*). While reading the *Vimalakīrti*, he attained an insight into the ground of consciousness. Hsüan-t'sê, a disciple of the patriarch, happened to call on him. They talked absorbingly on Buddhism, and Hsüan-t'sê found that Hsüan-chiao's remarks were in complete agreement with those of the Zen Fathers, though Chiao himself was not conscious of it. T'sê asked, "Who is your teacher in the Dharma?" Chia replied: "As regards my understanding of the sūtras of the Vaipulya class I have for each its regularly authorized teacher. Later while studying the *Vimalakīrti*, by myself I gained an insight into the teaching of the Buddha-mind, but I have nobody yet to confirm my view." T'sê said, "No confirmation is needed prior to Bhīshmasvara-rāja,[2] but after him those who have

---

[1] *See* First Series, p. 223.

[2] *Wei-yin-wang.* This may be considered to mean 'prior to the dawn of consciousness' or 'the time before any systematic teaching of religion started'.

satori by themselves with no master belong to the naturalistic school of heterodoxy." Chiao asked "Pray you testify." T'sê said, however: "My words do not carry much weight. At T'sao-ch'i the Sixth Patriarch is residing now, and people crowd upon him from all quarters to receive instruction in the Dharma. Let us go over to him". . . .'[1]

4. If the intensified Zen consciousness does not break out into the state of satori, we can say that the intensification has not yet attained its highest point; for when it does there is no other way left to it than to come to the final *dénouement* known as satori. This fact, as we have already seen, has been specially noticed by Tai-hui as characterizing the Zen experience. For, according to him, there is no Zen where there is no satori. That satori came to be recognized thus as the Zen experience *par excellence* at the time of Tai-hui and even previously, and that Tai-hui and his school had to uphold it so strongly against some tendencies which grew up among Zen followers and threatened to undermine the life of Zen, prove that the development of the koan exercise was something inevitable in the history of Zen consciousness—so inevitable indeed that if this failed to develop Zen itself would have ceased to exist.

6. *The Psychological Antecedent and the Content of the Zen Experience*

Since the early days of Zen, its practice has been mistakenly regarded as that of mere quietism or a kind of technics of mental tranquillization. Hence Hui-nêng's expostulation about it and Nan-yüeh's warning to Ma-tsu.[2] The sitting cross-legged is the form of Zen, while inwardly the Zen consciousness is to be nursed to maturity. When it is fully matured, it is sure to break out as satori, which is an

---

[1] This whole passage does not occur in the Tun-huang MS. It is probable that it was added at a much later date. But this fact does not affect the force of the argument advanced by Hsüan-t'sê.

[2] First Series, p. 236 *ff.*

insight into the Unconscious. There is something noetic in the Zen experience, and this is what determines the entire course of Zen discipline. Tai-hui was fully conscious of this fact and was never tired of upholding it against the other school.

That satori or Zen experience is not the outcome of quiet-sitting or mere passivity, with which Zen discipline has been confused very much even by the followers of Zen themselves, can be inferred from the utterances or gestures that follow the final event. How shall we interpret Lin-chi's utterance, 'There is not much in the Buddhism of Huang-po'? Again, how about his punching the ribs of Tai-yü? These evidently show that there was something active and noetic in his experience. He actually grasped something that met his approval.

There is no doubt that he found what he had all the time been searching for, although at the moment when he began his searching he had no idea of what it meant—for how could he? If he remained altogether passive, he could never have made such a positive assertion. As to his gesture, how self-assuring it was, which grew out of his absolute conviction! There is nothing whatever passive about it.[1]

The situation is well described by Dai-o Kokushi when he says: 'By a "special transmission outside the sūtra-teaching" is meant to understand penetratingly just one

[1] One day St. Francis was sitting with his companions when he began to groan and said, 'There is hardly a monk on earth who perfectly obeys his superior.' His companions much astonished said, 'Explain to us, Father, what is perfect and supreme obedience.' Then, comparing him who obeys to a corpse, he said: 'Take a dead body and put it where you will, it will make no resistance: when it is in one place it will not murmur; when you take it away from there it will not object; put it in a pulpit, it will not look up but look down; wrap it in purple and it will only look doubly pale.' (Paul Sabatier's *Life of St. Francis*, pp. 260-1.) While it is difficult to tell what is the real purport of this, it may appear as if St. Francis wished his monks to be literally like a corpse; but there is something humorous about the remark when he says, 'Put it in a pulpit. . . .' The Zen Buddhist would interpret it as meaning to keep one's mind in a perfect state of perspicuity which perceives a flower as red and a willow-tree as green, without putting anything of its own confused subjectivity into it. A state of passivity, indeed, and yet there is also fullness of activity in it. A form of passive activity, we may call it.

phrase by breaking both the mirror and the image, by transcending all forms of ideation, by making no distinction whatever between confusion and enlightenment, by paying no attention to the presence or the absence of a thought, by neither getting attached to nor keeping oneself away from the dualism of good and bad. The one phrase which the follower of Zen is asked to ponder (*kung-fu*) and find the final solution of is "Your own original features even before you were born of your parents."

'In answering this one ought not to cogitate on the meaning of the phrase, nor try to get away from it; do not reason about it, nor altogether abandon reasoning; respond just as you are asked and without deliberation, just as a bell rings when it is struck, just as a man answers when he is called by name. If there were no seeking, no pondering, no contriving as to how to get at the meaning of the phrase, whatever it may be, there would be no answering—hence no awakening.'

While it is difficult to determine the content of Zen experience merely by means of those utterances and gestures which involuntarily follow the experience—which is, indeed, a study in itself—I give in the appendices some of them which are culled indiscriminately from the history of Zen.[1] Judging from these utterances, we can see that all these authors have had an inner perception, which put an end to whatever doubts and mental anxieties from which they may have been suffering; and further, that the nature of this inner perception did not allow itself to be syllogistically treated, as it had no logical connection with what has preceded it.

Satori as a rule expresses itself in words which are not intelligble to the ordinary mind; sometimes the expression is merely descriptive of the experience-feeling, which naturally means nothing to those who have never had such feelings within themselves. So far as the intellect is con-

---

[1] Some have already been given in my *Essays in Zen Buddhism*, Vol. 1, pp. 248 *et seq.*, where I have collected more of these utterances as they stand in the original.

cerned, there is an unsurpassable gap between the antecedent problem and its consequent solution; the two are left logically unconnected. When Lin-chi asked about the ultimate principle of Buddhism, he was given thirty blows by his master Huang-po. After he had attained satori and understood the meaning of his experience, he merely said, 'There is not much in Huang-po's Buddhism.' We are left ignorant as to what this 'not much' really is. When this 'what' was demanded by Tai-yü, Lin-chi simply poked his ribs.

These gestures and utterances do not give the outsider any clue to the content of the experience itself. They seem to be talking in signs. This logical discontinuity or discreteness is characteristic of all Zen teaching. When Ch'ing-ping[1] was asked what the Mahāyāna was, he said, 'The bucket-rope.' When asked about the Hīnayāna, he replied: 'The coin-string'; about the moral impurities (*āsrava*), 'The bamboo-basket'; about the moral purities (*anāsrava*), 'The wooden dipper'. These answers are apparently nonsensical, but from the Zen point of view they are easily digested, for the logical discontinuity is thereby bridged over. The Zen experience evidently opens a closed door revealing all the treasures behind it. It suddenly leaps over to the other side of logic and starts a dialectics of its own.

Psychologically, this is accomplished when what is known as 'abandonment', 'or 'throwing oneself over the precipice', takes place. This 'abandonment' means the moral courage of taking risks; it is plunging into the unknown which lies beyond the topography of relative knowledge. This unknown realm of logical discontinuity must be explored personally; and this is where logic turns into psychology, it is where conceptualism has to give way to life-experience.

We cannot, however, 'abandon' ourselves just because we wish to do so. It may seem an easy thing to do, but after all it is the last thing any being can do, for it is done only when we are most thoroughly convinced that there is no

---

[1] *Ch'ing-ping ling-tsun*, 845–919. As regards his interview with *T'sui-wei*, see elsewhere.

other way to meet the situation. We are always conscious of a tie, slender enough to be sure, but how strong when we try to cut it off! It is always holding us back when we wish to throw ourselves at the feet of an all-merciful One, or when we are urged to identify ourselves with a noble cause or anything that is grander than mere selfishness. Before being able to do this there must be a great deal of 'searching', or 'contriving', or 'pondering'.[1] It is only when this process is brought to maturity that this 'abandoning' can take place. We can say that this 'contriving' is a form of purgation.

When all the traces of egotism are purged away, when the will-to-live is effectively put down, when the intellect gives up its hold on the discrimination between subject and object, then all the contrivances cease, the purgation is achieved, and the 'abandonment' is ready to take place.[2]

All Zen masters are, therefore, quite emphatic about completing the whole process of 'contriving and searching'. For an abandonment to be thoroughgoing, it is necessary for the preliminary process to be also thoroughgoing. The masters all teach the necessity of going on with this 'searching' as if one were fighting against a deadly enemy, or 'as if a poisonous arrow were piercing a vital part of the body, or as if one were surrounded on all sides by raging flames, or as if one had lost both his parents, or as if one were disgraced owing to one's inability to pay off a debt of a thousand pieces of gold'.

Shōichi Kōkushi, the founder of Tōfukuji monastery, advises one to 'think yourself to be down an old deep well; the only thought you then have will be to get out of it, and

---

[1] The Christians would say, 'a great deal of seeking, asking, and knocking'.

[2] James gives in his *Varieties of Religious Experience* (pp. 321 *ff.*) the story of Antoinette Bourignon, who, finding her spiritual obstacle in the possession of a penny, threw it away and started her long spiritual journey thus absolutely free from earthly cares. 'A penny' is the symbol of the last thread of egotism which so effectively ties us up to a world of relativity. Slender though the thread is, it is sufficiently strong for all of us. The cutter is given to the student of Zen in the shape of a koan, as will be seen later on.

71

you will be desperately engaged in finding a way of escape; from morning to evening this one thought will occupy the entire field of your consciousness'. When one's mind is so fully occupied with one single thought, strangely or miraculously there takes place a sudden awakening within oneself. All the 'searching and contriving' ceases, and with it comes the feeling that what was wanted is here, that all is well with the world and with oneself, and that the problem is now for the first time successfully and satisfactorily solved. The Chinese have the saying, 'When you are in an *impasse*, there is an opening.' The Christians teach, 'Man's extremity is God's opportunity.'

The main thing to do when a man finds himself in this mental extremity is to exhaust all his powers of 'searching and contriving', which means to concentrate all his energy on one single point and see the farthest reach he can make in this frontal attack. Whether he is pondering a knotty problem of philosophy, or mathematics, or contriving a means of escape from oppressive conditions, or seeking a passage of liberation from an apparently hopeless situation, his empirical mind, psychologically speaking, is taxed to its limit of energy; but when the limit is transcended a new source of energy in one form or another is tapped.

Physically, an extraordinary amount of strength or endurance is exhibited to the surprise of the man himself; morally, often on a battlefield a soldier manifests great courage, performing deeds of audacity; intellectually, a philosopher, if he is a really great one, clears up a new way of looking at Reality; religiously, we have such spiritual phenomena as conversion, conformation, reformation, salvation to the Christians, and satori, enlightenment, intuition, *parāvṛitti*, etc., to the Buddhists.

All these various orders of phenomena are explainable, as far as psychology goes, by the same law; accumulation, saturation, and explosion. But what is peculiar to the religious experience is that it involves the whole being of the individual, that it affects the very foundation of his character. And besides, the content of this experience may be described in the terminology of either Christian faith or Buddhist philosophy, according to the nature of its antecedents, or according to the surroundings and education of the particular individual concerned. That is, he interprets the experience in conformity to his own intellectual resources, and to him this interpretation is the best and the only plausible one to be given to the facts in hand.

He cannot accept them in any other light, for to do so will be the same as rejecting them as illusive and devoid of meaning. As Buddhism has no such creeds as are cherished by Christians, who are Christians because of their intellectually conforming themselves to the theology and tradition of their forefathers, Buddhists give their religious experience an altogether different colouring. Especially to Zen followers such terms as divine grace, revelation, mystic union, etc., are foreign and sound quite unfamiliar. No matter how closely psychologically related one experience may be to the other, Buddhist or Christian, it begins to vary widely as soon as it is subsumed under categories of the Christian or the Buddhist ideology.

As stated before, the antecedents of the experience are thus designated by Zen masters altogether differently from those of the Christian mystics. Stigmata, ligature, expurgation, road of the cross, the anguish of love, etc.—all such terms have no meaning in Zen experience. The antecedents required by the latter are concentration, accumulation, self-forgetting, throwing oneself down the precipice, going over to the other side of birth-and-death, leaping, abandonment, cutting off what precedes and what follows, etc. There is here absolutely nothing that may be called religious by those who are familiar only with the other set of phraseology.

To make clearer this psychological process of 'self-forgetting' and 'cutting off both the past and the future', let me cite some of the classical examples.

The monk Ting came to Lin-chi and asked, 'What is the essence of Buddhism?' Chi came down from his straw

73

chair, seized the monk, gave him a slap, and let him go. Ting stood still. A monk nearby said, 'O Ting, why don't you make a bow?' Ting was about to bow when he came to a realization.[1]

This is the brief statement in the language of Lin-chi of the event that happened to Ting. Brief though it is, we can gather from it all that is essential, all that we need to know concerning Ting's Zen experience. First of all, he did not come to Lin-chi casually. There is no doubt that his question was the outcome of a long pondering and an anxious search after the truth. Before the koan system was yet in vogue, Zen followers did not definitely know how to ask a question, as we saw in the case of Lin-chi.

Intellectual puzzles are everywhere, but the difficulty is to produce a question which is vital and on which depends the destiny of the questioner himself. When such a question is brought to light, the very asking is more than half the answering. Just a little movement on the part of the master may be sufficient to open up a new life in the questioner. The answer is not in the master's gesture or speech; it is in the questioner's own mind which is now awakened. When Ting asked the master about the essence of Buddhism, the question was no idle one; it came out of his inmost being, and he never expected to have it answered intellectually.

When he was seized and slapped by the master, he was probably not at all surprised, in the sense that he was taken aback and at a loss what to do; but he was surprised in this sense that he was entirely put out of the beaten track of logic where he was most likely still lingering, although he was not conscious of it himself. He was carried away from the earth where he used to stand and to which he seemed to be inevitably bound; he was carried away he knew not where, only that he was now lost to the world and to himself. This was the meaning of his 'standing still'. All his former efforts to find an answer to his question were put to naught; he was at the edge of the precipice to which he clung with all his remaining strength, but the master

[1] *Lin-chi-lu.*

74

relentlessly pushed him over. Even when he heard the voice of the attending monk calling out to him, he was not fully awakened from his stupefaction. It was only when he was about to make the usual bows that he recovered his sense— the sense in which logical discontinuity was bridged over and in which the answer to his question was experienced within himself—the sense in which he read the ultimate meaning of all existence, having nothing further to seek.

This *dénouement*, however, could not have been attained had it not been preceded by the regular course of concentration, accumulation, and abandonment. If Ting's question had been an abstract and conceptual one which had no roots in his very being, there could not have been truth and ultimacy in his understanding of the answer.

To give another illustration which will be illuminating when considered in connection with Ting, Yün-mên[1] (*d.* 949) was the founder of the school bearing his name. His first master was Mu-chou, who had urged Lin-chi to ask Huang-po concerning the essence of Buddhism. Mên was not satisfied with his knowledge of Buddhism which had been gained from books, and came to Mu-chou to have a final settlement of the intellectual balance-sheet with him. Seeing Mên approach the gate, Mu-chou shut it in his face. Mên could not understand what it all meant, but he knocked and a voice came from within:

'Who are you?'

'My name is Yün-mên. I come from Chih-hsing.'

'What do you want?'

'I am unable to see into the ground of my being and most earnestly wish to be enlightened.'

Mu-chou opened the gate, looked at Mên, and then closed it. Not knowing what to do, Mên went away. This was a great riddle, indeed, and some time later he came back to Mu-chou. But he was treated in the same way as before. When Yün-mên came for a third time to Mu-chou's gate, his mind was firmly made up, by whatever means, to have a talk with the master. This time as soon as the

[1] *Yün-mên lu.*

gate was opened he squeezed himself through the opening. The intruder was at once seized by the chest and the master demanded: 'Speak! Speak!' Mên was bewildered and hesitated. Chou, however, lost no time in pushing him out of the gate again, saying, 'You good-for-nothing fellow!' As the heavy gate swung shut, it caught one of Mên's legs, and he cried out: 'Oh! Oh!' But this opened his eyes to the significance of the whole proceeding.

It is easy to infer from this record that Yün-mên's Zen experience had a long and arduous preliminary course, although there is in the record no allusion to his psychological attitude towards the whole affair. His 'searching and contriving' did not of course begin with this experience; it came to an end when he called on Mu-chou. He knew no means of escape from the dilemma in which he found himself; his only hope was centred in Mu-chou. But what answer did he get from the master? To be looked at and shut out—what relation could this have to his earnest questioning about his inner self?

On his way home he must have pondered the new situation to the limit of his mental capacity. This pondering, this searching must have been intensified by his second visit to the master, and on the third visit it was fast approaching a culmination, and most naturally ended dramatically. When he was requested by Mu-chou to speak out if he had anything to say, to utter a word if there was something that required expression, his Zen consciousness became fully matured, and only a touch was needed to change it into an awakening. The needed touch came in the form of an intense physical pain. His cry, 'Oh! Oh!' was at the same time the cry of satori, an inner perception of his own being, whose depth now for the first time he has personally sounded so that he could really say, 'I know, for I am it!'

(This psychological process has been depicted here somewhat conjecturely, but it will grow more convincing later when the psychology of the koan exercise is described according to the various records left by the masters, and also according to the directions given by them to their devotees.)

## 7. Technique of Zen Discipline in its Early History

As can readily be conceived from the foregoing delinea-
tion of the satori psychology, it is, indeed, no easy task to
develop the Zen consciousness into this culminating stage.
In the early days of Zen Buddhism in China there were
enough original minds who looked for a first-hand experience, and who never flinched from the hazardous adventure
into the *terra incognita* of Zen mysticism.

The masters at that time had no special system for leading them to the final experience except giving them some
indications in gestures or words, both of which, being altogether unapproachable, repelled rather than attracted the
truth-seekers. The path was strewn with thistles and
brambles instead of flowers, and they had to risk so much
when they wandered out into it. It was, therefore, natural
that there were only a few out of the many disciples that
gathered about a master who attained satori. Out of the
five hundred or a thousand pupils that are said to have
come to a mountain monastery presided over by a fully-
qualified Zen master, there were less than ten whose eyes
were said to have been opened to gaze into the mysterious
values of Zen. Zen was an aristocratic form of Buddhism.
Its ideal was to have one great master-mind which towered
far above the ordinary, rather than to have many medio-
crities.

The masters thus made the path of Zen as steep and as
stormy as they could so that only the tough-hearted could
scale it to the summit. This was not intentional, of course,
on their part; they had no malicious or selfish will to keep
the treasure among themselves; they naturally wanted to
see their teaching embraced as widely as possible among
their fellow-beings; they never seemed to get tired in its
propagation, but when they wanted to be true to their insight they could not stoop to appeal to popular taste, that is,
they could not give up their vocation for mere reputation
and cheap appreciation. Ching-t'sên of Chang-sha used to

*Cherishors*

say that, 'If I were to demonstrate the truth of Zen in its absolute aspect, the front court of my monastery would see weeds growing rampant.'

On the other hand, the world is generally filled with imitators, counterfeiters, dealers in second-hand articles, this not only in the commercial world but in religious circles also. Perhaps more so in the latter, because here it is less easy to distinguish the genuine from the spurious. When other practical circumstances are added to the difficulties inherent in Zen which make for its exclusion, solitude, and gradual disappearance from the world, we can see how mortified the masters must have been over the actual situation in which they often found themselves. That is, they could not sit quiet in their mountain retreats and watch the declining of the Zen spirit. There were imitators enough who swallowed the literature and left the spirit behind. *Christians*

Moreover, since Hui-nêng, the sixth patriarch, there had been a steady growth of Zen literature, and the way in which Zen expressed itself grew more delicate, subtle, and varied. Gradually the one school of Hui-nêng divided itself into several branches so that in early Sung, that is, in the eleventh century, there were five of them flourishing. The time was fast approaching when Zen masters were not content just to wait and see Zen consciousness develop of its own accord. They recognized the need of some system to accelerate the development and to effect its healthful propagation and continued prosperity. They thought it was their duty to see that their Zen experience be successively transmitted from master to disciple without interruption. But before we speak of the development of this system let us first see how Zen was taught in the early days of its history.

As we know already from the examples of Lin-chi, Yün-mên, the monk Ting, and Tê-shan, the master had no special contrivance or method by which the mind of the disciple could be matured for the experience. Each no doubt occasionally gave sermons and discourses on Zen in his Dharma Hall; he also demonstrated it in most practical ways for the sake of his disciples. Zen was not a conceptual plaything with them but a vital fact which intimately concerned life itself—even in raising a finger, in sipping a cup of tea, in exchanging greetings, and so on. And to awaken the consciousness of his disciples to the truth of Zen, it was most natural for the masters to make use of every opportunity in their daily life. The following interviews recorded of the ancient masters[1] will fully illustrate what I mean.

When Hui-nêng saw Nan-yüeh approach, he asked:
'Whence comest thou?'
'I come from Tung-shan.'
'What is it that thus cometh?'

It took Nan-yüeh six years to solve this object lesson and say, 'Even when it is said to be something, the mark is already missed!'

A monk came to Ch'i-an of Yen-kuan and asked, 'Who is Vairocana Buddha?'
Said the master, 'Kindly pass that pitcher over here.'
The monk took it to the master, who then asked the monk to put it back where he got it from. He did so and then asked the master again about the Buddha.
The master replied, 'Long gone is he!'

Wu-yeh of Fêng-chou was a stalwart, athletic monk. When he came to Ma-tsu the latter remarked:
'What a magnificent structure with no Buddha in it!'
Wu-yeh made a bow and said, 'As to the literature of the Triple Vehicle, I have a general knowledge of it, but I have not yet been able to understand the teaching of Zen according to which mind is the Buddha.'
Replied the master, 'The mind that does not understand is the Buddha; there is no other.'
Yeh asked again: 'The First Patriarch is said to have brought a secret message from India. What was it?'
Ma-tsu said, 'Monk, I am very busy just now, you may come some other time.'

[1] From the *Chuan-têng-lu.*

# SÁKYA AS ASCETIC

## Ascribed to JASOKU SOGA

The verse by Ikkyü (1394–1481):

"For six years he has fought with cold and hunger which
     has penetrated even to the marrow of his bones;
Self-mortification is the most profound teaching of the
     Buddhas and Patriarchs.
Believe me, there is no Sakya nature-made,
The masters of the world are also rice-bags [when left
     to themselves]."

*Ikkyu Sojun*

*One early autumn day, the second year of
     Kosho (A.D. 1456).*

By "Self-mortification" Ikkyu no doubt means the intensification of "an inquiring spirit," for mere asceticism will be of no avail in the study of Zen. "Rice-bags," even as well are, turn into Buddhas, when the inner spirit asserts itself in spite of all its encumbrances and obstructions, which are imposed on us in the form of mind and matter.

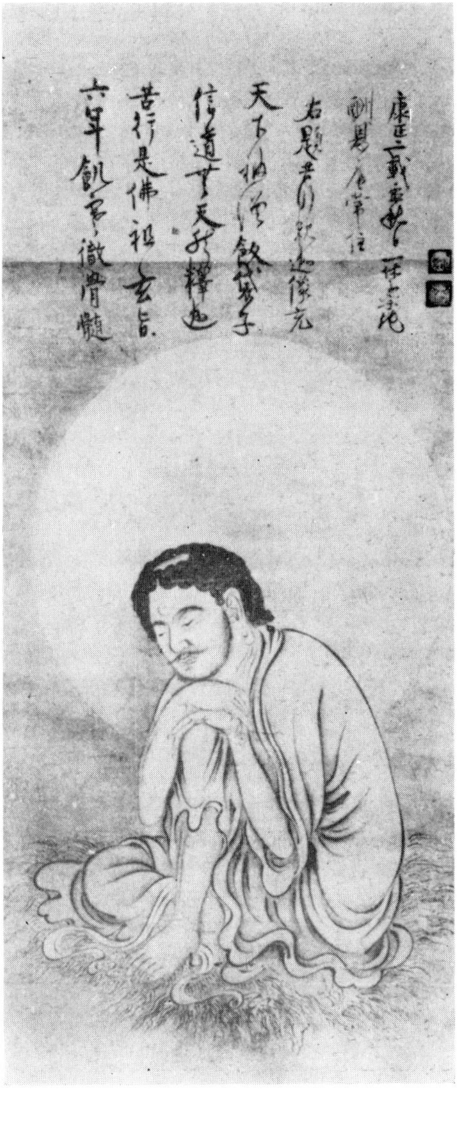
苦行是佛祖玄旨
六年飢寒徹骨髓

# SHIH-KUNG AND SAN-PING

## By Motonobu Kano

Shih-kung was a hunter before he was ordained as a Zen monk under Ma-tsu. He disliked very much Buddhist monks who were against his profession. One day while chasing a deer he passed by the cottage where Ma-tsu resided. Ma-tsu came out and greeted him. Shih-kung the hunter asked, "Did you see some deer pass by your door?"

"Who are you?" asked the master.

"I am a hunter."

"Do you know how to shoot?"

"Yes, I do."

"How many can you shoot down with one arrow?"

"One with one arrow."

"Then you do not understand how to shoot," declared Ma-tsu.

"You know how to shoot?" asked the hunter.

"Yes, most certainly."

"How many can you shoot down with one arrow?"

"I can shoot down the entire flock with one arrow."

"They are all living creatures; why should you destroy the whole flock at one shooting?"

"If you know that much, why don't you shoot yourself?"

"As to shooting myself, I do not know how to proceed."

"This fellow," exclaimed Ma-tsu, all of a sudden, "has put a stop today to all his past ignorance and evil passions!"

Thereupon, Shih-kung the hunter broke his bow and arrows and became Ma-tsu's pupil.

When he became a Zen master himself, he had a bow with an arrow ready to shoot, with which his monks were threatened when they approached him with a question. San-ping was one so treated. Shih-kung exclaimed, "Look out for the arrow!" Ping opened his chest and said, "This is the arrow that kills; where is the one that resuscitates?" Kung struck three times on the bow-string; Ping made a bow. Said Kung, "I have been using one bow and two arrows for the past thirty years, and today I have succeeded in shooting down only a half of a wise man." Shih-kung broke his bow and arrows once more, and never used them again.[1]

---

[1] *Chuan-téng Lu*, VI and XIV.

Yeh was about to leave the room when the master called out, 'O monk!'

Yeh turned back.

'What is it?' the master said.

This awakened Wu-yeh's mind to the full understanding of Zen, and he made his bows.

'O this stupid fellow! What is the use of your making bows?' were the master's last words.

Têng Yin-fêng[1] was standing beside Shih-t'ou who was cutting weeds. When Shih-t'ou moved a bundle of grass in front of Feng, the latter said:

'You only know how to cut this down, but not the other one.'

Shih-t'ou held up the sickle.

Fêng snatched it from him and assumed the posture of a mower.

T'ou remarked, 'You cut the other one down, but know not how to cut this one down.'

Fêng made no answer.

When Wei-shan was one day in attendance on his master, Pai-chang, the master asked him:

'Who are you?'

'Ling-yu, sir.'

'Dig into the ashes and see if there is any fire in the fire-place.'

---

[1] When Fêng was about to pass away at the Vajra Cave, of Wu-tai Shan, he said: 'I have myself seen the masters pass away lying or sitting but not standing. Do you know any masters who passed away standing?' The monks said, 'Yes, there is the record of such.' 'Do you then know one who passed away standing on his head?' 'No, never yet,' was the answer. Whereupon Fêng stood on his head and passed away. His garment remained attached to his body. When people carried his body to the crematory it kept its extraordinary position unchanged. It was an object of wonder and admiration. The master had a sister who was a nun, and she happened to be among the interested crowd. She approached the corpse of the brother and reproached him saying, 'O brother! While still alive, you have not observed the laws, and after death you still try to play a trick on people.' She then poked the brother with her hand, and the dead body went down on the ground with a thud.

Shan dug into the fire-place, and said, 'No fire, sir.'

Pai-chang rose from his seat, dug deeper into the ashes, and, finding a little piece of live charcoal, held it up, and showing it to Shan, said:

'Is this not a live one?'

This opened Shan's eye.

Tai-an studied the Vinaya texts at Huang-po Shan, which, however, failed to satisfy him, for he had as yet no approach to the ultimate meaning of Buddhist truth. He went about on his disciplinary pilgrimage and came to Pai-chang. Tai-an remarked, 'I have been seeking for the Buddha, but do not yet know how to go on with my research.'

Said the master, 'It is very much like looking for an ox when riding on one.'

'What shall a man do after knowing him?'

'It is like going home on the back of an ox.'

'May I be further enlightened as to the care I shall have to bestow on the whole matter?'

Pai-chang said, 'It is like a cowherd looking after his cattle, who using his staff keeps them from wandering into another's pasture.'

When Kao was still a novice and not yet fully ordained, he came to Yao-shan.

Yao-shan said, 'Whence comest thou?'

'From Nan-yüeh, sir.'

'Whither goest thou?'

'To Chiang-ling for ordination.'

'What is your idea in getting ordained?'

'I wish to be free from birth-and-death.'

'Do you know,' said the master, 'there is one who, even without being ordained, is free from birth-and-death?'

Shan-tao was walking one day with his master in the mountains. The master, Shih-t'ou, saw the branches of a tree obstructing the pathway and requested Shan-tao to clear them away.

Said the disciple, 'I did not bring a knife with me.'

Shih-t'ou took out his own knife and held it out with the naked blade towards his disciple.

Shan-tao said, 'Please give me the other end.'

'What do you want to do with the other end?' asked the master.

This made Shan-tao wake to the truth of Zen.

From these examples taken at random from *The Transmission of the Lamp*, which is the first history of Zen, we can see that the method of the Zen masters was thoroughly practical but had no prescribed plan. If the pupil had no question of his own, the master would try to draw him out, not abstractly but out of life itself as they were living it. There were already some stock questions in circulation among followers of Zen, with which they approached the master, and there were also some favourite questions that were regularly asked by the masters. But there was nothing systematized either on the part of the master or the pupil as to the pursuance of the study of Zen.

One of the questions most frequently asked by the novitiate was concerned with the reason for Bodhidharma's visit to China. This was quite natural as Zen had originated in China with his coming from India, and those who wished to follow his steps could not but be eager to know the great message of Bodhidharma. On the other hand, the most popular question put by the masters was as to the whence and the whither of each new arrival at the monastery. 'Whence comest thou?' was not a question prompted by mere curiosity; for if we really know the whence and the whither we are already masters of Zen.

Besides these *bona fide* Zen followers, there were many Buddhist philosophers, especially in the earlier days of Zen in the T'ang dynasty, who being partial to their own philosophies were often in controversy with Zen masters. These interviews afford us an interesting spectacle which is always at the expense of the philosophers.

. . . . .

A monk came to Hui-chung and was asked, 'What is your business?'

'I discourse on the *Vajracchedikā Sūtra*.'

'Tell me what are the first two characters of the sūtra?'

'*Ju shih*' (thus, *evam*).[1]

Demanded the master, 'What does that mean?'

There was no answer.

A Buddhist philosopher called on Ma-tsu and said, 'May I ask what teaching is held by a Zen master?'

Ma-tsu, instead of answering him, proposed a counter-question, 'What teaching do you hold?'

'I have the honour of discoursing on more than twenty sūtras and śastras.'

'You are really a lion-child, are you not?'

'I feel complimented, sir.'

Ma-tsu gave out a soft long breath. Thereupon, the philosopher remarked, 'This is really it.'

'What does that mean?'

'This is the way the lion comes out of its den.'

The master remained silent.

'This also is really it,' remarked the philosopher.

'What does that mean?'

'This is the way the lion lies in his den.'

'When there is neither going-out nor coming-in, what becomes of it?'

The philosopher gave no answer. Later, when he left the master and was about to pass out of the gate, the master called out, 'O philosopher!' He turned back. Said the master, 'What is that?' There was no answer, which elicited this from Ma-tsu, 'Oh, that stupid teacher of the sūtras!'

A teacher of the *Avataṁsaka* came to see Hui-hai and asked, 'Master, do you believe that non-sentient beings are Buddhas?'

'No,' said the master, 'I do not believe so. If non-sentient

[1] Ju shih is the opening word of all the sūtras.

beings are Buddhas, living beings are worse off than the dead; dead donkeys, dead dogs will be far better than living human beings. We read in the sūtra that the Buddha-body is no other than the Dharma-body which is born of morality (*śīla*), meditation (*dhyāna*), and knowledge (*prajñā*), born of the three sciences (*vidyā*) and the six supernatural powers (*abhijñā*), born of all deeds of merit. If non-sentient beings are Buddhas, you, Reverend Sir, had better pass away this moment and attain Buddhahood.'

Another *Avataṁsaka* teacher called Chih came to Hui-hai and asked, 'Why do you not admit that the evergreen bamboos are all the Dharmakāya and that there are no thickly-blooming yellow flowers that are not Prajñā?'

Said the master: 'The Dharmakāya [in itself] has no form, but by means of the green bamboos it assumes a form; Prajñā [in itself] is devoid of sentiency, but facing the yellow flowers it functions. That there is Prajñā and Dharmakāya is not owing to the green bamboos and yellow flowers. Therefore, it is stated in the sūtra that the true Dharmakāya of the Buddha is like emptiness of space, and that like the moon reflected in water there are forms in response to individual objects. If the yellow flower is Prajñā, Prajñā is non-sentient; if the green bamboo is the Dharmakāya, the bamboo may know how to function in various relations. O Teacher, do you understand?'

'No, Master, I am unable to follow you.'

'If a man has an insight into the nature of his own being,' said the master, 'he will understand the truth in whatever way it is presented either affirmatively or negatively. He knows how not to get attached to either side since he has grasped the principle of things as they move on. But a man of no such spiritual insight is attached to the green bamboo or to the yellow flower when reference is made to either of them. He dallies with Dharmakāya when he discourses on it, he knows not what Prajñā is, even when he talks of it. Thus there is a constant wrangling among you teachers.'

.  .  .  .  .  .

This was the way Zen teaching was practised until about the tenth century. In order to facilitate the understanding of the state of affairs that had been going on during those years, let me cite what is known as 'The Eighteen kinds of Question', compiled by Shan-chao of Fên-yang.[1] He flourished towards the end of the tenth century and was a disciple of Shêng-nien of Shou-shan.[2] The classification is unscientific but the 'Questions' are illuminating in many ways as they illustrate how Zen was studied in those days.

1. The question asking for instruction. This is what is generally asked by a novice of the master, wishing to be enlightened on such subjects as Buddha, the signification of Bodhidharma's visit to China, the essence of the Buddhist teaching, the Dharmakāya, etc.

2. The question in which the questioner asks for the master's judgment by describing his own mental condition. When a monk said to Chao-chou, 'What do you say to one who has nothing to carry about?' he was analysing his own state of mind. To this Chao-chou replied, 'Carry it along.'

3. The question whereby the questioner attempts to see where the master stands. A monk came to Tung-fêng who lived in a mountain hut and asked him, 'If a tiger should suddenly appear here, what would you do?' The hut-keeper roared like a tiger; the monk behaved as if terrified; whereupon the keeper laughed heartily.

4. The question in which the questioner shows that he still has a doubt as to his attainment and expresses his desire for confirmation. A monk asked Tao-wu of T'ien-huang, 'What shall I do when there is still a shadow of doubt?' Wu replied, 'Even oneness when held on to is wide of the mark.'

5. The question whereby the questioner is anxious to find out the master's attitude. A monk asked Chao-chou, 'All things are reducible to the One; but where is the One

[1] *Jen t'ien yen mu*, 'Eyes of Men and Gods', Fas. II.
[2] A.D. 926–993.

reducible?' Chou said, 'When I was in the district of Ch'ing I had a robe made that weighed seven *chin*.'

6. The question asked by one who is at a loss as to how to go on with his study of Zen. A monk asked Hsing-hua: 'I am unable to distinguish black from white. Pray enlighten me somehow.' The question was hardly out when the master gave him a good slashing.

7. The question asked with the intention to probe into the attainment of the master. This kind of question must have been in vogue when the Zen monasteries were everywhere established and the monks travelled from one master to another. A monk asked Fêng-hsüeh, 'How is it that one who understands not, never cherishes a doubt?' Replied the master, 'When a tortoise walks on the ground, he cannot help leaving traces in the mud.'

8. The question of ignorance. This does not seem to differ from the sixth. A monk asked Hsüan-sha, 'I am a newcomer in the monastery; please tell me how to go on with my study.' 'Do you hear the murmuring stream?' 'Yes, master.' 'If so, here is the entrance.'

9. The question proposed by one who has his own view of Zen and wishes to see how the master takes it. 'As to worldly knowledge and logical cleverness, I have nothing to do with them; pray let me have a Zen theme.' When this was asked by a monk, the master gave him a hearty blow.

10. The question in which an ancient master's saying is referred to. A monk said to Yün-mên, 'What would one do when no boundaries are seen, however wide the eyes are open?' Said Mên, 'Look!'

11. The question containing words from the sūtras. 'According to the sūtra, all beings are endowed with the Buddha-nature; how is it then that they know it not?' 'They know,' replied Shou-shan.

12. The question containing references to a known fact. 'The ocean is said to contain the precious gem; how can a man lay hands on it?' Replied Fêng-hsüeh: 'When Wang-hsiang comes, its brightness is dazzling; when Li-lou goes, the waves roll as high as the sky. The more one tries to take

hold of it, the farther it vanishes; the more one attempts to see it, the darker it grows.'

13. The question that starts from an immediate fact of observation. 'I see that you belong to the Brotherhood, what is the Buddha? What is the Dharma?' San-shêng replied, 'This is the Buddha, this is the Dharma, knowest thou?'

14. The question containing a hypothetical case. 'This Buddha sits in the Hall; what is the other Buddha?' Ching-shan's answer was, 'This Buddha sits in the Hall.'

15. The question embodying a real doubt. 'All things are such as they are from the beginning; what is that which is beyond existence?' 'Your statement is quite plain; what is the use of asking me?' was a master's solution.

16. The question with an aggressive intent. 'The Patriarch came from India and what did he design to do here?' Mu-chou retorted, 'You tell; what did he design?' The monk gave no reply, so Mu-chou struck him.

17. The question plainly and straightforwardly stated. A non-Buddhist philosopher asked the Buddha, 'Words or no-words, I ask neither.' The Buddha remained silent. The philosopher said: 'The Blessed One is indeed full of mercy and compassion. He has cleared off clouds of confusion for my sake, showing me how to enter upon the path.'

18. The question not expressed in words. A non-Buddhist philosopher came to the Buddha and stood before him without uttering a word. The Buddha then said, 'Abundantly indeed, O philosopher!' The philosopher praised him, saying, 'It is all owing to the Blessed One's mercy that I now enter upon the path.'

From this somewhat confused classification we can see how varied were the questions asked and answered among the followers of Zen during the first five hundred years of its steady development after Bodhidharma. Especially is this true during the three hundred years after Hui-nêng, now generally recognized as the sixth patriarch.

## 8. *The Growth of the Koan System, and its Signification*

No doubt, in these long years of Zen history there was a genuine growth of Zen consciousness among Zen followers, but at the same time, as in everything else, there was a tendency which made for the evaporation of Zen experience into conceptualism. If things were allowed to go on much further in that direction, the genuine experience might entirely die away, and all the literature consisting chiefly of the sayings of the Zen masters would become either unintelligible or a matter of philosophical discussion.

This degeneration, this departure from life and experience, is a phenomenon everywhere observable in the history of religion. There is always in the beginning a creative genius, and a system grows out of his experiences. People of lesser capacity are gathered about him; he endeavours to make them go through the same experiences as his own; he succeeds in some cases, but failures generally exceed successes. Because most of us are not original and creative enough, we are satisfied with following the steps of a leader who appears to us to be so great and so far above. The system thus gradually becomes ossified, and unless there follows a period of revival, the original experiences rapidly die away. In the Chinese history of Zen, this period of decline, we can say, came with the invention of the koan exercise, although it is quite true that this invention was something inevitable in the history of Zen consciousness.

What the koan proposes to do is to develop artificially or systematically in the consciousness of the Zen followers what the early masters produced in themselves spontaneously. It also aspires to develop this Zen experience in a greater number of minds than the master could otherwise hope for. Thus the koan tended to the popularization of Zen and at the same time became the means of conserving the Zen experience in its genuineness. Aristocratic Zen was now turned into a democratic, systematized and, to a certain extent, mechanized Zen. No doubt it meant to that extent a deterioration; but without this innovation Zen might have died out a long time before. To my mind it was the technique of the koan exercise that saved Zen as a unique heritage of Far-Eastern culture.

In order to understand a little better the circumstances which necessitated the rise of koan, let me quote one or two of the masters who lived in the eleventh century. From them we can see that there were at least two tendencies that were at work undermining Zen. They were the doctrine and practice of absolute quietude, and secondly, the habit of intellection that was everywhere impressed upon Zen from the outside. Absolute quietism, which the masters were never tired of combating, was regarded from the outset of Zen history as the essence of Zen teaching; but this tendency, being the inevitable accompaniment of Zen practice, readily and frequently reasserted itself.

As to the intellectual understanding of Zen, the outsiders as well as some Zen advocates are constantly practising it against the experience of Zen. There is no doubt that herein lurks the most deadly enemy of Zen. If they are not effectually put down they are sure to raise their heads again and again, especially when Zen shows any symptoms of decline. Chên-ching K'ê-wên[1] says in one of his sermons: 'As far as Zen is concerned, experience is all in all. Anything not based upon experience is outside Zen. The study of Zen, therefore, must grow out of life itself; and satori must be thoroughly penetrating. If anything is left unexhausted there is an opening to the world of devils.

'Did not an ancient master say that numberless corpses are lying on the smooth, level ground, and also that they are really genuine ones who have passed through thickets of briars and brambles? Nowadays most people are led to imagine that Zen reaches its ultimate end when all the functions of body and mind are suspended, and concentration takes place in one single moment of the present in which

[1] 1024–1102.

91

a state of eternity-in-one-moment prevails—a state of absolute cessation, a state like an incense-burner in an old roadside shrine, a state of cold aloofness.

'It is most unfortunate that they are unable to realize that this state of concentration, however desirable it may be, when one becomes attached to it hinders the attainment of a true inner perception and the manifestation of the light which is beyond the senses.'

Tai-hui says in a letter to Chên-ju Tao-jên, who was one of his monk disciples: 'There are two forms of error now prevailing among followers of Zen, laymen as well as monks. The one thinks that there are wonderful things hidden in words and phrases, and those who hold this view try to learn many words and phrases. The second goes to the other extreme, forgetting that words are the pointing finger, showing one where to locate the moon. Blindly following the instruction given in the sūtras, where words are said to hinder the right understanding of the truth of Zen and Buddhism, they reject all verbal teachings and simply sit with eyes closed, letting down the eyebrows as if they were completely dead. They call this quiet-sitting, inner contemplation, and silent reflection. Not content with their own solitary practices, they try to induce others also to adopt and practise this wrong view of Zen. To such ignorant and simple-minded followers they would say, "One day of quiet-sitting means one day of progressive striving."

'What a pity! They are not at all aware of the fact that they are planning for a ghostly life. Only when these two erroneous views are done away with is there a chance for real advancement in the mastery of Zen. For we read in the sūtra that while one should not get attached to the artificialities and unrealities which are expressed by all beings through their words and language, neither should one adopt the other view which rejects all words indiscriminately, forgetting that the truth is conveyed in them when they are properly understood, and further, that words and their meanings are neither different nor not different, but are mutually related so that the one without the other is unintelligible. . . .'

There are many other passages expressing similar views in the sayings and discourses of the Zen masters of Tai-hui's day besides those given by him, and from them we can conclude that if Zen were left to its own course, it would surely have degenerated either into the practice of quiet-sitting and silent contemplation, or into the mere memorizing of the many Zen sayings and dialogues. To save the situation and to plan for a further healthy development of Zen, the Zen masters could do nothing better than introduce the innovation of the koan exercises.

What is a koan?

A koan, according to one authority, means 'a public document setting up a standard of judgment', whereby one's Zen understanding is tested as to its correctness. A koan is generally some statement made by an old Zen master, or some answer of his given to a questioner. The following are some that are commonly given to the uninitiated:

1. A monk asked Tung-shan, 'Who is the Buddha?' 'Three *chin* of flax.'

2. Yün-mên was once asked, 'When not a thought is stirring in one's mind, is there any error here?' 'As much as Mount Sumeru.'

3. Chao-chou answered, '*Wu*!' (*mu* in Japanese) to a monk's question, 'Is there Buddha-nature in a dog?' *Wu* literally means 'not' or 'none', but when this is ordinarily given as a koan, it has no reference to its literal signification; it is '*Wu*' pure and simple.

4. When Ming the monk overtook the fugitive Hui-nêng, he wanted Hui-nêng to give up the secret of Zen. Hui-nêng replied, 'What are your original features which you have even prior to your birth?'

5. A monk asked Chao-chou, 'What is the meaning of the First Patriarch's visit to China?' 'The cypress tree in the front courtyard.'

6. When Chao-chou came to study Zen under Nan-ch'üan, he asked, 'What is the Tao (or the Way)?' Nan-ch'üan replied, 'Your everyday mind, that is the Tao.'

7. A monk asked, 'All things are said to be reducible to the One, but where is the One to be reduced?' Chao-chou answered, 'When I was in the district of Ch'ing I had a robe made that weighed seven *chin*.'

8. When P'ang the old Zen adept first came to Ma-tsu in order to master Zen, he asked, 'Who is he who has no companion among the ten thousand things of the world?' Ma-tsu replied, 'When you swallow up in one draught all the water in the Hsi Ch'iang, I will tell you.'

When such problems are given to the uninitiated for solution, what is the object of the master? The idea is to unfold the Zen psychology in the mind of the uninitiated, and to reproduce the state of consciousness, of which these statements are the expression. That is to say, when the koans are understood the master's state of mind is understood, which is satori and without which Zen is a sealed book.

In the beginning of Zen history a question was brought up by the pupil to the notice of the master, who thereby gauged the mental state of the questioner and knew what necessary help to give him. The help thus given was sometimes enough to awaken him to realization, but more frequently than not puzzled and perplexed him beyond description, and the result was an ever-increasing mental strain or 'searching and contriving' on the part of the pupil, of which we have already spoken in the foregoing pages. In actual cases, however, the master would have to wait for a long while for the pupil's first question, if it were coming at all. To ask the first question means more than half the way to its own solution, for it is the outcome of a most intense mental effort for the questioner to bring his mind to a crisis. The question indicates that the crisis is reached and the mind is ready to leave it behind. An experienced master often knows how to lead the pupil to a crisis and to make him successfully pass it. This was really the case before the koan exercise came in vogue, as was already illustrated by the examples of Lin-chi, Nan-yüeh, and others.

As time went on there grew up many 'questions and answers' (*mondō* in Japanese) which were exchanged between masters and pupils. And with the growth of Zen literature it was perfectly natural now for Zen followers to begin to attempt an intellectual solution or interpretation of it. The 'questions and answers' ceased to be experiences and intuitions of Zen consciousness, and became subjects of logical inquiry. This was disastrous, yet inevitable. Therefore the Zen master who wished for the normal development of Zen consciousness and the vigorous growth of Zen tradition would not fail to recognize rightly the actual state of things, and to devise such a method as to achieve finally the attainment of the Zen truth.

The method that would suggest itself in the circumstances was to select some of the statements made by the old masters and to use them as pointers. A pointer would then function in two directions: (1) To check the working of the intellect, or rather to let the intellect see by itself how far it can go, and also that there is a realm into which it as such can never enter; (2) To effect the maturity of Zen consciousness which eventually breaks out into a state of satori.

When the koan works in the first direction there takes place what has been called 'searching and contriving'. Instead of the intellect, which taken by itself forms only a part of our being, the entire personality, mind and body, is thrown out into the solution of the koan. When this extraordinary state of spiritual tension, guided by an experienced master, is made to mature, the koan works itself out into what has been designated as the Zen experience. An intuition of the truth of Zen is now attained, for the wall against which the Yogin has been beating hitherto to no purpose breaks down, and an entirely new vista opens before him. Without the koan the Zen consciousness loses its pointer, and there will never be a state of satori. A psychological *impasse* is the necessary antecedent of satori.

Formerly, that is, before the days of the koan exercise, the antecedent pointer was created in the consciousness of the Yogin by his own intense spirituality. But when Zen became systematized owing to the accumulation of Zen literature in the shape of 'questions and answers' the indispensability of the koan had come to be universally recognized by he masters.

The worst enemy of Zen experience, at least in the beginning, is the intellect, which consists and insists in discriminating subject from object. The discriminating intellect, therefore, must be cut short if Zen consciousness is to unfold itself, and the koan is constructed eminently to serve this end.

On examination we at once notice that there is no room in the koan to insert an intellectual interpretation. The knife is not sharp enough to cut the koan open and see what are its contents. For a koan is not a logical proposition but the expression of a certain mental state resulting from the Zen discipline. For instance, what logical connection can there be between the Buddha and 'three *chin* of flax'? or between the Buddha-nature and '*Wu*'? or between the secret message of Bodhidharma and 'a cypress tree'? In a noted Zen textbook known as *Hekiganshu* (*Pi-yen-chi* in Chinese)[1] Yüan-wu gives the following notes concerning the 'three *chin* of flax', showing how the koan was interpreted by those pseudo-Zen followers who failed to grasp Zen:

'There are some people these days who do not truly understand this koan; this is because there is no crack in it to insert their intellectual teeth. By this I mean that it is altogether too plain and tasteless. Various answers have been given by different masters to the question, "What is the Buddha?" One said, "He sits in the Buddha Hall." Another said, "The one endowed with the thirty-two marks of excellence." Still another, "A bamboo-root whip." None, however, can excel T'ung-shan's "three *chin* of flax" as regards its irrationality, which cuts off all passage of

[1] This is one of the most favourite vademecums of Zen Buddhists. For further explanation see below.

speculation. Some comment that T'ung-shan was weighing flax at the moment, hence the answer. Others say that it was a trick of equivocation on the part of T'ung-shan; and still others think that as the questioner was not conscious of the fact that he was himself the Buddha, T'ung-shan answered him in this indirect way.

'Such [commentators] are all like corpses, for they are utterly unable to comprehend the living truth. There are still others, however, who take the "three *chin* of flax" as the Buddha [thus giving it a pantheistic interpretation]. What wild and fantastic remarks they make! As long as they are beguiled by words, they can never expect to penetrate into the heart of T'ung-shan, even if they live to the time of Maitreya Buddha. Why? Because words are merely a vehicle on which the truth is carried. Not comprehending the meaning of the old master, they endeavour to find it in his words only, but they will find therein nothing to lay their hands on. The truth itself is beyond all description, as is affirmed by an ancient sage, but it is by words that the truth is manifested.

'Let us, then, forget the words when we gain the truth itself. This is done only when we have an insight through experience into that which is indicated by words. The "three *chin* of flax" is like the royal thoroughfare to the capital; when you are once on it every step you take is in the right direction. When Yün-mên was once asked what was the teaching that went beyond the Buddhas and the patriarchs, he said "Dumpling". Yün-mên and T'ung-shan are walking the same road hand in hand. When you are thoroughly cleansed of all the impurities of discrimination, without further ado the truth will be understood. Later the monk who wanted to know what the Buddha was went to Chih-mên and asked him what T'ung-shan meant by "three *chin* of flax". Said Chih-mên, "A mass of flowers, a mass of brocade." He added, "Do you understand?" The monk replied, "No." "Bamboos in the South, trees in the North," was the conclusion of Mên.'

Technically speaking, the koan given to the uninitiated

is intended 'to destroy the root of life', 'to make the calculating mind die', 'to root out the entire mind that has been at work since eternity', etc. This may sound murderous, but the ultimate intent is to go beyond the limits of intellection, and these limits can be crossed over only by exhausting oneself once for all, by using up all the psychic powers at one's command. Logic then turns into psychology, intellection into conation and intuition. What could not be solved on the plane of empirical consciousness is now transferred to the deeper recesses of the mind. So, says a Zen master, 'Unless at one time perspiration has streamed down your back, you cannot see the boat sailing before the wind.' 'Unless once you have been thoroughly drenched in a perspiration you cannot expect to see the revelation of a palace of pearls on a blade of grass.'

The koan refuses to be solved under any easier conditions. But once solved the koan is compared to a piece of brick used to knock at a gate; when the gate is opened the brick is thrown away. The koan is useful as long as the mental doors are closed, but when they are opened it may be forgotten. What one sees after the opening will be something quite unexpected, something that has never before entered even into one's imagination. But when the koan is re-examined from this newly acquired point of view, how marvellously suggestive, how fittingly constructed, although there is nothing artificial here!

## 9. *Practical Instructions Regarding the Koan Exercise*

The following are some of the practical suggestions that have been given by Zen masters of various ages, regarding the koan exercise; and from them we can gather what a koan is expected to do towards the development of Zen consciousness, and also what tendency the koan exercise has come to manifest as time goes on. As we will see later on, the growth of the koan exercise caused a new movement among the Zen masters of the Ming dynasty to connect it with the Nembutsu,[1] that is, the recitation of the Buddha-name. This was owing to the presence of a common denominator between the psychological mechanism of the koan exercise and the recitation of the Buddha-name. (The subject will be given special treatment later on.)

A Zen master of Huang-po Shan, probably of early Sung, gives the following instruction in the study of Zen:

'O you brother-monks! You may talk glibly and perhaps intelligently about Zen, about Tao, and scoff at the Buddhas and patriarchs; but when the day comes to reckon up all your accounts, your lip-Zen will be of no avail. Thus far you have been beguiling others, but today you will find that you have been beguiling yourselves. O you brother-monks! While still strong and healthy in body try to have real understanding as to what Zen is. After all it is not such a difficult thing to take hold of the lock; but simply because you have not made up your minds to die in the last ditch, if you do not find a way to realization, you say, "It is too difficult; it is beyond my power." It is absurd! If you are really men of will, you will find out what your koan means. A monk once asked Chao-chou, "Has a dog the Buddha-nature?" to which the master answered, "*Wu!*" Now devote yourselves to this koan and try to find its meaning. Devote yourselves to it day and night, whether sitting or lying, whether walking or standing; devote yourselves to its solution during the entire course of the twelve periods. Even when dressing or taking meals, or attending to your natural wants, have your every thought fixed on the koan. Make resolute efforts to keep it always before your mind. Days pass, years roll on, but in the fullness of time when your mind is so attuned and recollected there will be a sudden awakening within yourselves—an awakening into the mentality of the Buddhas and the patriarchs. You will then, for the first time, and wherever you may go, never again be beguiled by a Zen master.'[2]

---

[1] *Nien-fo.*
[2] From the *Zenkwan Sakushin* ('Breaking Through the Zen Frontier Gate').

I-an Chên of Fo-chi monastery gives this advice:

'The old saying runs, "When there is enough faith, there is enough doubt which is a great spirit of inquiry, and when there is a great spirit of inquiry there is an illumination." Have everything thoroughly poured out that has accumulated in your mind—learning, hearing, false understanding, clever or witty sayings, the so-called truth of Zen, Buddha's teachings, self-conceit, arrogance, etc. Concentrate yourself on the koan, of which you have not yet had a penetrating comprehension. That is to say, cross your legs firmly, erect your spinal column straight, and paying no attention to the periods of the day, keep up your concentration until you grow unaware of your whereabouts, east, west, south, north, as if you were a living corpse.

'The mind moves in response to the outside world and when it is touched it knows. The time will come when all thoughts cease to stir and there will be no working of consciousness. It is then that all of a sudden you smash your brain to pieces and for the first time realize that the truth is in your own possession from the very beginning. Would not this be great satisfaction to you in your daily life?'

Tai-hui was a great koan advocate of the twelfth century. One of his favourite koans was Chao-chou's 'Wu', but he had also one of his own. He used to carry a short bamboo stick which he held forth before an assembly of monks, and said: 'If you call this a stick, you affirm; if you call it not a stick, you negate. Beyond affirmation and negation what would you call it?' In the following extract from his sermons titled *Tai-hui Pu-shuo*, compiled by T'su-ching, 1190, he gives still another koan to his gardener-monk, Ching-kuang.

'The truth (*dharma*) is not to be mastered by mere seeing, hearing, and thinking. If it is, it is no more than the seeing, hearing, and thinking; it is not at all seeking after the truth itself. For the truth is not in what you hear from others or learn through the understanding. Now keep yourself away from what you have seen, heard, and thought, and see

what you have within yourself. Emptiness only, nothingness, which eludes your grasp and to which you cannot fix
your thought. Why? Because this is the abode where the
senses can never reach. If this abode were within the
reach of your sense it would be something you could
think of, something you could have a glimpse of; it
would then be something subject to the law of birth and
death.

'The main thing is to shut off all your sense-organs and
make your consciousness like a block of wood. When this
block of wood suddenly starts up and makes a noise, that is
the moment you feel like a lion roaming about freely with
nobody disturbing him, or like an elephant that crosses a
stream not minding its swift current. At that moment there
is no fidgeting, nothing doing, just this and no more. Says
P'ing-t'ien the Elder:

> ' "The celestial radiance undimmed,
> The norm lasting for ever more;
> For him who entereth this gate,
> No reasoning, no learning."

'You should know that it is through your seeing, hearing,
and thinking[1] that you enter upon the path, and it is also
through the seeing, hearing, and thinking that you are pre-
vented from entering. Why? Let you be furnished with the
double-bladed sword that destroys and resuscitates life
where you have your seeing, hearing, and thinking, and
you will be able to make good use of the seeing, hearing, and
thinking. But if the sword that cuts both ways, that destroys
as well as resuscitates, is missing, your seeing, hearing, and
thinking will be a great stumbling-block, which will cause
you to prostrate again and again on the ground. Your
truth-eye will be completely blinded; you will be walking
in complete darkness not knowing how to be free and in-

[1] (Dṛiṣṭa-śruta-mata-yñāta). Abbreviated for 'the seen, heard, thought
and known'.

dependent. If you want, however, to be the free master of yourself by doing away with your seeing, hearing, and thinking, stop your hankering monkey-like mind from doing mischief; keep it quietly under control; keep your mind firmly collected regardless of what you are doing—sitting or lying, standing or walking, remaining silent or talking; keep your mind like a line stretched taut; do not let it slip out of your hand. Just as soon as it slips out of your control you will find it in the service of the seeing, hearing, and thinking. In such a case is there any remedy? What remedy is applicable here?

'A monk asked Yün-mên, "Who is the Buddha?" "The dried-up dirt-cleaner." This is the remedy; whether you are walking or sitting or lying, let your mind be perpetually fixed on this "dirt-cleaner". The time will come when your mind will suddenly come to a stop like an old rat who finds himself in a *cul-de-sac*. Then there will be a plunging into the unknown with the cry, "Ah, this!" When this cry is uttered you have discovered yourself. You find at the same time that all the teachings of the ancient worthies expounded in the Buddhist Tripitaka, the Taoist Scriptures, and the Confucian Classics, are no more than commentaries upon your own sudden cry, "Ah, this!" '

Tai-hui was never tired of impressing upon his disciples the importance of having satori which goes beyond language and reasoning and which bursts out in one's consciousness by overstepping the limits of consciousness. His letters and sermons are filled with advice and instructions directed towards this end. I quote one or two of them. That he was so insistent on this point proves that Zen in his day was degenerating to a form of mere quietism on the one hand and on the other to the intellectual analysis of the koans left by the old masters.

'The study of Zen must end in satori.[1] It is like a holiday race-boat which is ordinarily put away in some quiet corner, but which is designed for winning a regatta. This has been the case with all the ancient masters of Zen, for

[1] *Wu-ju.*

we know that Zen is really won only when we have satori. You have to have satori somehow, but you will never get what you want by trying to be quiet with yourself, by sitting like a dead man. Why? Does not one of the patriarchs say that when you attempt to gain quietness by suppressing activity your quietness will all the more be susceptible to disturbance? However earnestly you may try to quiet your confused mind, the result will be altogether contrary to what you expect to realize so long as your reasoning habit continues.

'Abandon, therefore, this reasoning habit; have the two characters, "birth" and "death", pasted on your forehead, and fix your attention exclusively on the following koan, as if you were oppressed under the obligation of a very heavy debt. Think of the koan regardless of what you are doing, regardless of what time of the day it is, day or night. A monk asked Chao-chou, "Has a dog the Buddha-nature, or not?" Said Chou, "*Wu!*" Collect your thoughts upon this "*Wu!*" and see what is contained in it. As your concentration goes on you will find the koan altogether devoid of taste, that is, without any intellectual clue whereby to fathom its content. Yet in the meantime you may have a feeling of joy stealing into your heart, which, however, is soon followed by another feeling, this time a feeling of disquietude. Paying no attention to this interweaving of emotions, exert yourself to go ahead with the koan, when you will become aware that you have pushed yourself like the old rat into a blind alley. A turning back will then be necessary, but this can never be accomplished by the weak-minded, who are ever faltering and hesitating.'

In another place Tai-hui says: 'Just steadily go on with your koan every moment of your life. If a thought rises, do not attempt to suppress it by conscious effort; only renew the attempt to keep the koan before the mind. Whether walking or sitting, let your attention be fixed upon it without interruption. When you begin to find it entirely devoid of flavour, the final moment is approaching; do not let it

slip out of your grasp. When all of a sudden something
flashes out in your mind, its light will illumine the entire
universe, and you will see the spiritual land of the Enlightened Ones fully revealed at the point of a single hair,
and the great wheel of the Dharma revolving in a single
grain of dust.'[1]

K'ung-ku Ching-hung[2] has a similar advice for monks.
He says:

'Chao-chou's "*Wu!*"', before you have penetrated into
its meaning, is like a silver mountain or an iron wall
[against which you stand nonplussed]. But as you go on
with "*Wu!*" day after day trying to get into its content,
and do not give even a moment's rest to yourself, the
supreme moment will inevitably come upon you, just as
a flood makes its own channel; and then you will see that
the iron wall and the silver mountain were not, after all,
very formidable. The main point is not to put any reliance
on learning, but to put a stop to all hankering, and to exert
yourself to the utmost to solve the great problem of birth
and death. Do not waste your time by merely thinking of
"*Wu!*" as if you were no more than a simpleton, make no
attempt to give a false solution to it by means of speculation
and imagination. Resolutely put yourself, heart and soul,
into the unravelling of the problem of "*Wu!*" When suddenly, as you let go of your hold, there comes a grand over-
turning of the whole system of consciousness, and for the
first time you realize in a most luminous manner what all
this finally comes to.'

The author of *The Mirror for Zen Students*[3] confirms all
that has already been quoted, and describes fully the
psychology of the koan exercise.

[1] Tai-hui's passages are taken from a collection of his letters, sermons,
discourses, and sayings known as his *Pu-shao*, *Yü-lu*, and *Shu*. He was
very well acquainted with the *Avataṁsaka* (or *Gaṇḍavyūha*), and there are
many allusions by him to its teachings, as we find in this last sentence
here.
[2] Still living in 1466.
[3] Compiled by T'ui-yin, a Korean Zen master of the Ming era (A.D.
1368–1650). The book appeared in 1579.

'What is required of Zen devotees is to see into the phrase[1] that liveth and not into the one which is dead. Try to search for the sense of the koan you have, putting your whole mental strength into the task like the mother-hen sitting on her eggs, like a cat trying to catch a rat, like a hungry one eagerly looking everywhere for food, like a thirsty one seeking for water, like a child thinking of its mother. If you exert yourself as seriously and as desperately as that, the time will surely come when the sense of the koan will dawn upon you.

'There are three factors making for success in the study of Zen: (1) great faith, (2) great resolution, and (3) great spirit of inquiry. When any one of these is lacking it is like a cauldron with a broken leg, it limps. At all moments of your life, regardless of what you are doing, exert yourself to see into the meaning of Chao-chou's "*Wu*". Keep the koan always before your mind and never release the spirit of inquiry. As the inquiry goes on steadily and uninterruptedly you will come to see that there is no intellectual clue in the koan, that it is altogether devoid of sense as you ordinarily understand that word, that it is entirely flat, devoid of taste, has nothing appetizing about it, and that you are beginning to have a certain feeling of uneasiness and impatience. When you come to this state it is the moment for you to cast aside the scabbard, throw yourself down into the abyss, and by so doing lay a foundation for Buddhahood.

'Do not think that the meaning of the koan is at the moment of your holding it up for solution; do not reason about it or exercise your imagination over it; do not wait for satori to come over you by clearing your mind of its confused ideas; only collect yourself on the unintelligibility

---

[1] That is, *chü*. The Zen masters generally distinguish two kinds of *chü*; the live one and the dead one. By the 'live *chü*' are meant such statements as give no clues whatever to their rational interpretations but put an end to the functioning of the empirical consciousness; whereas the 'dead *chü*' are those that lend themselves to logical or philosophical treatment and therefore that can be learned from others and committed to memory. This according to T'ui-yin.

of the koan over which the mind evidently has no control.[1] You will finally find yourself like an old rat getting into the furthest corner of the barn where it suddenly perceives by veering clear round the way of escape. To measure the koan by an intellectual standard, as you ordinarily do with other things, to live your life up and down in the stream of birth and death, to be always assailed by feelings of fear, worry, and uncertainty, all this is owing to your imagination and calculating mind. You ought to know how to rise above the trivialities of life, in which most people are found drowning themselves. Do not waste time asking how to do it, just put your whole soul into the business. It is like a mosquito biting at an iron bull; at the very moment the iron absolutely rejects your frail proboscis, you for once forget yourself, you penetrate, and the work is done.'

Sufficient authorities have now been quoted to show where lies the function of the koan in bringing about what is known as satori, and also to show what the Zen master

---

[1] In some of the Appendices I have given more advice regarding the Zen Yogin's attitude towards the koan, which afford interesting and illuminating materials for the psychological student of Zen consciousness. T'ui-yin cautions his koan students on the following ten points: (1) Do not calculate according to your imagination; (2) Let not your attention be drawn where the master raises his eyebrows or twinkles his eyes; (3) Do not try to extract meaning from the way the koan is worded; (4) Do not try to demonstrate on the words; (5) Do not think that the sense of the koan is to be grasped where it is held out as an object of thought; (6) Do not take Zen for a state of mere passivity; (7) Do not judge the koan with the dualistic standard of *yu* (*asti*) and *wu* (*nāsti*); (8) Do not take the koan as pointing to absolute emptiness; (9) Do not ratiocinate on the koan; and (10) Do not keep your mind in the attitude of waiting for satori to turn up. The koan exercise is confused with so-called meditation, but from all these warnings given by an old master regarding the exercise it is evident that Zen is not an exercise in meditation or in passivity. If Zen is to be properly understood by its students, Eastern and Western, this characteristic aspect of it must be fully comprehended. Zen has its definite object, which is 'to open our minds to satori' as we say, and in order to bring about this state of consciousness a koan is held out before the mental eye, not to meditate on, nor to keep the mind in a state of receptivity, but to use the koan as a kind of pole with which to leap over the stream of relativity to the other side of the Absolute. And the unique feature of Zen Buddhism is that all this is accomplished without resorting to such religious conceptions as sin, faith, God, grace, salvation, a future life, etc.

had in mind when he first began to exercise the minds of his disciples towards the maturing of their Zen consciousness. In the way of summary I conclude this part of the present chapter with a passage from the writings of Hakuin, who is father of the modern Japanese Rinzai school of Zen. In this we will see how the psychology of Zen has been going on without much change for more than a thousand years, since the days of Hui-nêng and his Chinese followers.

'If you want to get at the unadulterated truth of egolessness, you must once for all let go your hold and fall over the precipice, when you will rise again newly awakened and in full possession of the four virtues of eternity, bliss, freedom, and purity, which belong to the real ego. What does it mean to let go of your hold on the precipice? Suppose a man has wandered out among the remote mountains, where no one else has ever ventured. He comes to the edge of a precipice unfathomably deep, the rugged rock covered with moss is extremely slippery, giving him no sure foothold; he can neither advance nor retreat, death is looking at him in the face. His only hope lies in holding on to the vine which his hands have grasped; his very life depends on his holding on to it. If he should by carelessness let go his hold, his body would be thrown down to the abyss and crushed to pieces, bones and all.

'It is the same with the student of Zen. When he grapples with a koan single-handedly he will come to see that he has reached the limit of his mental tension, and he is brought to a standstill. Like the man hanging over the precipice he is completely at a loss what to do next. Except for occasional feelings of uneasiness and despair, it is like death itself. All of a sudden he finds his mind and body wiped out of existence, together with the koan. This is what is known as "letting go your hold". As you become awakened from the stupor and regain your breath it is like drinking water and knowing for yourself that it is cold. It will be a joy inexpressible.'

## 10. *Various Generalizations on the Koan Exercise*

To recapitulate: The innovation of the koan exercise was inevitable owing to the following circumstances:

1. If the study of Zen had run its natural course it would soon have come to its own extinction owing to the aristocratic nature of its discipline and experience.

2. As Zen gradually exhausted its creative originality in two or three hundred years of development after the time of Hui-nêng, the sixth patriarch, it found that a new life must be awakened in it, if it were to survive, by using some radical method which would vigorously stir up the Zen consciousness.

3. With the passing of the age of creative activity there was an accumulation of materials known as 'stories' (*hua-t'ou*), or 'conditions' (*chi-yüan*), or 'questions and answers' (*mên-ta*), which made up the bulk of Zen history; and this tended to invite intellectual interpretation, ruinous to the maturing of the Zen experience.

4. The rampant growth of Zen quietism since the beginning of Zen history most dangerously threatened the living experience of Zen. The two tendencies, quietism or the school of 'silent illumination', and intuitionalism or the school of noetic experience, had been from the beginning, covertly if not openly, at war with each other.

Because of these conditions, the koan exercise adopted by the Zen masters of the tenth and the eleventh century was designed to perform the following functions:

1. To popularize Zen in order to counteract native aristocracy which tended to its own extinction;

2. To give a new stimulus to the development of Zen consciousness, and thus to accelerate the maturing of the Zen experience;

3. To check the growth of intellectualism in Zen;

4. To save Zen from being buried alive in the darkness of quietism.

From the various quotations which have been given

concerning the koan exercise, the following psychic facts may be gathered:

1. The koan is given to the student first of all to bring about a highly wrought-up state of consciousness.

2. The reasoning faculty is kept in abeyance, that is, the more superficial activity of the mind is set at rest so that its more central and profounder parts which are found generally deeply buried can be brought out and exercised to perform their native functions.

3. The effective and conative centres which are really the foundations of one's personal character are charged to do their utmost in the solution of the koan. This is what the Zen master means when he refers to 'great faith' and 'great spirit of inquiry' as the two most essential powers needed in the qualification of a successful Zen devotee. The fact that all great masters have been willing to give themselves up, body and soul, to the mastery of Zen, proves the greatness of their faith in ultimate reality, and also the strength of their spirit of inquiry known as 'seeking and contriving', which never suspends its activity until it attains its end, that is, until it has come into the very presence of Buddhatā itself.

4. When the mental integration thus reaches its highest mark there obtains a neutral state of consciousness which is erroneously designated as 'ecstasy' by the psychological student of the religious consciousness. This Zen state of consciousness essentially differs from ecstasy in this: Ecstasy is the suspension of the mental powers while the mind is passively engaged in contemplation; the Zen state of consciousness, on the other hand, is the one that has been brought about by the most intensely active exercise of all the fundamental faculties constituting one's personality. They are here positively concentrated on a single object of thought, which is called a state of oneness (*ekāgra*). It is also known as a state of daigi or 'fixation'.[1]

This is the point where the empirical consciousness with all its contents both conscious and unconscious is about to

[1] *Tai-i* in Chinese. First Series, p. 254.

tip over its border-line, and get noetically related to the Unknown, the Beyond, the Unconscious. In ecstasy there is no such tipping or transition, for it is a static finality not permitting further unfoldment. There is nothing in ecstasy that corresponds to 'throwing oneself down the precipice', or 'letting go the hold'.

5. Finally, what at first appears to be a temporary suspense of all psychic faculties suddenly becomes charged with new energies hitherto undreamed of. This abrupt transformation has taken place quite frequently by the intrusion of a sound, or a vision, or a form of motor activity. A penetrating insight is born of the inner depths of consciousness, as the source of a new life has been tapped, and with it the koan yields up its secrets.

A philosophical explanation of these psychic facts is offered by Zen Buddhists in the following manner. It goes without saying that Zen is neither psychology nor philosophy, but that it is an experience charged with deep meaning and laden with living, exalting contents. The experience is final and its own authority. It is the ultimate truth, not born of relative knowledge, that gives full satisfaction to all human wants. It must be realized directly within oneself: no outside authorities are to be relied upon. Even the Buddha's teachings and the master's discourses, however deep and true they are, do not belong to one so long as they have not been assimilated into his being, which means that they are to be made to grow directly out of one's own living experiences. This realization is called satori. All koans are the utterances of satori with no intellectual mediations; hence their uncouthness and incomprehensibility.

The Zen master has no deliberate scheme on his part to make his statements of satori uncouth or logically unpalatable; the statements come forth from his inner being, as flowers burst out in spring-time, or as the sun sheds its rays. Therefore to understand them we have to be like flowers or like the sun; we must enter into their inner being. When we reproduce the same psychic conditions out of which the Zen masters have uttered these koans, we shall know them. The masters thus avoid all verbal explanations, which only serve to create in the minds of his disciples an intellectual curiosity to probe into the mystery. The intellect being a most obtrusive hindrance, or rather a deadly enemy, at least in the beginning of Zen study, it must be banished for a while from the mind. The koan is, indeed, a great baffler to reasoning. For this reason, Zen is ever prone to give more value to the psychic facts than to conceptualism. As the facts are directly experienced and prove quite satisfactory, they appeal irresistibly to the 'seeking and contriving' mind of the Zen follower.

As facts of personal experience are valued in Zen, we have such koans as Yün-mên's 'dried up dirt-cleaner,' or Chao-chou's 'cypress-tree', T'ung-shan's 'three *chin* of flax', etc., which are all familiar incidents in everyone's life. Compared with the Indian expressions such as 'All is empty, unborn, and beyond causation' or 'The whole universe is contained in one particle of dust', how homely the Chinese are!

Owing to this fact, Zen is better designed to exclude the intellect and to lead our empirical consciousness to its deeper sources. If a noetic experience of a radically different order is to be attained, which sets all our strivings and searchings at rest, something that does not at all belong to the intellectual categories is to be devised. More precisely speaking, something illogical, something irrational, something that does not yield itself to an intellectual treatment is to be the special feature of Zen. The koan exercise was thus the natural development of Zen consciousness in the history of human strivings to reach the ultimate. By means of the koan the entire system of our psychic apparatus is made to bear upon the maturing of the satori state of consciousness.

## 11. *Personal Records of the Zen Experiences*

Some personal records of the function which is performed by the koan exercise in the maturing of the Zen consciousness are given here. Three of such were already given in the First Series of my *Zen Essays* (pp. 251-258). They are a psychological study by themselves, but my object here is to demonstrate the role of the koan exercise in the practice of Zen and the wisdom of this system as innovated by the Sung masters.

Tê-i of Mêng-shan,[1] who was the eighth descendant of Fa-yen of Wu-tsu Shan (died 1104), tells the following story of his experiences in Zen:

When I was twenty years old I became acquainted with Zen, and before I was thirty-two I had visited seventeen or eighteen Zen masters asking them as to their method of discipline, but none were able to enlighten me on the most important point. When later I came to the master Huan-shan he told me to see into the meaning of '*Wu*' (*mu*), and added, 'Be vigilant over your "*Wu*" through all the periods of the day, as constantly vigilant as a cat is when she tries to catch a rat, or as a hen is while sitting on the eggs. As long as you have as yet no insight, be like a rat gnawing at the coffin-wood and never vacillate in your exertion. As you go on with your task like that, the time will surely come when your mind will become enlightened.'

Following this instruction, I steadily applied myself to the work, day and night. Eighteen days thus elapsed. Suddenly, when I was taking tea, I came upon the meaning of Kāśyapa's smile, which was elicited when the Buddha produced a flower before a congregation of his disciples. I was overjoyed; I wished to find out whether my under-

[1] All the quotations cited here are taken from the *Zenkwan Sakushin* ('Aids to Breaking Through the Frontier Gate of Zen'). For the biographical records of these masters see a history of Zen called the *Hui-yüan hsü-liao*.

standing was correct and called upon a few masters of Zen. They, however, gave me no definite answer; some told me to stamp the whole universe with the stamp of Sāgara-mudrā-samādhi, and not to pay attention to anything else. Believing this, I passed two years. In the sixth month of the fifth year of Ching-ting (1265), I was in Chung-ch'ing, Szŭ-ch'uan, and, suffering a great deal from dysentery, was in a most critical condition. No energy was left in me, nor was the Sāgaramudrā of any avail at this hour. Whatever understanding of Zen I had all failed to support me. The tongue refused to speak, the body to move; all that remained was to greet death. The past unrolled itself before me—the things I had done, as well as the situations I had been in; I was thus in a ghastly state of despondency and completely at a loss as to how to escape from its torture.

At last, determining to be master of myself, I managed to make my will. I then got up quietly, lit some incense, arranged the invalid cushions; I made bows to the Triple Treasure and also to the Nāga gods, and silently confessed my previous sins before them. I prayed that if I were to pass away at this time I might be reborn through the power of Prajñā in a good family and become a monk in my early years. But if I should be cured of this disease I wanted to become a monk at once and devote the rest of my life entirely to the study of Zen. If an illumination should come I would help others even as myself to get enlightened.

After making this prayer, I set up 'Wu' before my mind and turned the light within myself. Before long I felt my viscera twist for a few times, but I paid no attention; it was after some time that my eyelids became rigid and refused to blink, and later on I became unconscious of my own body; the 'Wu' alone occupied my consciousness. In the evening I arose from my seat and found that I was half cured of the disease; I sat down again until the small hours of the morning when the physical disorder completely disappeared. I was myself again, well and in good spirits.

In the eighth month of the same year I went to Chiang-ling and had my head shaved [i.e. became a monk]. Before the year was over, I went on a pilgrimage, and while cooking rice I found out that the koan exercise must be carried on uninterruptedly and with continuous effort. I then settled myself at Huang-lung.

When I felt sleepy for the first time I exercised my will to resist it and kept on sitting, when the sleepiness was easily vanquished. When I became sleepy a second time, I drove it away in a similar manner. A third attack was too strong; I got down from my seat and made bows to the Buddha, which revived me. I resumed my seat and the process had to be repeated. But when at last I had to sleep I used a pillow and slept a little; later my elbow was substituted for the pillow, and finally I altogether avoided lying down. Two nights were thus passed; on the third night I was so fatigued that I felt as if my feet did not touch the ground. Suddenly a dark cloud that seemed to obstruct my vision cleared away, and I felt as if I had just come from a bath and was thoroughly rejuvenated.

As to the koan, a state of mental fixation prevailed, and the koan occupied the centre of attention without any conscious striving on my part for it. All external sensations, the five passions, and the eight disturbances, no longer annoyed me; I was as pure and transparent as a snow-filled silver bowl or as the autumnal sky cleared of all darkening clouds. The exercise thus went on quite successfully but as yet with no turning point.

Later I left this monastery and travelled to Chê. On the way I experienced many hardships and my Zen exercise suffered accordingly. I came to the Ch'êng-t'ien monastery which was presided over by the master Ku-ch'an, and there took up my temporal habitation. I vowed to myself that I would not leave this place until I realized the truth of Zen. In a little over a month I regained what I had lost in the exercise. It was then that my whole body was covered with boils; but I was determined to keep the discipline even at the cost of my life.

This helped a great deal to strengthen my spiritual powers, and I knew how to keep up my seeking and striving (*kung-fu*) even in illness. Being invited out to dinner I walked on with my koan all the way to the devotee's house, but I was so absorbed in my exercise that I passed by the house without even recognizing where I was. This made me realize what was meant by carrying on the exercise even while engaged in active work. My mental condition then was like the reflection of the moon penetrating the depths of a running stream the surface of which was in rapid motion, while the moon itself retained its perfect shape and serenity in spite of the commotion of the water.

On the sixth of the third month I was holding '*Wu*' in my mind as usual while sitting on the cushion, when the head-monk came into the meditation hall. Accidentally he dropped the incense-box on the floor, making a noise. This at once opened my mind to a new spiritual vista, and with a cry I obtained a glimpse into my inner being, capturing the old man Chao-chou [the author of the '*Wu*']. I gave voice to the following extempore stanza:

'Unexpectedly the path comes to an end;
When stamped through, the waves are the water itself.
They say, old Chao-chou stands supremely above the rest,
But nothing extraordinary I find in his features.'

During the autumn I interviewed masters of high reputation such as Hsüeh-yen, T'ui-kêng, Shih-fan, and Hsü-chou. The last-mentioned advised me to go to Huan-shan. When I saw Shan, he asked, 'The light, serenely illuminating, fills all the universe to its furthest limits— are these not the words of the literati Chang-cho?' I was about to open my mouth when Shan gave a '*Ho!*' (*Kwatz!*), and dismissed me unceremoniously. This upset me, and since then my thoughts were concentrated on this attitude of the master. Walking or sitting, eating or drinking, my mind was occupied with it.

Six months passed when, one day in the spring of the following year, I was returning from an out-of-town trip and was about to climb a flight of stone steps, when the

solid ice that had been clogging my brain for so long unexpectedly melted away, and I forgot that I was walking
on the roadway. I immediately went to the master, and
when he repeated his former question I overturned his seat.
I now thoroughly understood the koan, whose knots had
been so hard to untie.

O Brothers! Be thoroughgoing in your Zen exercise.
If I had not been taken ill when at Chung-ch'ing my life
might have been almost wasted. The main thing is to be
introduced to a master with really spiritual insight. Consider how earnestly and steadily the ancient masters devoted themselves both day and night to the study of Zen in
order to grasp the ultimate truth of it.

．　　　．　　　．　　　．　　　．

Yüan-chon Hsüeh-Yen Tsu-ch'in (died 1287), who was a
disciple of Wu-chou Shih-fan (died 1249), has this to tell
about his experiences:

I left my home when I was five years old, and while
under my master, by listening to his talks to visitors, I began
to know that there was such a thing as Zen, and gradually
came to believe in it, and finally made up my mind to
study it. At sixteen I was ordained as a regular monk and at
eighteen started on a Zen pilgrimage. While staying under
Yüan of Shuang-shan I was kept busy attending to the
affairs of the monastery from morning to evening, and was
never out of the monastery grounds. Even when I was in
the general dormitory or engaged in my own affairs, I kept
my hands folded over my chest and my eyes fixed on the
ground without looking beyond three feet.

My first koan was '*Wu*'. Whenever a thought was stirred
in my mind, I lost no time in keeping it down, and my consciousness was like a cake of solid ice, pure and smooth,
serene and undisturbed. A day passed as rapidly as the
snapping of the fingers. No sound of the bell or the drum
ever reached me.

At nineteen I was staying at the monastery of Ling-yin

when I made the acquaintance of the recorder Lai of Ch'u-chou. He gave me this advice: 'Your method has no life in it and will achieve nothing. There is a dualism in it; you keep movement and quietude as two separate poles of thought. To exercise yourself properly in Zen you ought to cherish a spirit of inquiry (*i-ch'ing*); for according to the strength of your inquiring spirit will be the depth of your enlightenment.' Thus advised, I had my koan changed to 'the dried-up dirt-wiper'. I began to inquire (*i*) into its meaning in every possible manner and from every possible point of view. But being now annoyed by dullness and now by restlessness, I could not get even a moment of serene contemplation. I moved to Ching-tzŭ monastery where I joined a company of seven, all earnest students of Zen. Sealing up our bedding we determined not to lie down on the floor. There was a monk called Hsiu who did not join us, but who kept sitting on his cushion like a solid bar of iron; I wanted to have a talk with him, but he was forbidding.

As the practice of not lying down was kept up for two years I became thoroughly exhausted both in mind and body. At last I gave myself up to the ordinary way of taking rest. In two months my health was restored and my spirit reinvigorated once more by thus yielding to nature. In fact the study of Zen is not necessarily to be accomplished by merely practising sleeplessness. It is far better to have short hours of a sound sleep in the middle of the night when the mind will gather up fresh energy.

One day I happened to meet Hsiu in the corridor, and for the first time I could have a talk with him. I asked, 'Why was it that you avoided me so much last year when I wished to talk with you?' He said, 'An earnest student of Zen begrudges even the time to trim his nails; how much more the time wasted in conversation with others!' I said, 'I am troubled in two ways, by dullness and restlessness, how can I get over them?' He replied: 'It is owing to your not being fully determined in your exercise. Have the cushion high enough under you, and keeping your spinal column upright, throw all the spiritual energy you possess into the koan it-self. What is the use of talking about dullness and restless-ness?'

This advice gave me a new turn to my exercise, for in three days and nights I came to realize a state in which the dualism of body and mind ceased to exist. I felt so trans-parent and lively that my eyelids were kept open all the time. On the third day I was walking by the gate still feeling as I did when sitting cross-legged on the cushions. I happened to meet Hsiu, who asked, 'What are you doing here?' I answered, 'Trying to realize the truth (*tao*).' 'What do you mean by the truth?' he asked. I could not give him a reply, which only increased my mental annoyance.

Wishing to return to the meditation hall I directed my steps towards it, when I encountered the head-monk. He said, 'Keep your eyes wide open and see what it all means.' This encouraged me. I came back into the hall and was about to go to my seat when the whole outlook changed. A broad expanse opened, and the ground appeared as if all caved in. The experience was beyond description and alto-gether incommunicable, for there was nothing in the world to which it could be compared. Coming down from the seat I sought Hsiu. He was greatly pleased, and kept repeating: 'How glad I am! How glad I am!' We took hold of each other's hands and walked along the willow embankment outside the gate. As I looked around and up and down, the whole universe with its multitudinous sense-objects now appeared quite different; what was loathsome before, together with ignorance and passions, was now seen to be nothing else but the outflow of my own inmost nature which in itself remained bright, true, and transparent. This state of consciousness lasted for more than half a month.

Unfortunately, as I did not happen to interview a great master of deeper spiritual insight at the time, I was left at this stage of enlightenment for some time. It was still an imperfect stage which if adhered to as final would have obstructed the growth of a truly penetrating insight; the sleeping and waking hours did not yet coalesce into a unity. Koans that admitted some way of reasoning were intelligible enough, but those that altogether defied it, as if they were a wall of iron blocks, were still quite beyond my reach. I passed many years under the master Wu-chun, listening to his sermons and asking his advice, but there was no word which gave a final solution to my inner disquietude, nor was there anything in the sūtras or the sayings of the masters, as far as I read, that could cure me of this heart-ache.

Ten years thus passed without my being able to remove this hard inner obstruction. One day I was walking in the Buddha Hall at T'ien-mu when my eyes happened to fall on an old cypress-tree outside the Hall. Just seeing this old tree opened a new spiritual vista and the solid mass of obstruction suddenly dissolved. It was as if I had come into the bright sunshine after having been shut up in the darkness. After this I entertained no further doubt regarding life, death, the Buddha, or the Patriarchs. I now realized for the first time what constituted the inner life of my master Wu-chun, who indeed deserved thirty hard blows.

T'ien-shan Ch'iung, who was disciple of Tê-i of Mêng-shan, has the following to record:

When I was thirteen years old I came to know something about Buddhism; at eighteen I left home and at twenty-two was ordained a monk. I first went to Shih-chuang where I learned that the monk Hsiang used to look at the top of his nose all the time and that this kept his mind transparent. Later, a monk brought from Hsüeh-yen his 'Advice Regarding the Practice of Meditation (za-zen)'. By this I found that my practice was on a wrong track. So I went to Hsüeh-yen, and following his instructions exercised myself exclusively on 'Wu'. On the fourth night I found myself perspiring, but my mind was clear and lucid. While in the Hall I never conversed with others, wholly devoting myself to zazen.

Later on I went to the master Miao of Kao-fêng, who

said this to me: 'Let there be no intermission in your exercise during the twelve periods of the day. Get up in the small hours of the morning and seek out your koan at once so that it will be held all the time before you. When you feel tired and sleepy, rise from your seat and walk the floor, but even while walking do not let your koan slip away from your mind. Whether you are eating, or working, or engaged in monastery affairs, never fail to keep your koan before you. When this is done by day and night, a state of oneness will prevail, and later your mind will surely open to enlightenment.' I then kept up my exercise according to this advice, and surely enough I finally achieved a state of oneness. On the twentieth of March Yen gave me a sermon to this effect:

'Brethren, when you feel too drowsy after a long sitting on the cushions, come down on the floor, have a run around the hall, rinse your mouth, and bathe your face and eyes with cold water; after that resume your sitting on the cushions. Keeping your spinal column straight up like an outstanding precipice, throw all your mental energy on the koan. If you go on like this for seven days, I can assure you of your coming to enlightenment, for this is what happened to me forty years ago.'

I followed this advice and found my exercise gaining more light and strength than usual. On the second day I could not close my eyelids even if I wanted to; on the third day I felt as if I were walking in the air; and on the fourth day all worldly affairs ceased to bother me. That night I was leaning against the railing for a while, and when I examined myself I found that the field of consciousness seemed to be all empty, except for the presence of the koan itself. I turned around and sat on the cushion again, when all of a sudden I felt as if my whole body from head to foot were split like a skull; I felt as if I were taken out of an abysmal depth and thrown up into the air. My joy knew no bounds!

My experience was presented to Yen, but it did not meet his full approval. He advised me to go on with my exercise as before. When I asked for further instruction, among other things he gave me this: 'If you really wish to attain the highest truth of Buddhism, there is still something lacking in your understanding, there ought to be a really final stroke. Say to yourself, "Where do I lack this finality?"' I could not believe his words, and yet there was a shadow of doubt lurking in my mind. So I went on stolidly with my zazen every day as before for about six months more.

One day I had a headache and was preparing a medicine when a monk known as Chiao the Red-nosed asked me how I understood the story of Prince Nata?[1]

Thus asked, I remembered that I was once asked by the senior monk Wu about the same story, but failed to give him a reply. This remembrance at once led to the solution.

Later on, after Yen had passed away, I went to Mêng-shan, and Shan asked, 'Where in the study of Zen do you consider yourself to have reached its consummation?' I did not know what to say. Shan then told me to exercise myself in tranquillization so that all the dust of worldliness might be thoroughly removed. But whenever I entered his room and tried to say a word he at once remarked, 'Something lacking.' One day I began my zazen at four in the afternoon and continued until four in the morning, and through sheer power of concentration I reached an exquisite state of ecstasy. Coming out of it I saw the master and told him about it. He then asked, 'What is your original self?' I was about to speak when he shut the door in my face.

After this I exerted myself more and more in zazen and was able to experience many exquisite states of mind. Though I had to see my former master pass away before I had penetrated into the details of Zen, yet fortunately

---

[1] 'Prince Nata rending himself asunder gives his flesh back to his mother and his bones to his father and then manifesting his own original body and by his miraculous powers preaches the Dharma for the benefit of his parents.' This is one of the well-known koans. The idea is to make the student interview this 'original body' shorn of all its trappings, physical, mental, or spiritual.

through the guidance of the present master I have been led into deeper realizations. In truth, when one is earnest and resolute enough, realizations will come to one frequently and there will be a stripping-off at each step forward.

One day when I was looking at the 'Inscriptions'[1] by the third patriarch, in which I read, 'When one returns to the root, the meaning is realized, but when one follows only the appearance, the substance is lost', then there was another stripping-off. The master Shan said: 'The study of Zen is like the polishing of a gem; the more polished the brighter the gem, and when it becomes thus brighter, let it still be polished up. When there is the more stripping-off of its outer coatings, this life of yours will grow worth more than a gem.'

But whenever I attempted to utter a word, the master would at once declare, 'Something lacking.' One day when deeply absorbed in meditation, I came across this 'something lacking'. All the bonds that had hitherto bound my mind and body were dissolved at once, together with every piece of my bones and their marrow. It was like seeing the sun suddenly bursting through the snow-laden clouds and brightly shining. As I could not contain myself, I jumped down at once from the seat, and running to the master took hold of him, exclaiming, 'Now, what am I lacking?' He gave me three slaps and I bowed to him profoundly. Said the master, 'O T'ien-shan, for many years you have exerted yourself for this very thing. Today, at last, you have it.'

Wu-wên T'sung of Hsiang-shan succeeded Ch'ing as a Zen master, and the following is his Zen experience:

Tu-wêng was the first master I saw in my study of Zen; he had me inquire into the meaning of 'Neither mind, nor Buddha, nor a thing, this.' Later we formed a group of six including Yün-fêng and Yüeh-shan, so that we might be a stimulation to one another in the Zen exercise. Next I saw the master Chiao Wu-nêng, who gave me '*Wu!*' Next I went

[1] The First Series, p. 196.

to Chang-lu where, again, I had friends together in order to encourage one another. I happened to meet the brother-monk Ching of Huai-shan, who asked, 'What is your understanding of Zen after several years of study?' I replied, 'Not a thought stirring all day.' Ching asked further, 'Where does this notion of yours originate?' I felt as if I knew but I was not quite sure how to answer him. Seeing that I had no insight into the gist of the matter, Ching told me that I was all right as far as my tranquillization went, but that I had no hold of the thing in its activity. This surprised me and I begged him to advise me as to how my exercise should be carried on so as to have an insight into the matter. Said Ching: 'Don't you know what Ch'uan-lao says? "If one wants to have an understanding in the matter, look at the North Star by turning around towards the south",' and without making further remarks he went away.

Thus questioned, I did not know what to say. Whether walking or sitting my mind refused to dwell on anything else, and for several succeeding days '*Wu*', was dropped and this 'North Star seen in the south' occupied my attention exclusively. One day I found myself in the shaving-room where I was sitting with others on a block of wood; the 'doubt' (*i*) firmly took hold of me and time passed without my knowing, and it was about meal time when without premonition I felt my mind broadening out, becoming clear, light, and serene. It seemed my whole mental system was broken up and its coatings were all stripped off; the entire world with all its objects, sentient and non-sentient, vanished before me; and there was a vast vacuity.

After a while I was awakened, feeling perspiration running down my whole body, and I knew what was meant by seeing the North Star in the south. I met Ching, and he asked, 'Who is it that comes this way?' I replied, 'Neither the self nor the other.' He said, 'If it is neither the self nor the other, what is it after all?' 'One who eats when hungry and sleeps when tired out,' I answered. Ching then made me express the experience in verse, which I did, and everything went on with no impediment. But still there was something final, and I was impressed that I had not yet grasped it.

Later on, I went into the mountains of Hsiang-yen where I passed the summer. The mosquitoes were terrible and I could not keep my hands in position. Then I thought of the ancient masters who had sacrificed their very lives for the sake of the Dharma—why then should I be bothered by mosquitoes? I made up my mind not to be disturbed by them any longer. Firmly setting my teeth, clenching my fists, I held up the 'Wu' before me and made a most desperate fight against the insects. While I was thus subjecting myself to a test of endurance it so happened that my body and mind finally attained a state of quietude. It felt as if the whole building with all its walls had crashed down leaving me in a vast void—an experience which nothing earthly could describe. My sitting lasted from about seven in the morning until two in the afternoon. I then realized that Buddhism contains the whole truth and that it is altogether due to our not being thorough enough in the attempt to grasp it that we sometimes imagine Buddhism to be misleading.

While my understanding of Zen was clear and full, there was yet something not quite thoroughly exhausted in the hidden and almost inapproachable recesses of my consciousness; so I retired again into the mountains for six years in Kwang-chou, for another six years in Li-an, and finally for three years again in Kwang-chou, when I was released in the fullest sense of the term.

12. *The Importance and the Function of the Spirit of Inquiry*

As has already been stated, the preparatory equipment of the Zen devotee before he takes up the koan exercise is:

1. To awaken a most sincere desire to be delivered from the bondage of karma, from the pain of birth and death;

2. To recognize that the aim of the Buddhist life consists

in attaining enlightenment, in maturing a state of consciousness known as satori;

3. To realize the futility of all intellectual attempts to reach this aim, that is, to solve in a most living manner the ultimate problem of existence;

4. To believe that the realization of satori means the awakening of Buddhatā which lies deeply buried in all minds;

5. To be in possession of a strong spirit of inquiry which will ever urge a man to experience within himself the presence of Buddhatā. Without this fivefold equipment he may not hope to carry out the koan exercise successfully to its end.

Even when he is thus mentally qualified, he may not believe the koan to be the most efficient means to reach the goal. It may be that he is more attracted to the Shingon or T'ien-tai method of discipline, or to the recitation of the Buddha's name as in the Pure Land sects, or to the repetition of the Daimoku as in the Nichiren sect. This is where what may be termed his religious idiosyncrasies rule, which are due to his previous karma. In this case, he cannot be a successful follower of Zen, and his emancipation will have to be effected in some other way.

Even among Zen followers there are some who are no believers in the koan, regarding it as something artificially contrived; indeed, they even go further and declare satori itself to be a sort of excrescence which does not properly belong to the original system of Zen. Most Japanese adherents of the Sōtō school of Zen belong to this class of koan denouncers. This divergence of views as to the efficacy of the koan exercise and the experience of satori comes rather from the differences of philosophical interpretation given to Zen by the followers of the Sōtō and the Rinzai. As far as the practice of Zen is concerned, both the Sōtō and the Rinzai are descendants of Bodhidharma and Hui-nêng.

However this may be, one must believe in the koan if he is to disciplined in it and awakened by it to satori. Now the question is: How is a koan—at least the first koan—to be brought up into the field of consciousness so as to occupy its centre when one undertakes to solve its meaning? It evidently has no logical connotation, for its express purpose is to cut off every passage to speculation and imagination. For instance, when '*Wu*' or '*Mu*' is given to a Zen Yogin, how is he expected to deal with it? There is no doubt that he is not to think about it, for no logical thinking is possible. '*Wu*' does not yield any meaning inasmuch as it is not to be thought of in connection with the dog, nor for that matter with the Buddha-nature, either; it is '*Wu*' pure and simple. The koan neither denies nor asserts the presence of Buddha-nature in the dog, although Chao-chou used the '*Wu*' on being asked about the Buddha-nature. When the '*Wu*' is given as a koan to the uninitiated, it stands by itself; and this is exactly what is claimed from the beginning by Zen masters, who have used it as an eye-opener.

So with 'the Cypress-tree'. It is simply 'the Cypress-tree', and has no logical connection with the question: 'What is the idea of the First Patriarch's visit to China?' Nor does it at all refer to the pantheistic view of existence, which is sometimes thought to be the world-conception of the Buddhists. This being the case, what mental attitude shall we take to the koan when it is given us as the key to the secrets of Zen?

Generally, the Chinese characters used in describing the mental attitude towards a koan are: *t'i-ch'i*, *t'i-szŭ*, *t'i-to*, *chu*, meaning, 'to lift', 'to hold up', 'to raise'; *k'an*, 'to see', 'to regard', 'to hold before the eye'; *san*, 'to be concerned with', 'to be in', 'to consult', 'to refer to'; *san-chiu* or *t'i-chiu*, 'to investigate', 'to inquire into'; *kung-fu*, 'to seek a clue', 'to search for a solution', 'to exercise one's mind on a subject'; *yai*, to 'examine'. All these terms purport to mean 'to keep a koan continually before one's mental eye so as to make one endeavour to find a clue to its secrets'.

These two processes, the holding up and the striving, may be considered one; for the sole object of holding up a koan before the mind is to see into its meaning. As this goes on, the meaning searched after objectively in '*Wu*', 'Cypress-tree', or 'three *chin* of flax', exfoliates itself, not from the koan indeed, but from within the Yogin's own mind. This is the moment when the koan becomes perfectly identified with the searching and striving mind, and the meaning yields itself through this identification.

It may not thus be proper to say that the koan is understood, for at the moment of understanding there is no koan separate from the mind. Nor is it proper to assert that it is the mind that understands itself, for the understanding is a reflection, an aftermath; a mind is the reconstruction of the understanding. There is as yet no judgment here, no subject, no predicate; there is simply the exclamation, 'Ah!' The Chinese terms used in this connection are quite graphic: *hê ti i hsia* or *p'ên ti i fa*, which means 'one outbursting cry'. The moment is thus: 'the bursting of the bag', 'the breaking up of the tar-casket', 'a sudden snapping', 'a sudden bursting', 'the bursting of the bamboo with a crack', 'the breaking up of the void', etc.

The word 'concentration' has been used very much in the koan exercise; but, in fact, concentration is not the main point, though it inevitably follows. The thing most essential in the exercise is the will to get into the meaning—we have at present no suitable expression—of the koan. When the will or the spirit of inquiry is strong and constantly working, the koan is necessarily kept without interruption before the eye, and all the other thoughts that are not at all cogent are naturally swept off the field of consciousness. This exclusion and sweeping off is a byproduct, it is more or less accidental. This is where the koan exercise is distinct from mere concentration and also from the Indian form of Dhyāna, that is, meditation, abstraction, or thought-cessation.

Two forms of concentration may be distinguished now; the one brought about as it were mechanically, and the other resulting inevitably, but in essence accidentally, from the intensification of an inquiring spirit. When concentration followed by identification is once attained either way, it necessarily ends in the final outburst of satori. But genuine Zen always requires the presence of a spirit of inquiry, as is shown in the following quotations.

# WEI-SHAN TURNING DOWN THE PITCHER

Ascribed to MOTONOBU KANO

Wei-shan Ling-yu (A.D. 771-853) was a disciple of Pai-chang. While he was studying Zen under the master, the monastery had a visitor from the south of the Lake. He was known as Szu-ma the ascetic and had a singular knowledge of what might in a sense be called "human geography" and also of phrenology in its wider application. He discovered in the South a certain mountain, Wei-shan, which he thought was a fine site for a big monastery capable of boarding one thousand and five hundred monks. He asked Pai-chang for somebody who could establish such an institution at Wei-shan.

Pai-chang, recommending himself for the undertaking, said, "Do you think I can fill the position?" Szu-ma said, "No," and explained the reason why: "You are a 'bony' person while Wei-shan is a 'fleshy' mountain. If you were to preside over the proposed monastery, the monks who would gather about you might not exceed one thousand."

Pai-chang then proposed a monk called Hua-lin, who occupied the first seat at his monastery. Szu-ma made Hua-lin clear his throat and then walk several steps. This stange test proved that Hua-lin was unsatisfactory. Pai-chang now called in Ling-yu who was the head-monk of the kitchen. As soon as he came into the room, Szu-ma the ascetic announced him to be the very person for the work, and Pai-chang agreed. Ling-yu was to be depatched to Wei-shan.

When Hua-lin learned of it, he protested, "How can I, the head-monk of the whole monastery, give away this work to my brother Yu?" Pai-chang then suggested this scheme to settle the difficult question in hand: "We will call a general meeting of the monks and see which of you will give the best answer to my question." When they all had gathered, the master produced the pitcher before them and said, "Do not call this a pitcher; what would you call it?" Hua-line said, "You cannot call it a block of wood." The master did not quite approve of this statement, and Ling-yu was beckoned to express his view. He came forward, and, gently pushing the pitcher down, left the room. Pai-chang smilingly declared: "The head-monk has lost the game!"

It may be added that Wei-shan was still a wild mountain in those days, and it took several years before Ling-yu had any disciple of his own and a monastery. In the meantime, his friends were monkeys and deer and his food consisted principally of nuts.[1]

*Chuan-téng Lu*, IX.

# MAÑJUŚRI INCARNATE AS THE GOD OF LITERATURE

### By MINCHO
### *(1352–1431)*

The idea that the Buddha and the Bodhisattva incarnate themselves in all possible forms of existence in order to save all beings, is characteristic, as is well known, of the Mahayana. The figure represented here is the Bodhisattva Mañjuśri in one of his transformation-bodies, for he is said once to have appeared in the history of Japan as the god of literature. In China, Wu-tai Shan is supposed to be Mañjuśri's favourite abode, and O-mi Shan shelters Samantabhadra. In the Third Series of my *Zen Essays*, both Samantabhadra and Mañjuśri will be shown in more of their transformation-bodies.

As was noticed elsewhere, the Buddhist life is closely knitted with nature, its concerns are not with humanity only, but with the whole universe, the plum-blossoms, the hanging vines, and the fierce, crouching beast (here meant for a lion), are all destined for Buddhahood, when they are once embraced by the Prajña (wisdom) and Karuna (love) of the Bodhisattva. Mañjuśri is not a being apart from the rest of us. As soon as we are awakened to his Enlightenment which is our own Bodhicitta, we are transformed and share in his transformation-body, each of us in his own way. The reason why the Bodhisattvas later came to be most intimately connected with our life on earth, not always as objects of worship, but as workers and participants in this worldly life, will be more graphically illustrated in the later Essays.

Tai-hui, who was one of the earlier advocates of the koan, was always emphatic about this point; for we find references to it everywhere in his discourses known as *Tai-hui's Sermons*.[1] Consider such statements as the following: 'Single out the point where you have been in doubt all your life and put it upon your forehead.' 'Is it a holy one, or a commonplace one? Is it an entity, or a non-entity? Press your question to its very end. Do not be afraid of plunging yourself into a vacuity: find out what it is that cherishes the sense of fear. Is it a void, or is it not?'

Tai-hui never advises us just to hold up a koan before the mind; he tells us, on the contrary, to make it occupy the very centre of attention by the sheer strength of an inquiring spirit. When a koan is backed up by such a spirit, it is, he says, 'like a great consuming fire which burns up every insect of idle speculation that approaches it'. Without this stimulating spirit of inquiry philosophically coloured, no koan can be made to hold up its position before the consciousness. Therefore, it is almost a common-sense saying among Zen masters to declare that, 'In the mastery of Zen the most important thing is to keep up a spirit of inquiry; the stronger the spirit the greater will be the satori that follows; there is, indeed, no satori when there is no spirit of inquiry; therefore begin by inquiring into the meaning of a koan.'

According to Kao-fêng Yüan-miao,[2] we have this:

'The koan I ordinarily give to my pupils is: "All things return to the One; where does the One return?" I make them search after this. To search after it means to awaken a great inquiring spirit for the ultimate meaning of the koan. The multitudinousness of things is reducible to the One, but where does this One finally return? I say to them: Make this inquiry with all the strength that lies in your personality, giving yourself no time to relax in this effort. In whatever physical position you are, and in whatever business you are employed, never pass your time idly. Where

[1] *Tai-hui p'u-shuo.*
[2] 1238-1295.

does the One finally return? Try to get a definite answer to this query. Do not give yourself up to a state of doing nothing; do not exercise your fantastic imagination, but try to bring about a state of perfect identification by pressing your spirit of inquiry forward, steadily and uninterruptedly. You will be then like a person who is critically ill, having no appetite for what you eat or drink. Again you will be like an idiot, with no knowledge of what is what. When your searching spirit comes to this stage, the time has come for your mental flower to burst out.'

Ku-yin Ching-ch'in, late in the fifteenth century, has this to say regarding the koan exercise:

' "Searching and contriving" (*kung-fu*) may best be practised where noise and confusion do not reach; cut yourself off from all disturbing conditions; put a stop to speculation and imagination; and apply yourself wholeheartedly to the task of holding on to your koan, never letting it go off the centre of consciousness, whether you are sitting or lying, walking or standing still. Never mind in what condition you are placed, whether pleasing or disagreeable, but try all the time to keep the koan in mind, and reflect within yourself who it is that is pursuing the koan so untiringly and asking you this question so unremittingly.

'As you thus go on, intensely in earnest, inquiring after the inquirer himself, the time will most assuredly come to you when it is absolutely impossible for you to go on with your inquiry, as if you had come to the very fountain of a stream and were blocked by the mountains all around. This is the time when the tree together with the entwining wistaria breaks down, that is, when the distinction of subject and object is utterly obliterated, when the inquiring and the inquired are fused into one perfect identity. Awakening from this identification, there takes place a great satori that brings peace to all your inquiries and searchings.'

T'ien-ch'i Shui's[1] advice to students of Zen is this:

'Have your minds thoroughly washed off of all cunning and crookedness, sever yourselves from greed and anger which

[1] From Chu-hung's *Biographies of the Famous Zen Masters of Ming.*

rise from egotism, and let no dualistic thoughts disturb you any longer so that your consciousness is wiped perfectly clean. When this purgation is effected, hold up your koan before the mind: "All things are resolvable into the One, and when is this One resolved? Where is it really ultimately resolved?"

'Inquire into this problem from beginning to end, severally as so many queries, or undividedly as one piece of thought, or simply inquire into the whereabouts of the One. In any event, let the whole string of questions be distinctly impressed upon your consciousness so as to make it the exclusive object of attention. If you allow any idle thought to enter into the one solid uninterruptible chain of inquiries, the outcome will ruin the whole exercise.

'When you have no koan to be held before your minds, there will be no occasion for you to realize a state of satori. To seek satori without a koan is like boiling sands which will never yield nourishing rice.

'The first essential thing is to awaken a great spirit of inquiry and strive to see where the One finally resolves itself. When this spirit is kept constantly alive so that no chance is given to languor or heaviness or otioseness to assert itself, the time will come to you without your specially seeking it when the mind attains a state of perfect concentration. That is to say, when you are sitting, you are not conscious of the fact; so with your walking or lying or standing, you are not at all conscious of what you are doing; nor are you aware of your whereabouts, east or west, south or north; you forget that you are in possession of the six senses; the day is like the night, and *vice versa*. But this is still midway to satori, and surely not satori itself. You will have yet to make another final and decided effort to break through this, a state of ecstasy, when the vacuity of space will be smashed to pieces and all things reduced to perfect evenness. It is again like the sun revealing itself from behind the clouds, when things worldly and super-worldly present themselves in perfect objectivity.'

According to Ch'u-shan Shao-ch'i:[1]

[1] Chu-hung's *Biographies*.

'It is necessary for the uninitiated to have a kind of too wherewith to take hold of Zen; and it is for this reason that they are told to practise the Nembutsu, that is, to be thinking of the Buddha. The Buddha is no other than Mind, or rather, that which desires to see this Mind. Where does this desire, this thought, take its rise? From the Mind, we all say. And this Mind is neither a mind, nor a Buddha, nor a something. What is it then?

'To find it out, let them abandon all that they have accumulated in the way of learning, intellection, and knowledge; and let them devote themselves exclusively to this one question, "Who is it that practises the Nembutsu (*namu-amida-butsu*)?" Let this inquiring spirit assert itself to the highest degree. Do not try to reason it out; do not assume a state of mere passivity for satori to come by itself; do not allow yourself to cherish false thoughts and imaginations; do not let ideas of discrimination assert themselves. When your striving and seeking is constant, permitting no breaks and interruptions, your Dhyāna will naturally be matured, and your inquiring spirit (*i-t'uan*) brought up to the inevitable crisis. You will then see that Nirvāṇa and Saṁsāra, the land of purity and the land of defilement, are mere idle talk, and that there is from the beginning nothing requiring explanation or commentary, and further that Mind is not a somewhat belonging to the realm of empirical consciousness and therefore not an object of mental comprehension.'[1]

Tu-fêng Chi-shan,[2] who flourished in the latter half of the fifteenth century, used to advocate strongly the awakening of an inquiring spirit, as is seen in the following passage:[3]

[1] *Pu-k'ê-tê, anupalabdha* in Sanskrit.
[2] His stanza on the Zen experience is recorded in Chu-hung's *Biographies of the Famous Zen Masters of Ming*:
   'Here rules an absolute quietness, all doings subside;
   Just a touch, and lo, a roaring thunder-clap!
   A noise that shakes the earth, and all silence;
   The skull is broken to pieces, and awakened I am from the dream!'
[3] Quoted in the *Ch'an-kuan ts'ê-chin* ('Aids to Breaking Through the Frontier Gate of Zen').

'If you are determined to escape birth and death, a great believing heart is first of all to be awakened and great vows to be established. Let this be your prayer: So long as the koan I am holding this moment is not solved, so long as my own face which I have even prior to my birth is not seen, so long as the subtle deeds of transmigration are not destroyed, I make up my mind most resolutely not to abandon the koan given me for solution, not to keep myself away from truly wise teachers, and not to become a greedy pursuer of fame and wealth; and when these determinations are deliberately violated, may I fall in the evil paths. Establishing this vow, keep a steady watch over your heart so that you will be a worthy recipient of a koan.

'When you are told to see into the meaning of "*Wu*" the essential thing to do in this case is to let your thought be focussed on the "why" of the Buddha-nature being absent in the dog. When the koan deals with the oneness of all things, let your thought be fixed on the "where" of this oneness. When you are told to inquire into the sense of the Nembutsu, let your attention be principally drawn on the "who" of the Nembutsu. Thus, turning your light of reflection inwardly, endeavour to enter deeply into a spirit of inquiry. If you feel that you are not gaining strength in this exercise, repeat the whole koan as one complete piece of statement from the beginning to the end. This orderly pursuance of the koan will help you to raise your spirit of inquiry as to the outcome of it. When this spirit is kept alive without interruption and most sincerely, the time will come to you when you perform, even without being aware of it, a somersault in the air. After experiencing this you may come back to me and see how my blows are dealt out.'

K'ung-ku Lung[1] seems to be an advocate of the Nembutsu as well as the koan, but as far as he advises his pupils to exercise themselves on a koan, he upholds the spirit of inquiry to be the sustaining force in the exercise. For he says that the koan is to be 'silently inquired into' (*mo-mo t'san chiu*), that the '*Wu*' is to be 'made lucid' (*ming*) by

[1] From Chu-hung's *Biographies*.

'furiously' (*fên-fên-jan*) attending to it; that students of Zen should apply themselves to this thought, 'This mind is kept working while the body continues its Māyā-like existence, but where is it to rest when the dead body is cremated?' To find out where the oneness of things ultimately lies, the student must reflect within himself and inquire into the problem so as to locate definitely its whereabouts.[1]

All these masters belonging to late Yüan and early Ming, when the koan system became a definitely settled method in the mastery of Zen, agree in keeping up a strong inquiring spirit as regards the meaning of the koan or the spirit itself that thus inquires. The koan is not just to be held up before the mind as something that gathers up like a magnet all one's mental energies about it; the holding must be sustained and nourished by the strong undercurrent of spiritual energy without whose backing the holding becomes mechanical and Zen loses its creative vitality.

We may question: Why is not the mechanical method also in full accord with the spirit of Zen? Why is the inquiring method to be preferred? Why is it necessary to keep up the spirit of inquiry throughout the koan exercise? Has it anything to do with the nature of satori itself that emerges from the exercise? The reason why the masters have all emphasized the importance of the inquiring spirit is, in my view, owing to the fact that the koan exercise started first to reproduce the Zen consciousness, which had grown up naturally in the minds of the earlier Zen devotees. Before these earlier men had taken to the study of Zen, they were invariably good students of Buddhist philosophy; indeed, they were so well versed in it that they finally became dissatisfied with it; for they came to realize that there was something deeper in its teachings than mere

---

[1] Chu-hung comments on Lung's view of the Nembutsu: When the question is concerned with the Nembutsu, Lung is not so particular about cherishing a spirit of inquiry as was generally done in his day. For he states in one of his letters that while, according to the master Yu-t'an, one is advised to inquire into the 'who' of the Nembutsu, this inquiring form of Nembutsu is not absolutely necessary, for just to practise it in one's ordinary frame of mind will be enough.

analysis and intellectual comprehension. The desire to penetrate behind the screen was quite strong in them.

What is the Mind, or the Buddhatā, or the Unconscious that is always posited behind the multitudinousness of things, and that is felt to be within ourselves? They desired to grasp it directly, intuitively, as the Buddhas of the past had all done. Impelled by this desire to know, which is the spirit of inquiry, they reflected within themselves so intensely, so constantly, that the gate was finally opened to them, and they understood. This constant knocking at the gate was the antecedent condition that always seemed to be present and that resulted in the maturing of their Zen consciousness.

The object of the Zen exercise is to bring about this intense state of consciousness, in a sense artificially, for the masters could not wait for a Zen genius to rise spontaneously,[1] and therefore sporadically, from among their less spiritually-equipped brothers. Unless the aristocratic nature of Zen was somewhat moderated, so that even men of ordinary capacity could live the life of a Zen master, Zen itself might rapidly disappear from the land where Bodhidharma and his followers had taken such special pains to make its root strike in deeply. Zen was to be democratized, that is, systematized.

Pao-nêng Jên-yang[2] says in one of his sermons: 'Should-

[1] According to Kung-ku Lung: 'Anciently, there were probably some who had satori without resorting to the koan exercise, but there are none nowadays who can ever attain satori without strenuously applying themselves to the exercise.'

[2] Pao-nêng Jên-yang was a disciple of Yang-ch'i Fang-hui (died 1046). Before he became a Zen devotee he was a great scholar of T'ien-tai philosophy. When he came to Hsüeh-tou, who was a great figure in the Yün-mên school of Zen, the master at once recognized in him a future Zen master. To stimulate him, Hsüeh-tou addressed him sarcastically, 'O you great college professor!' The remark stung Jên-yang to the quick, and he determined to surpass in Zen even this great master. When he finally became a master himself, as Hsüeh-tou had expected, he once appeared in the pulpit and said: 'Behold, I am now in the tongue-pulling hell!' So saying, he was seen as if pulling out his tongue with his own hand and exclaimed: 'Oh! Oh! This hell is meant for liars.' Another time, seeing his attendant-monk offering incense to the Buddha, preparatory for a regular discourse to be given by the master, he said, 'Monks, my attendant has already given you a sermon,' and without another word he came down from the pulpit.

ering a bag, holding a bowl, I have been pilgrimaging for more than twenty years all over the country and visited more than a dozen masters of Zen. But at present I have no special attainment to call my own. If I have, I can tell you, I am not much better than a piece of rock devoid of intelligence. Nor had those reverend masters of Zen whom I visited any special attainment which might benefit others. Ever since I remain a perfect ignoramus with no knowledge of anything, with no intelligence to understand anything. I am, however, satisfied with myself. Inadvertently carried by the wind of karma I find myself at present in the country of Chiang-nêng, and have been made to preside over this humble monastery and to lead others, mixing myself with people of the world. Here thus as a host I serve all the pilgrims coming from various parts of the country. There is enough of salt, sauce, porridge, and rice with which to feed them sufficiently. My time, thus engaged, is passed quietly, but as to the truth of Buddhism there is not even a shadow of it to dream of.'

If all Zen masters held themselves on to this exalted view of Zen Buddhism, who would ever be able to succeed them and uninterruptedly transmit to posterity their experience and teaching?

Shih-t'ien Fa-hsün (1170–1244) says:[1]

'Very few indeed there are who can walk the path of our
    Fathers!
In depth and steepness it surpasses an abysmal pit;
Uselessly I extend the hand to help the passengers;
Let the moss in my front court grow as green as it chooses.'

This view of Zen is what we must expect of course of a genuine Zen master, but when the moss of the Zen courtyard is never disturbed by the footsteps of any human beings, what will become of Zen? The path must be made walkable, to a certain extent at least; some artificial means

[1] From his *Sayings*, Vol. II.

must be devised to attract some minds who may one day turn out to be true transmitters of Zen.[1]

The rise of the koan exercise was altogether a natural growth in the history of Zen. Being so, the function of a first koan must be to reproduce as it were artificially the same state of consciousness that was experienced by the earlier masters in a more spontaneous way. This means to bring the spirit of inquiry into a point of concentration or 'fixation'. The koan shows no logical clue to take hold of in an intellectual and discursive manner, and therefore an uninitiated Yogin has to turn away from logic to psychology, from ideation to personal experience, from what is his own only superficially to his inmost being.

The koan does not, indeed, make light of reasoning, that is, it does not try to check it by force; but as the koan stands before the Yogin like 'an iron wall and a silver mountain' against any advance of speculation or imagination, he has no choice but to abandon reasoning. He must find some other means of approach. He cannot yield up his spirit of inquiry, for it is that which makes him stronger and more determined than ever to break through the iron wall. When the koan is properly presented, it never crushes this spirit but gives it greater stimulation.

It was because of this inquiring mind that the earlier Zen devotees became dissatisfied with all the intellectual explanations of things, and that they came finally to a master and knew what they wanted of him. Without this perpetual urge from within, they might have remained well contented with whatever philosophical teachings were given them in the sūtras and śastras. This urge from within was thus never to be ignored even when the koan exercise came to replace the more spontaneous rise of Zen consciousness. San-ch'ing or i-ch'ing, which is no other than this urge or this inquiring spirit, is therefore now always kept in the foreground in the study of Zen. The master's advice:

[1] That Zen was something unapproachable from its first appearance in China can easily be evinced from the legend that Bodhidharma kept up his lonely silent meditation for nine years.

'See where you are going to rest after death, after crema-
tion!'; or 'Exerting all your mental energies, inquire into
the final abode where the oneness of things returns'; or
'Awaken a great spirit of inquiry and see where the One
returns; do not let this spirit vacillate or falter'; or 'See
what kind of mental attitude it is, see what meaning is
yielded here, be decided to search out all that is contained
therein'; or 'Ask of your self, inquire into your self, pursue
your self, investigate within your self, and never let others
tell you what it is, nor let it be explained in words.'

When a Yogin grapples with the koan in this manner,
he is ever alive to the spirit of Zen, and so is the koan. As
the problem is a living one and not at all a dead one, satori
which follows must also be a really living experience.

Metaphysically stated, we can say that a persistent
appeal to the spirit of inquiry is based on a firm faith in
the working of Buddhatā in every individual being. It is in
fact this Buddhatā itself that leads us to inquire into the
abode of the One. The keeping up of an inquiring spirit
in Zen devotees means no less than the self-assertion of
Buddhatā. Hence the statement that 'the greater the faith
the stronger the spirit of inquiry, and the stronger the
spirit of inquiry the deeper the attainment of satori'.[1]

Faith and an inquiring spirit are not contradictory terms,
but are complementary and mutually conditioning. The
reason why the old masters were so persistent in keeping up
a great spirit of inquiry in the koan exercise becomes now
intelligible. Probably they were not conscious of the logic
that was alive behind their instruction. The presence of
Buddhatā could only be recognized by a perpetual knocking at a door, and is not this knocking an inquiring into?
The Chinese character which I have rendered 'spirit of
inquiry' literally means 'to doubt' or 'to suspect', but in the
present case 'to inquire' will be more appropriate. Thus
tai-i will mean 'great mental fixation resulting from the
utmost intensification of an inquiring spirit'.

[1] Quoted by Fo-chi I-an Chên in a Zen history entitled *Hui-yüan
hsü-liao*.

Hakuin writes in one of his letters, in which he treats of the relative merits of the Nembutsu[1] and the koan: 'In the study [of Zen] what is most important is the utmost intensification of an inquiring spirit. Therefore, it is said that the stronger the inquiring spirit, the greater the resulting satori, and that a sufficiently strong spirit of inquiry is sure to result in strong satori. Further, according to Fo-kuo, the greatest fault [with Zen devotees] is the lack of an inquiring spirit over the koan. When their inquiring spirit reaches its highest point of fixation there is a moment of outburst. If there are a hundred of such devotees, nay a thousand of them, I assure you, every one of them will attain the final stage. When the moment of the greatest fixation presents itself, they feel as if they were sitting in an empty space, open on all sides and extending boundlessly; they do not know whether they are living or dead; they feel so extraordinarily transparent and free from all impurities, as if they were in a great crystal basin, or shut up in an immense mass of solid ice; they are again like a man devoid of all sense; if sitting, they forget to rise, and if standing, they forget to sit.

'Not a thought, not an emotion is stirred in the mind which is now entirely and exclusively occupied with the koan itself. At this moment they are advised not to cherish any feeling of fear, to hold no idea of discrimination, but to go on resolutely ahead with their koan, when all of a sudden they experience something akin to an explosion, as if an ice basin were shattered to pieces, or as if a tower of jade had crumbled, and the event is accompanied with a feeling of immense joy such as never before has been experienced in their lives. . . . Therefore, you are instructed to inquire into the koan of "*Mu*" (*wu*) and see what sense there is in it. If your inquiring spirit is never relaxed, always intent on "*Mu*" (*wu*) and free from all ideas and emotions and imaginations, you will most decidedly attain the stage of great fixation. . . . This is all due to the presence of an inquiring spirit in you; for without that the climax will never

[1] Literally, 'thinking of the Buddha'.

be reached, and, I assure you, an inquiring spirit is the wings that bear you on to the goal.'[1]

One of the practical reasons why the mechanical method of holding the koan which is not accompanied by a spirit of inquiry is disclaimed by the masters, is that the devotee's mind becomes concentrated on mere words or sounds. This, however, may not be an altogether bad thing, as we may see later on, only that we cannot be sure of reaching, as maintained by Hakuin and others, the stage of the greatest fixation prior to the outburst of satori.

The presence of an inquiring spirit paves the way much more readily and surely to satori, because satori is what gives satisfaction to the inquiring spirit, but chiefly because the inquiring spirit awakens the faith which lies at the basis of our being. The Zen masters say, 'Where there is faith (hsin), there is doubt (i)', that is, where there is faith, there is an inquiring spirit, for doubting is believing. Let it be remarked that doubting or inquiring in Zen does not mean denying or being sceptical, it means desiring to see, to come in direct contact with the object itself, putting aside all that stands between the seer and the object. The devotee as yet has no idea as to the what of the object he wishes to see, but he believes in its existence or presence within himself. Mere description or intellectual explanation does not satisfy him, his faith is not thereby confirmed. The desire for confirmation, to see his faith solidly or absolutely established, as in the case of sense-perception, means the awakening of an inquiring spirit, and the importance of this is steadily maintained by Zen masters. If so, the mechanical repetition of the koan must be said not to be in accord with the spirit of Zen.

In a book called *Po-shan's Admonitions Regarding the Study of Zen* (*Po-shan san-ch'an ching-yü*),[2] which belongs to late Ming, the question of an inquiring spirit (*i-ch'ing*) is discussed in detail. The following is an abstract.

---

[1] From Hakuin's work known as *Orate-gama*, to which references are frequently made in this book.

[2] Wu-i Yüan-lai (1575–1630) is the author.

In striving (*kung-fu*) to master Zen, the thing needed is to cherish a strong desire to destroy a mind subject to birth and death. When this desire is awakened, the Yogin feels as if he were enveloped in a blazing fire. He wants to escape it. He cannot just be walking about, he cannot stay quietly in it, he cannot harbour any idle thoughts, he cannot expect others to help him out. Since no moment is to be lost, all he has to do is to rush out of it to the best of his strength and without being disturbed by the thought of the consequence.

Once the desire is cherished, the next step is more technical in the sense that an inquiring spirit is to be awakened and kept alive, until the final moment of solution arrives. The inquiry is concerned with the whence of birth and the whither of death, and to be constantly nourished by the desire to rise above them. This is impossible unless the spirit of inquiry is matured and breaks itself out to a state of satori.

The method of maturing consists chiefly in:

1. Not caring for worldly things.
2. Not getting attached to a state of quietude.
3. Not being disturbed by pluralities of objects.
4. Being constantly watchful over oneself, behaving like a cat who is after a mouse.
5. Concentrating one's spiritual energy on the koan.
6. Not attempting to solve it intellectually where there are no such cues in it.
7. Not trying to be merely clever about it.
8. Not taking it for a state of doing-nothing-ness.
9. Not taking a temporary state of transparency for finality.
10. Not reciting the koan as if it were the Nembutsu practice or a form of Dhāraṇī.

When these cautions are properly followed, the Yogin is sure to bring the spirit of inquiry to a state of maturity. If not, not only the spirit refuses to be awakened, but the Yogin is liable to get into wrong ways and will never be able to rise above the bondage of birth and death, that is, to realize the truth of Zen.

The wrong ways into which the Yogin may fall are:

1. Intellectualism, wherein the koan is forced to yield up its logical contents.

2. A pessimistic frame of mind whereby the Yogin shuns such environments as are unfavourable to quiet contemplation.

3. Quietism, by which he tries to suppress ideas and feelings in order to realize a state of tranquillization or perfect blankness.

4. The attempt to classify or criticize according to his own intellectualistic interpretation all the koans left by the ancient masters.

5. The understanding that there is something inside this body of the various combinations, whose intelligence shines out through the several sense-organs.

6. And which by means of the body functions to perform deeds good or bad.

7. Asceticism, in which the body is uselessly subjected to all forms of mortification.

8. The idea of merit by the accumulation of which the Yogin desires to attain Buddhahood or final deliverance.

9. Libertinism, in which there is no regulation of conduct, moral or otherwise.

10. Grandiosity and self-conceit.

These, in short, are the ways of those whose spirit of inquiry is not sincere and therefore not in accordance with the spirit of the koan exercise.

It is by means of this *i-ch'ing*, 'spirit of inquiry', that we finally attain Hakuin's *daigi* (*tai-i*), 'great fixation' or 'a state of oneness', where a mountain is not seen as such, nor a sheet of water as such, for the reason that pluralities lose their meaning and appear to the Yogin in their aspect of sameness. But that too is merely a stage in his progress towards the final realization, in which a mountain is a

# HSIANG-YEN AND THE BAMBOOS

## By Motonobu Kano

The story is told in the First Series of *Zen Essays*, p. 226. The following *mondo* may interest the reader who has seen how Hsiang-yen came to his realisation.

Yen asked a monk, "Where do you come from?"

"I come from Wei-shan."

"What instructions does the master give out these days?"

"When a man come to him," said the monk, "and asks what is the idea of the first Patriarch's coming from the West, he raises his *hossu*."

Hsiang-yen, after listening to the report, asked: "How do the Brethren there understand the master?"

'They argue that the master's idea is to reveal Mind by means of form, to manifest Reason by means of matter."

Hsiang-yen said, "Your understanding ought to be a direct one. If it is not, what is the use of reasoning about it?"

The monk then asked Yen how he understood Wei-shan the master. Yen raised the *hossu*.[1]

[1] *Chuan-téng Lu*, XI.

# LING-YÜN AND THE PEACH-BLOSSOMS

By Motonobu Kano

Ling-yün was a disciple of Wei-shan Ling-yu. While studying with him, Ling-yün had an insight into the truth of Zen by accidently watching the peaches in bloom. The following is his verse composed at the time:

> "For thirty years I have been in search of
>     the swordsman;
> Many a time have I watched the leaves decay
>     and the branches shoot!
> Ever since I saw for once the peaches in
>     bloom,
> Not a shadow of doubt do I cherisht[1]

[1] *Chuan-téng Lu*, XI.

mountain and a sheet of water a sheet of water. When this state of great fixation is held as final, there will be no up-turning, no outburst of satori, no penetration, no insight into Reality, no severing the bonds of birth and death.

PART II

### 1. *The Koan Exercise and the Nembutsu*

We are now in the position to see in what relation the koan exercise stands to the practice of the Nembutsu. Chinese Buddhism has developed along the two lines of Zen and Nembutsu, and to treat of their relationship means to gain knowledge concerning some of the fundamental psychological facts of the Buddhist life, and also, as I wish to maintain, of all the religious life.

Among the circumstances that led to the mechanical treatment of the koan, we may mention the prevalence of the Nembutsu in Yüan and Ming. The Nembutsu literally means, 'to think of the Buddha', and consists particularly in the recitation of the name of Amitābha Buddha (*o-mi-to-fo* in Chinese).

Historically, we can trace the origin of the Nembutsu teaching in the very early days of Buddhism in India. In China the first known group of Nembutsu devotees was the White Lotus Society led by Hui-yüan (died 416). The gradual democratization of the Buddhist faith down through the successive dynasties favoured the spread of the Nembutsu all over China and alongside of the more aristocratic Zen. Superficially considered, the Nembutsu is the very opposite of Zen, for when Zen depends on nobody outside one's self, the Nembutsu puts its reliance exclusively on the Buddha. But when the psychology of the Nembutsu is analysed there is something in the recitation of the Buddha's

name as practised by the Pure Land followers, which corresponds to the holding of a koan in Zen. It was owing to this
psychological common ground that their mutual approach
was possible, Zen to Nembutsu and Nembutsu to Zen.

The Nembutsu was by no means mechanical in the
beginning. Thinking of the Buddha came first and the
invocation by name followed. But as in everything else, the
content that first determined the form is later determined
by the form; that is, the order is reversed. The Buddha's
name may be invoked by a devotee without necessarily his
thinking of the Buddha, of his excellent virtues, of his
saving vows; but as he repeats the name it calls up in him
all the memories and images concerning the Buddha, and
without his being conscious of it, he is ever more absorbed
in the contemplation of the Adored One. The invocation
that was started mechanically is now turned in a direction
that was not previously so designed.

The new psychology thus ushered in began to influence
the adherents of the koan in late Yüan, and there were some
Zen masters who took a decided stand against it. They saw
the danger of the koan turning into a Nembutsu recitation,
for in that case both the spirit of Zen and the reason for the
koan exercise would be destroyed.

Even when the practice of the Nembutsu grew quite
universal in the fifteenth century, invading even the Zen
monasteries, the masters resisted the practice, advising
their pupils to see *who* it is that calls upon the Buddha or
recites his name. For instance, Tu-fêng Chi-shan,[1] who
probably died towards the end of the fifteenth century,
said: 'The main thing is to understand the ultimate meaning of life; therefore, exert yourself and spare no effort to
see *who* it is that does the invoking of the name. The word
*Who* is most important; concentrate yourself on this one
word.'

Ch'u-shan Shao-ch'i (1404–1473) writes to one of his
disciples: 'The idea of the invocation is to know that the

[1] In *The Reputed Zen Masters of the Ming Dynasty*, compiled by Chu-
hung.

147

Buddha is no other than your own mind; but what is this mind? See into the *whence* of your thought which makes you utter the name of the Buddha; where does it originate? But you must go even farther than this and make inquiries as to the *who* of this person who wants to see into the whence of a thought. Is it mind, or Buddha, or matter? No, it is none of these, say the masters. What is it, then?'

This is the way the masters dealt with the Nembutsu in connection with the koan exercise if one wanted to master Zen. An inquiring spirit was by no means to be lost sight of. The following quotations from the Yüan and Ming Zen teachers show which way the wind was blowing in the thought world of the fourteenth and the fifteenth centuries. T'ien-ju Wei-tsê, who flourished early in the fourteenth century, was a great figure during the Yüan dynasty, and there is no doubt that the Nembutsu movement was going on quite strongly then and encroaching upon the realm of Zen. Wei-tsê could not ignore it and wished to define clearly where Zen differed from Nembutsu and how far the one agreed with the other. In the second volume of his *Sayings* (*yü-lu*) it is written:

'There are some these days among the laity as well as in the Brotherhood who desire by means of the Nembutsu to be born in the Land of Purity and wonder if the Nembutsu is not to be distinguished from Zen. In my view, they fail to recognize that Zen and Nembutsu are not the same and yet are the same; for the object of Zen is to understand what life means, and the object of the Nembutsu is also that. Zen directly points to the mind in every one of us, declaring that to see into the nature of every being means attaining Buddhahood; whereas the Nembutsu aims at reaching the Land of Purity which is no other than one's own mind, and seeing into the original nature of every being which is Amitābha himself.

'If this is so, how can one differentiate Nembutsu from Zen? We read in a sūtra that it is like entering into a great city which is provided with gates on its four sides; people coming from different quarters will find their own entrance as there is more than one gate. But, once in, they are in the same city. Zen and Nembutsu each appeals to a special type of character; that is all.

'In the Nembutsu you can distinguish between that which is effective and that which is not. Why? If the devotee's invocation does not go farther than his lips while his mind is not at all thinking of the Buddha, this kind of invocation is not effective. If on the other hand his lips and his mind are conjointly working towards the Buddha as his name is recited, so that his mind always works in union with the Buddha, his Nembutsu will surely bring its result. Suppose here is a man carrying a rosary in his hand and reciting the Buddha's name with his lips; but if in the meantime his thoughts are all in confusion, running wild in every direction, he is the one whose invocation is on his lips only and not in his mind. He is uselessly fatiguing himself, his labour comes to naught. It is far better to be thinking of the Buddha in the mind even though the lips are not moving, for such is the real follower of the Nembutsu.

'Do we not read in a sūtra that all the Tathāgatas in the ten quarters are lovingly thinking of all beings just as a mother does of her children; for beings that are drowning in the ocean of birth and death are like children who are wandering in strange foreign countries. The Buddha like a loving mother thinks of them, and though he may not be talking about his compassionate feeling, his heart never ceases thinking of his lost children. If the children thought of their mother in the same way, will not they, mother and children, some day come face to face?

'Therefore, the sūtra says that if the hearts of all beings long for the Buddha and think of him they will surely see him either in the present or in the future. The present means this life, the future means the life to come. If this is so, he who intensely longs for the Buddha and thinks of him, will most assuredly come into his presence. What then is the difference between coming into the presence of the Buddha and attaining satori by the study of Zen?

'Says the Master Huan-chu: The study of Zen aims at

elucidating the meaning of birth and death, whereas the Nembutsu proposes to get settled with the question of death and birth; choose either one of the pathways, for there is no disputation to be aroused about them. Quite true, there is no disputation between the two, but do not allow yourself to keep both with you. Let the Zen devotee keep himself exclusively to Zen, and let the one who recites the Nembutsu keep exclusively to the Nembutsu. If the mind is divided between the two, neither will be attained. There is a comparision drawn by an old master between such a divided mind and a man who tries to be in two boats simultaneously and is in neither. So far, there is no harm, perhaps, but a worse case may come to him at any moment, for he may fall between the two boats if he does not look out for himself.

'As for myself, I do not know much, but this I can tell, that in the Nembutsu just these four syllables are held up: *O-mi-to-fo* (*a-mi-da-butsu* in Japanese), which indicates no way, at least to Zen beginners, as to how to proceed with it. They are naturally at a loss, and fail to know what to do with the subject. But in the study of the koan you are told that you are each in possession of "the original face" which is the same as it is in all the Buddhas, only that in us it is not recognized. Try and see into it all by yourself without depending on anyone else. In this it may be said that you have a kind of clue whereby to go on with your Zen.'

One of the first Zen masters to introduce the idea of Nembutsu into Zen was Yang-ming Yen-shou.[1] He laid great importance on Zen Yogins devoting themselves to the practice of the Nembutsu to this extent, that he declared that those who follow Zen without Nembutsu may fail nine out of ten in their attainment of the final goal, whereas those who practise Nembutsu will all without exception come to realization; but the best are those who practise Zen and Nembutsu, for they will be like a tiger provided with horns. What Yang-ming exactly means by this statement is not easy to comprehend, for he does not tell us as to its

[1] Died 975.

practical side; that is, how to practise both Zen and Nembutsu at the same time. Did he mean to practise the Nembutsu after the attainment of Zen, or *vice versa*? Until this practical question is definitely settled, we may not venture either to refute or to defend Yang-ming.

This much we can say, that the Nembutsu had been making steady progress even among followers of Zen as early as the tenth century, and Yang-ming, as one of the greatest syncretists China ever produced, attempted to include into his system of Zen philosophy every school of Buddhism, and the Nembutsu naturally came to be fused into it. Besides, there was another strong reason why Zen had to listen to the appeal of the Nembutsu, which was this. Zen being too philosophical (though not in the ordinary sense of the term) exposed itself to an utter disregard of the emotional side of life. Zen indulges itself in excessive satori, so to speak, and as the result it frequently dries up its tears which must be shed over ignorance, over the miseries of life, over the world filled with iniquity. Thus Zen holds out no hope for a land of bliss and purity which is so vividly felt by the followers of Nembutsu. Did Yang-ming mean this when he said that Zen must be accompanied by the Nembutsu? The following remarks made by K'ung-ku Ching-lung, who flourished early in the fifteenth century, seem at least partly to point this interpretation. He says:

'Those who practise Zen are so exclusively devoted to Zen, thinking that they are thus exerting themselves to the attainment of quietude and nothing else: as to invoking the name of the Buddha in order to be born in the Land of Purity and worshipping him and reciting the sūtras in the morning and evening, they practise nothing of the sort. Such devotees may be called those who have Zen but have no Nembutsu. Yet really those followers of Zen are not of the right kind; they are mere sticklers of the koan exercise, they are quite like a stick or stone or brick. When they are attacked by this form of mental disease, they cannot be saved, except perhaps only one out of ten.

'Zen is a living spirit; it is like a gourd floating on water, when you touch it it dances most lively. Therefore, it is said that regard should be paid to the living spirit of the masters and not to their dead words. But there are others who practising Zen do not slight the teaching of the Nembutsu school and will regularly attend the morning and evening services. Indeed, the truth of Zen is met with anywhere you go if you only look for it. Hsüeh-fêng laboured hard as cook wherever he went, and Yang-chi busied himself as overseer of the monastery; they never made light of their daily life while innerly they devoted themselves to Zen. Yang-ming mastered the Zen of his teacher, Tê-shao, and yet was well disposed to propagate the doctrine of the Pure Land school. Is he not one who innerly was round and outwardly square? Innerly, he was all that could be desired of a Bodhisattva, and outwardly, acted as if he were one who belonged to the Śrāvakas. He is one who has both Zen and Nembutsu.'[1]

There is something lame in this interpretation, but the fact is not to be denied that the Nembutsu was rapidly undermining the strongholds of Zen in those days, and we will presently see that in the psychology of the Nembutsu there is a factor that can readily ally itself with the koan exercise in its mechanical phase. For in spite of this attitude of K'ung-ku towards the Nembutsu as a kind of Śrāvaka practice, he proceeds to uphold it as of the same efficiency as the koan exercise in the realization of the true Buddhist life.

In K'ung-ku's letter to another of his disciples, which was evidently written in answer to an inquiry concerning the practice of Nembutsu, the author advises him just to say the Nembutsu not necessarily with a philosophical attitude of mind; that is, with no inquiring spirit. The main point in the Nembutsu is to have a believing heart and quietly say it without troubling oneself about things of this world. Ku says:

'The doctrine of the Nembutsu is the shortest road to the realization of the Buddhist life. Be convinced of the

---

[1] From a letter to one of his disciples as quoted in Chu-hung's *Ming Masters*.

unrealness of this bodily existence, for to get attached to the vanities of this worldly life is the cause of transmigration. What is most desirable is the Land of Purity and what is most dependable is the Nembutsu. No matter how you are thinking of the Buddha, intensely or leisurely, no matter how you are invoking his name, whether loudly or softly, do not allow yourself to be constrained by any rule, but keep your mind unruffled, restful, and in silent contemplation. When it attains a state of unity undisturbed by environment, some day an accident will unexpectedly cause in you a sort of mental revolution, and thereby you will realize that the Pure Land of Serene Light is no less than this earth itself, and Amitābha Buddha is your own mind. But you must be careful not to let your mind expectantly wait for such a momentous event, for this will prove a hindrance to the realization itself.

'The Buddha-nature is a spontaneous generation in the sense that it is not a product of intellection, nor of imagination. When I say this, however, you may take it for a state of unconsciousness, which is another great error to be avoided. The only thing that is essential in this connection is to have a believing heart and not to allow any unnecessary and disturbing thoughts to become mixed in it. As you go on thus in the practice of Nembutsu while you may have no chance of attaining satori in this life, you will after death surely be reborn in the Pure Land, where by going up various grades you will finally arrive at the position which never turns back.

'The master Yu-t'an makes people hold this: "Who is it that practises the Nembutsu? What is it that is my own nature, which is, Amitābha?" This may be called the Nembutsu said in a strained state of mind or the Nembutsu accompanied with an inquiring spirit. It is not necessary for you to follow this method; just say your Nembutsu in an ordinary frame of mind.'

K'ung-ku's advice that the Nembutsu is not necessarily to be backed by an intensification of an inquiring spirit opens the way to the mechanical method of invocation.

This is what made Hakuin and his school rise furiously against some of the Chinese Zen masters of the fourteenth century and after.

Chu-hung, the author of the *Ming Masters*, the *Frontier Gate of Zen*, and many other works, who was also bitterly attacked by Hakuin, comments on K'ung-ku Ching-lung: 'Most Zen teachers tell people to see who he is that invokes the Buddha's name, but Ching-lung states that this is not absolutely necessary. As medicine is to be prescribed according to disease, so is the truth to be taught according to capacity. Each of these two is justifiable and there is no option to be made between them.'[1]

This method of invocation endorsed by such masters as Ching-lung and Chu-hung is based on psychological facts, and the subject may better be approached now from the viewpoint of the Nembutsu and not from that of Zen. Let us then see what is really meant by the Nembutsu.

## 2. *Nembutsu (nien-fo) and Shōmyō (ch'êng-ming)*

*Nembutsu* or *buddhānusmṛiti* literally means 'to think of the Buddha', or 'to meditate on the Buddha', and is counted as one of the six subjects of meditation in the *Mahāvyutpatti*. The six are as follows: 1. *Buddhānusmṛiti*; 2. *Dharma*; 3. *Samgha* (Brotherhood); 4. *Śīla* (morality); 5. *Tyāga* (giving up); and 6. *Devatā* (gods). It is also one of the five subjects of mental discipline known as *Wu t'ing hsin*; that is, objects by thinking of which the mind is kept away from erroneous views. The five are: 1. Impurity of the body, the thought of which reacts against greed and lust; 2. Compassion, as against anger; 3. Causation, as against infatuation or folly; 4. The six elements, as against the notion of an ego-substance; and 5. Breathing exercise, as against mental perturbation. Though I am unable to find out exactly how it came to pass, the fourth subject (that is, the six elements: earth, water, fire, air, the void, and consciousness) is

[1] *Biographies of the Famous Ming Masters.*

replaced by 'meditation on the Buddha' (*nembutsu*) in Chih-chê's commentary on the *Saddharmapuṇḍarīka*. According to a work belonging to the T'ien-tai school of Chih-chê, this meditation is considered to counteract mental heaviness, evil thoughts, and physical calamities.

It is a very natural thing for the Buddhists to meditate on their teacher, whose great personality impressed them in some way more than did his teaching. When they were not feeling energetic in their search after the truth, or when their minds were disturbed by all kinds of worldly temptation, the best way to strengthen their moral courage was, no doubt, to think of their teacher. In the beginning the Nembutsu was a purely moral practice, but as the mysterious power of a name came to claim a stronger hold on the religious imagination of the Indian Buddhists, the thinking of the Buddha as a person endowed with great virtues ceased and gave way to the uttering of his name. As a philosopher says, *Nec nomen Deo quaeras ; Deus nomen est.* Name is as good as substance; in some cases it works far more efficaciously than that for which it stands, for when we know the name, we can put a god into service. This has been so from the earliest days of every religious history all the world over. When Amitābha Buddha obtained his enlightenment he wished to have his name (*nāmadheya*) resound throughout the great chiliocosms, so that he might save any being that heard his name.[1]

But the sūtra[2] makes no reference yet to the uttering of his name only. The phrases used are: *daśabhiś cittotpādaparivartaiḥ*,[3] which forms the nineteenth vow of the

[1] See the *Sukhāvatīvyūha Sūtra*.

[2] This is one of the three principal sutras belonging to the Pure Land school. The three are: 1. *Sukhāvatīvyūha*, which treats of the Land of Bliss inhabited by Amitābha Buddha, and of the forty-eight (forty-three in the Sanskrit text) vows of the same Amitābha; 2. *Sūtra of the Meditations on Buddha Amitāyus*, in which Queen Vaidehī is instructed by Śākyamuni to practise sixteen forms of meditation regarding the Land of Bliss and its Lord; and 3. *The Sūtra of Amitābha*, which is generally known as the *Smaller Sukhāvatīvyūha*, as it also describes the Land of Bliss. Amitāyus (Eternal Life) and Amitābha (Infinite Light) refer to one and the same Buddha.

[3] Max Muller, p. 15, l. 4.

Sanskrit text, meaning 'Ten times repeating the thought [of the Pure Land]'; *prasannacittā mām anusmareyuh*,[1] which is the eighteenth vow of the Sanskrit text, meaning 'Remembered me with pure thoughts'; or *antaśa ekacittotpādam api adhyāśayena prasādasahagatena cittam utpādayanti*,[2] '[All beings] raise their thought, even for once only, raise their thought, with devotion and serenity.' *Cittotpāda* or *anusmṛiti*, 'thinking of [the Buddha]' is not the same as 'uttering the name'.

The *Pratyutpanna-samādhi-Sūtra* which was translated into Chinese as early as the second century by Lokaraksha, in which mention is also made of Amitābha Buddha in the West, and which is consequently regarded as one of the authoritative sources of the Pure Land school, refers to the name of the Buddha, saying 'The Bodhisattva, who hearing the name of the Buddha Amitābha wishes to see him, may see him by constantly thinking of the region where he is.' The term used here is 'thinking' (*nien* in Chinese) and not 'uttering'. Whenever the Buddha becomes an object of meditation, no matter to what school the devotee may belong, Hīnayāna or Mahāyāna, Zen or Shin, he has been thought of as a personality, not only physically, but as spiritually inspiring.

In the *Sūtra of the Meditation on the Buddha of Eternal Life*, however, the devotees are taught to say 'Adoration to Buddha Amitābha'; for when they utter this Buddha-name they will be liberated from sins committed in their lives for fifty billions of kalpas. Again, if a dying man cannot think of the Buddha owing to intense pain, he is told just to utter the name of the Buddha of Eternal Life (*Amitāyus*). In the *Smaller Sukhāvatīvyūha*, or *Sūtra of Amitāyus*, the author advises people to hold in mind (*manasikara*) the name of the blessed Amitāyus the Tathāgatā, which will make them depart with a tranquil mind from this life, when the time comes.

In accordance with these instructions in the sūtras,

[1] Max Muller, p. 14, l. 15.
[2] Max Muller, p. 47, ll. 2, 3.

Nāgārjuna writes in his *Commentary on the Daśabhūmika* (Chapter V, 'On Easy Practice') that if one wishes quickly to reach the stage of no-turning-back, he should hold the Buddha's name in mind full of reverent thought. There may be some difference, as far as words go, between 'holding in mind' and 'uttering' or 'invoking', but, practically, holding the Buddha's name in mind is to utter it with the lips, silently or audibly. The shifting of the centre of devotional attention from thinking to utterance, from remembrance to invocation, is a natural process.

Tao-ch'o[1] quotes a sūtra in his *Book of Peace and Happiness*,[2] which is one of the principal sources of the Pure Land doctrine. All the Buddhas save beings in four ways: 1. By oral teachings such as are recorded in the twelve divisions of Buddhist literature; 2. By their physical features of supernatural beauty; 3. By their wonderful powers and virtues and transformations; and 4. By their names, which, when uttered by beings, will remove obstacles and assure their rebirth in the presence of the Buddha.

To this Tao-ch'o adds: 'To my mind the present age belongs to the fourth five-hundred-years after the Buddha, and what we have to do now is to repent our sins, to cultivate virtues, and to utter the Buddha's name. Is it not said that even once thinking of Amitābha Buddha and uttering his name cleanses us from all our sins committed while transmigrating for eighty billion kalpas? If even one thought achieves this, how much more if one constantly thinks of the Buddha and repents one's [sinful deeds]!' All the Nembutsu followers who came after him have eagerly accepted his teaching, and *nembutsu* (*nien-fo*), 'thinking of the Buddha', has become identified with *shōmyō* (*ch'êngming*), 'uttering the name'.

In fact, uttering the name contains more and functions more effectively than thinking of the various excellent spiritual virtues and physical qualities with which the Buddha is endowed. The name represents all that can be

---

[1] 562–645, one of the foremost devotees of the Pure Land teaching.
[2] *An-lê-chi.*

predicated of the Buddha. The thinking of him means holding up his image in mind, and all kinds of hallucinations are apt to appear before the eye. In the case of the name, the mental operations tend more towards intellection, and a different psychology obtains here.

Here we can distinguish two ways in which the Buddha-name can be invoked; that is, when the name is announced, there are two attitudes on the part of the devotee towards the object of his adoration. In one case, the invocation takes place with the idea that *nomen est numen*, or as a sort of magical formula. The name itself is regarded as having some mysterious power to work wonders. For instance, we read in the *Saddharmapuṇḍarīka*, Chapter XXIV, where the worship of Avalokiteśvara is upheld:

'[Goblins and giants] would, by virtue of the name of Bodhisattva-Mahāsattva Avalokiteśvara being pronounced, lose the faculty of sight in their designs.' Or, 'Be not afraid, invoke all of you with one voice the Bodhisattva-Mahā-sattva Avalokiteśvara, the giver of safety, then you shall be delivered from this danger by which you are threatened at the hands of robbers and enemies.'

In these cases the name of Avalokiteśvara has undoubtedly a magical power not only over one's enemies, but also over impure passions, hatred, infatuation, etc. It further enables the devotee to get whatever happiness he desires. The gāthās in this chapter describe all the virtues issuing from him, and what the devotee has to do is just to think of him; that is, to utter his name. It was quite natural in the light here shed by the name of Avalokiteśvara that scholars of Shin Buddhism had once a heated discussion regarding the wonderful saving power of Amitābha, asking whether it comes from his name or from his vows.

The other attitude which may be assumed by the devotee towards the invocation, or Nembutsu, is especially represented by T'ien-ju Wei-tsê, a Zen master of the Yüan dynasty of the fourteenth century. He states in his *Some Questions Regarding the Pure Land Answered*:

'The Nembutsu consists in intensely thinking of the

thirty-two marks of excellence possessed by the Buddha, by holding them in mind in a state of concentration, when one will see the Buddha all the time whether his eyes are closed or open. This seeing the Buddha while still in this life may also take place when the Buddha is invoked by name, which is held fast in the mind. This way of coming into the presence of the Buddha by invoking him by name is better than the Nembutsu. When you practise this invocation, the mind must be kept under full control so that it will not wander about; let your thought dwell without interruption on the name of the Buddha, audibly repeat O-mi-to-fo[1] (or nembutsu). Each sound must be distinctly presented to the mind. Do not mind how many times the name is repeated, for the main thing is to have thought and will, mind and lips, all in perfect union.'

In the first case the name itself is regarded as having a wonderful power, especially over human affairs; it is a magic formula. When Amitābha wished to have his name resound all over the universe, did he want it to be a sort of talisman, or did he want it to be a moral force; that is, symbolic of something that is desirable in human life, so that whenever his name was heard his virtues and merits would be remembered, and would serve to incite the hearers to follow his example? Most likely the latter was in his mind. When the name is uttered, all that it stands for is awakened in the mind of the utterer; not only that, but finally his own mind will thereby open up its deepest resources and reveal its inmost truth which is no other than the reality of the name; that is, Amitābha himself.

In the second case, the name is pronounced not necessarily as indicative of things that are therein suggested, but in order to work out a certain psychological process thus set up. The name of the Buddha may now even be mechanically repeated without reference to the bearer of the name himself as an objective reality. This is what has actually taken place later in the history of the koan exercise. The following incident which took place in the mind of an old

[1] A-mi-da-butsu.

miser under the instruction of Hakuin, founder of the modern Japanese Rinzai School of Zen Buddhism, will supply us with a good illustration of what I mean by the psychological process induced by the recitation of the Buddha-name.

One of the numerous lay-disciples of Hakuin was worried over his old miserly father whose mind so bent on making money was not at all disposed towards Buddhism. He wanted Hakuin to suggest some method to turn his father's thought away from avarice. Hakuin suggested this proposal: Let the miserly old gentleman say the Nembutsu whenever he thinks of it, and have a penny paid for each recital. If he said the Nembutsu for one hundred times a day, he would have one hundred pennies for it.

The old man thought that it was the easiest way in the world to earn his pocket money. He came each day to Hakuin to be paid for his Nembutsu as he was perfectly regular in his account, so much for so many repetitions. He was enchanted with his earnings. But after a while he ceased to come to Hakuin for his daily payment. Hakuin sent for the son to learn what was the matter with the father. It was found that the father was now so engrossed in saying the Nembutsu that he forgot to make a record of it. This was what Hakuin was all the time expecting of him. He told the devoted son to leave his father alone for some time and see what would become of him now. The advice was followed, and in a week the father himself came up to Hakuin with beaming eyes, which told at once what a blissful spiritual experience he had gone through. There was no doubt that he had a kind of satori.

The mechanical repetition of the Nembutsu, that is, the rhythmic though monotonous utterance of the Buddha name, 'na-mu-a-mi-da-bu', 'na-mu-a-mi-da-bu' . . . over again and again, tens of thousands of times, creates a state of consciousness which tends to keep down all the ordinary functions of the mind. This state is very much akin perhaps to that of hypnotic trance, but fundamentally different from the latter in that what grows out of the Nembutsu consciousness is a most significant insight into the nature of Reality and has a most enduring and beneficial effect on the spiritual life of the devotee. In a hypnotic trance there is nothing of the sort, for it is a diseased state of mind bearing no fruit of a permanent value.

As regards the difference between the koan exercise and the Nembutsu, as was already repeatedly pointed out, in the one it consists in the absence of the intellectual element, and in the other in the presence of an inquiring spirit.

### 3. The Value of Shōmyō ('Uttering the Name') in the Jōdo school

After the decease of the Buddha the earnest desire of his followers was to see him again. They could not persuade themselves to think that such a great personality as the Buddha had completely passed away from among them. The impression he had left in their minds was too deep to be wiped off so soon and so easily. This is generally the case with any great soul. We are loath to consider his physical death the ending of all that constituted him, all that belonged to him; we want to believe that he is still alive among us, not in his former worldly fashion but in some way, perhaps in the way we like to designate spiritual. Thinking so, we are sure to see him somewhere and sometime.

This was true with the Christ as with the Buddha. But the Buddha had been living among a people who were trained in all kinds of concentration called Samādhi, and who were also perfect masters of practical psychology. The result was the production of such sūtras as the *Meditation Sūtra* (*Kwangyo*) or the *Pratyutpannasamādhi Sūtra* (*Hanjusammai*), in which directions are given in detail for having a personal interview with the Buddha or the Buddhas. First, there must be an intense thinking of the past master, an earnest longing to see him once more, and then, the spiritual exercise in which the thinking and longing is to be visualized —this is the natural order of things.

This visualization seems to have taken two courses as time went on: the one was nominalistic[1] and the other idealistic. It is of significance that these two tendencies are traceable in one and the same sūtra which is entitled *Sapta-śatikā-prajñā-pāramitā Sūtra*,[2] which was translated into Chinese by Man-t'o-lo-hsein of Fu-nan-kuo in A.D. 503, of the Liang dynasty. The sūtra belongs to the Prajñāpāramitā class of Mahāyāna literature and is considered to be one of the earliest Mahāyāna texts. It contains the essence of Prajñā-pāramitā philosophy, but what strikes us as strange is that the two tendencies of thought, nominalistic and idealistic, apparently contradicting each other, are presented here side by side. I suspect the later incorporation of the passages referring to the nominalistic current of thought which is made so much of by the expositors of the Pure Land teaching. However this may be, the visualizing process of meditation is generally superseded in this sūtra by the idealization of Buddhahood, which is typical of all the Prajñā texts.

In the opening passage of this sūtra, Mañjuśrī expresses his desire to interview the Buddha in his true aspect, thus:

'I desire to see the Buddha as he is in order to benefit all beings. I see the Buddha in the aspect of suchness (*tathatā*), of no-other-ness, of immovability, of doing-nothing-ness; I see the Buddha as free from birth and death, from form and no-form, from spatial and temporal relations, from duality and non-duality, from defilement and purity. Thus seen, he is in his true aspect and all beings are thereby benefited.

---

[1] It is not quite proper to use a scholastic term in this connection, but my idea is to distinguish here the aspect of the Nembutsu exercise in which the significance of the name is held up more emphatically against all other considerations. By 'nominalism', therefore, I wish to indicate roughly the principle operating in the emphatical upholding of the name as efficacious to mature the Samādhi of Oneness, or in being born in the Pure Land of Amitābha. 'Idealism' or 'conceptualism' will then mean the attitude of Prajñāpāramitā philosophers who endeavour to describe the ultimate nature of Reality by means of highly abstract, conceptualistic terms which are generally negativistic.

[2] There are three Chinese translations of this sūtra, the first of which appeared in A.D. 503 and the last in A.D. 693. It is generally known as a sūtra on Prajñāpāramitā expounded by Mañjuśrī. The Buddhist Tripitaka, Taisho Edition, Nos. 232, 233, and 220 (7).

'By seeing the Buddha in this manner [the Bodhisattva] is freed from both attachment and non-attachment, both accumulation and dissipation. . . .

'While thus seeing the Buddha for the sake of all beings, his [Bodhisattva's] mind is not attached to the form of all beings. While teaching all beings so as to make them turn towards Nirvāṇa, he is not attached to the form of Nirvāṇa. While arranging varieties of things in order for the sake of all beings, the mind does not recognize them [as having individual realities].'

In another version by Saṁghapāla, which appeared a few years later than Man-t'o-lo's, we have this:

'Buddha asked: Do you really wish to see the Buddha?

'Mañjuśrī said: The Dharmakāya of the Buddha is not really to be seen. That I come to see the Buddha here is for the sake of all things. As to the Dharmakāya of the Buddha, it is beyond thinkability, it has no form, no shape, it is neither coming nor departing, neither existent nor non-existent, neither visible nor invisible, it is such as it is, it is reality-limit. This light [that emanates from the Buddha giving a supernatural power to those who can perceive it] is Prajñāpāramitā, and Prajñāpāramitā is the Tathāgata, and the Tathāgata is all beings; and it is in this way that I practise Prajñāpāramitā.'

In Man-t'o-lo's translation, this Prajñāpāramitā is defined to be 'limitless, boundless, nameless, formless, beyond speculation, with nothing to depend on, with no anchorage, neither offensive nor blessed, neither darkening nor illuminating, neither divisible nor countable. . . . And when this is experienced, one is said to have attained enlightenment.'

The thought expressed here is in perfect agreement with what generally characterizes the philosophy of the *Prajñā-pāramitā Sūtras*. The Buddha here is described in highly abstract terms by a series of negations. While the idea Buddha thus does not appear to go beyond verbalism (*adhivacana*), he is after all more than a mere name (*nāmad-heya*). Any amount of negations, it is true, fails to make one grasp the suchness of Buddhahood, but this does not of course mean that the Buddha, or what is the same thing, Prajñāpāramitā or supreme enlightenment, can be realized by merely repeating his name. If this is possible, the uttering of the Buddha-name must be considered in some other light; that is, not in the sense of abstract negation, but in the psychological process started by the repetition itself. It is interesting to see this shifting of thought from conceptualism to psychological realism. Let us see what Mañjuśrī has further to say about supreme enlightenment to be attained by means of the Buddha-name (*nāmadheya*).

In the second half of the *Saptaśatikā-Prajñāpāramitā* (Man-t'o-lo version) a Samādhi known as *i-hsing*[1] is mentioned, whereby the Yogin realizes supreme enlightenment and also comes into the presence of the Buddhas of the past, present, and future. The passage in the Man-t'o-lo runs as follows:

'Again, there is the Samādhi *i-hsing*; when this Samādhi is practised by sons and daughters of good family, supreme enlightenment will speedily be realized by them.

Mañjuśrī asked, 'Blessed One, what is this *i-hsing* Samādhi?'

The Blessed One said: 'The Dharmadhātu is characterized with oneness, and as the Samādhi is conditioned by [this oneness of] the Dharmadhātu it is called the Samādhi

[1] 'Samādhi of One Deed (?)', in Man-t'o-lo's version, is the 'Samādhi of One Form Array' (*ekanimitta* (?) *vyūhasamādhi*) in Hsüan-tsang's translation. In the Sanskrit text now extant this Samādhi is called *ekavyūhasamādhi*. *Vyūha* is generally rendered as *chuang-yen* in Chinese, meaning 'embellishment', 'array', or 'arrangement in order'. The sense is, however, not to arrange things merely for the sake of decoration; it is to fill the abstract barrenness of Reality with multiplicities, and it may be regarded sometimes as synonymous with 'individualization', or 'particular objects'. *Ekavyūha*, therefore, may mean 'one particular object' and *ekavyūha-samādhi* 'a samādhi with one object in view'. It is difficult to take *hsing* to be equivalent to *vyūha*, for *hsing* is usually *caryā*.

The passage containing the account of the *i-hsing* samādhi is missing in Saṁghapāla's translation, which fact suggests its later addition. Probably the earlier text of the *Saptaśatikā-Prajñāpāramitā Sūtra* thoroughly retained the characteristic features of Prajñā-pāramitā philosophy with no admixture of the visualizing meditation and also of the nominalistic trend of thought.

of Oneness (*i-hsing*). If sons and daughters of good family wish to enter upon this Samādhi of Oneness they must listen to the discourse on Prajñāpāramitā and practise it accordingly; for then they can enter upon the Samādhi of Oneness whereby they will realize the Dharmadhātu in its aspect of not-going-back, of not-being-destroyed, of unthinkability, of non-obstruction, of no-form.

'If sons and daughters of good family wish to enter upon the Samādhi of Oneness, let them sit in a solitary place, abandon all thoughts that are disturbing, not become attached to forms and features, have the mind fixed on one Buddha, and devote themselves exclusively to reciting (*ch'êng*) his name (*ming*, or *nāmadheya*), sitting in the proper style in the direction where the Buddha is, and facing him squarely. When their thoughts are continuously fixed on one Buddha, they will be able to see in these thoughts all the Buddhas of the past, present, and future. . . .'[1]

In Man-t'o-lo's text there is a strange mixture of Prajñāpāramitā philosophy proper with the visualization of the Buddha by means of his name, which is recited with singleness of thought. Hsüan-tsang's text refers to reflecting on the personality of personal features of the Buddha in connection with holding his name, which to a certain extent contradicts the idea of the first text. For the first one emphasizes the uttering of the name with no allusion whatever to visualizing the personal marks of Buddhahood, and yet it promises the Yogins their seeing not only one Buddha whose name they recite but all the Buddhas of the past, present, and future. And this is indeed the point upon which

---

[1] In the Hsüan-tsang version no reference is made to the recitation (*ch'êng*), thus: 'If sons and daughters of good family wish to enter upon this Samādhi, let them retire to a solitary place away from confusions, and sit cross-legged without thinking of forms of any kind; let them, in order to benefit all sentient beings, single-mindedly and collectively take hold of the [Buddha's] name and reflect well on his personality, while turning in the direction where the Buddha is and facing him in the proper attitude. To have their thoughts continually fixed on this one Buddha is thereby to see all the Buddhas of the past, present, and future.'

In the Sanskrit *Saptaśatikā*, we have simply '*tasya nāmadheyaṁ grahitavyan*'.

the Pure Land followers lay great emphasis in their teaching; that is, the sutra's preference given to verbal or nominalistic recitation rather than reflection or visualization.

In the *Pratyutpanna-samādhi Sūtra*[1] also, the visualizing meditation singularly blends with the nominalistic trends of thought. The subject of discourse here as given to the Bodhisattva Bhadrapāla is how to realize a Samādhi known as Pratyutpanna, in which all the Buddhas of the ten quarters come and stand before the Yogin ready to answer all the questions he may ask them. The Yogin's qualifications are:

1. He must have great faith in the Buddha; 2. He must exert himself to the farthest extent of his spiritual energy; 3. He must be provided with a thorough understanding of the Dharma; and 4. He must always be associated with good friends and teachers. When these conditions are fulfilled, the Samādhi is matured, and then, first, because of the sustaining power of the Buddha which is added to the Yogin; secondly, because of the virtue of the Samādhi itself; and, thirdly, because of the virtue inherent in the accumulated stock of merit, all the Buddhas appear before the Yogin in such a manner as images are reflected in a mirror.

In the beginning the Yogin hears of the name of the Buddha Amitābha and his Land of Purity. By means of this name, he visualizes all the excellent and extraordinary features belonging to the Buddha, such as his thirty-two major marks of manhood and eighty minor ones. The Yogin will also visualize all the resplendent glories of the Buddha while reflecting (*nien*) on his name with singleness of thought.

When this exercise attains its fullness, the Yogin's mind is purged of all its impurities. As it grows pure, the Buddha is

[1] This is also known as the *Bhadrapāla Bodhisattva Sūtra* because this is the name of the interlocutor in the sūtra. There are four extant Chinese translations of it. The first one was done by Lou-chia-ch'ien as early as A.D. 179. It is one of the authoritative sources of the Pure Land teaching. See also pp. 182 f.

reflected in it, and the mind and the Buddha are finally identified, as if the mind is looking at itself or the Buddha at himself, and yet the Yogin is not conscious of this fact of self-identification. To be thus unconscious is Nirvāṇa. When there is the slightest stirring of a thought the identification scale is tipped, and there starts a world of infatuations.

Strictly speaking, it is doubtful whether the sūtra makes so much of the name and its recitation as is maintained by the followers of the Pure Land. As far as we can see, the visualization plays as much importance as thinking of the name. It is true that without a name our minds are unable to take hold of anything; even when there is really something objectively in existence, so long as it remains un-named it has no reality for us. When a thing gets its name, its relations with other things are defined and its value fully appreciated. Amitābha is non-existent when we can-not invoke him by a name; naming is creating, so to speak. But, on the other hand, mere naming does not prove to be so efficient, is not so effect-producing, as when there is back of it a corresponding reality. Mere uttering the name 'water' does not quench the thirst; when it is visualized and there is a mental picture of a spring it produces a more physiologically realistic effect; but it is only when there is real fresh water before us which is quaffed that the thirst actually eases.

By means of sheer will and imagination, the mental picture can attain the highest degree of intensification, but there is naturally a limit to human powers. When this limit is reached, a leap into the abyss is possible only by the sus-taining power which is now added to the Yogin by the Buddhas of the ten quarters. Thus the name, reflection or visualization and actualization are the natural order of things playing the most important role in the system of the Pure Land teaching.

It was owing to Shan-tao's[1] pietistic synthesis that the visualizing meditation, the nominalistic attitude, and the

[1] Died A.D. 681.

rebirth in the Pure Land were made to form a system, which was to be put into active service by means of the Nembutsu; that is, by constantly and singlemindedly pronouncing the name of Amitābha Buddha. After him, visualization gradually ceased to be upheld and nominalism came to reign over the entire school of the Pure Land. In China the koan exercise had about this time probably been gaining influence along with the prevalence of nominalism, but in Japan the establishment of the Pure Land school as an independent sect greatly helped the growth of the Nembutsu; that is, the vocal Nembutsu.

The transition of emphasis from idealism to nominalism, from the singleminded thinking to the vocal recitation, may be traced in the following passage from the *An-lê-chi* of Tao-ch'o, who answers the question how the Nembutsu is to be practised:

'It is like a man travelling through the wilderness who happens to be attacked by a highwayman. The latter savagely threatens the traveller at the point of the sword and if his order is not obeyed, is ready to murder him. The traveller fleeing away from the impending peril observes a stream before him. Before reaching it, he reflects: "When I come to the river, should I cross it with my dress on or not? As to undressing myself there may not be time enough for it. But even when I jump into it with all my things on, my head and neck may not be safe enough from the attack." At this critical moment he has indeed no other thought than devising the way to get to the other side of the river. His mind is exclusively devoted to it. It is the same with the devotee of the Nembutsu. When he thinks of the Buddha Amitābha, his mind should be exclusively occupied with the thought, so that it has no room left for anything else.

'Whether he thinks (*nien*) of the Dharmakāya of the Buddha, or of his supernatural powers, or of his Prajñā, or of the light issuing from his hair-tuft, or of his physical features, or of his Original Vow, let the devotee uninterruptedly pronounce (*ch'êng*) the name of the Buddha with singleness of thought so that no room is left in his mind for anything else, and he is sure to be reborn in the presence of the Buddha.'

At such a critical moment as described here it is doubted whether the devotee has enough room left in his mind to do any sort of reflection. All that he can do will be pronouncing the name of the Buddha, for he cannot have any psychological time which is to be devoted to thinking of the Buddha's virtues or powers or features. In this case his Nembutsu (*nien-fo*, literally, 'thinking of the Buddha') cannot be more than a *shōmyō* (*ch'êng-ming*, literally, 'pronouncing or uttering the name'). For in the pronouncing of the name of the Buddha, that is, in reciting the Nembutsu, his whole being is absorbed; this is all he can do consciously, there can be no other thoughts in his field of consciousness.

Shan-tao distinguishes, in his commentary on the *Sūtra of Meditations*, two kinds of devotional practice for the Nembutsu devotee, 'proper' and 'mixed'. The 'proper practice' consists in thinking (*nien*) of the name of the Buddha Amitābha with singleness of thought. But here too 'thinking of the name' has no meaning except when the name is deliberately pronounced. This kind of thinking is effective only when the vocal nerves and muscles are set in motion in accompaniment with the mental representation. In fact, it is doubtful whether any thinking, high or low, can be carried on without its muscular accompaniment, however slight and imperceptible it may be.

Adding to this psychological fact, the Pure Land philosophers propose the theory that the name (*nāmadheya*) is the repository of all the virtues belonging to the Buddha, that is to say, of all the inner attainments and virtues belonging to one Amitābha Buddha such as the fourfold knowledge, the triple body, the tenfold power, the fourfold fearlessness, etc. Together with all his external functions and virtues including his excellent features, his illuminating rays of light, his discourses on the Dharma, his deeds of salvation, etc.—they are all included in the name of the Buddha

Amitābha.[1] Thus, as we see further on, psychology and philosophy have combined to lay entire stress of the Nembutsu teaching on the pronouncement of the name.

In the *Wūjō-yōshyu* (Fas. II, Part 1), compiled by Genshin (942-1017), who was one of the forerunners of the Jōdo (Pure Land) school of Buddhism in Japan, the author raises the question: 'Is Nembutsu-samādhi to be gained by mere meditation or by vocal recitation?' The answer is given by a quotation from Chisha-daishi's *Maka-shikwan* (Chih-chê Tai-shih's *Mo-hê-chih-kuan*)[2] Fas. II, Part 1: 'Sometimes recitation and meditation go on hand in hand, sometimes meditation precedes and recitation follows, sometimes recitation comes first and then meditation. When recitation and meditation go on thus in constant succession and without interruption each thought as well as each sound is fixed on Amitābha.'[3] In this, the vocal Nembutsu is not yet brought out sufficiently prominently.

It was Hōnen (1133-1212) who, following the teaching of Shan-tao, emphasized the Nembutsu; that is, the recitation of the Buddha's name. This was regarded as the most important practice in the Pure Land school when the devotees wished to be re-born in the Land of Amida. Praising his virtues, making offerings, bowing before him, reading the sutras, and meditating on him—these were by no means to be slighted, but the chief act of piety consisted

---

[1] From Hōnen's *Passages Relative to the Nembutsu and Original Vows* (*Senjyaku nembutsu-hongwanshu*), Fas. I. In this Hōnen attempts to explain his position as founder of the Nembutsu school in Japan.

[2] The Taisho Tripitaka, No. 1911.

[3] Soon after this, Genshin quotes another authority in the Jōdo teaching, Huai-kan: 'According to the *Sūtra of the Meditations*, this one harassed to the extreme has no time to think of the Buddha; but being advised by good friends he recites the name of the Buddha Amitābha, and thereby he is enabled to keep up his recitation uninterruptedly and with sincerity of heart.—In a similar manner, let those who wish to attain a Samādhi in the Nembutsu keep up their recitation audibly without stopping, and they will surely realize the Samādhi and see the holy congregation of the Buddhas right before them as in the daylight.—The louder you recite the name of the Buddha at the top of your voice the easier the attainment of the Samādhi of the Nembutsu. When your recitation is not loud enough, the mind is liable to distraction. This will be found out by the Yogin himself without being told by others.'

in the recitation (ch'êng-ming). By constantly uttering his name with devotion, in whatever posture one may be in, whether sitting or standing, lying down or walking, he will surely, after some time has elapsed, be taken by Amida into his abode of happiness. For this, according to the masters of the Jōdo school, is in full accordance with the teachings of the sūtras; that is to say, with the original vows of the Buddha.

To confirm this view, Hōnen again quotes Shan-tao, according to whom the Nembutsu is easier to practise than any other deeds of devotion. The question as to why meditation is set aside in preference to singleminded recitation is answered thus: 'It is because sentient beings are all very heavily handicapped with hindrances, and the world in which they are living is full of subtle temptations; it is because their mind is too disconcerted, and their intelligence too clumsy, and their spirit too wandering. Meditation, therefore, is not theirs. Taking pity on them, the Buddha advises them to concentrate on reciting his name, for when this is practised without interruption the devotee is sure of his rebirth in the Land of Amida.'

Hōnen then proceeds to state that thinking or meditating is reciting, the two being the same; that to think of Amida is to recite his name and *vice versa*. *Nembutsu*, 'thinking of the Buddha', has thus come to be completely identified with *shōmyō*, 'reciting or pronouncing the name'; meditation has turned into recitation. What may be termed the Buddhist philosophy of nominalism has come to occupy the minds of the Pure Land devotees, for they now realize the presence in the name of something that goes altogether beyond conception. My object is now to study the psychological signification of this vocal Nembutsu and to see in what relationship it stands to the koan exercise as practised by followers of Zen.

4. *The Psychology of the Shōmyō Exercise, and Where it Becomes Related to the Koan Exercise*

With the vocalization of the Nembutsu on the one hand, Hōnen and his predecessors have not forgotten on the other hand to emphasize the importance and necessity of a believing heart. Meditating on the Buddha, as one in possession of all the virtuous qualities and also of the thirty-two marks of a great being, requires no doubt a great deal of concentration and may be beyond the psychic powers of an ordinary man. Compared to that, the recitation of the name is indeed much easier.

A name is something like an algebraic symbol; as *a* or *b* or *c* may stand for any kind of number, the name Amida may be regarded as representing everything that is contained in the conception of the Buddha, not only of one Amida, but of all the Buddhas, whose number is beyond calculation. When a man pronounces this name he digs down deeply into the content of his religious consciousness. Mere utterance, however, will be of no consequence, being devoid of sense; the uttering must be the outcome of deep thinking, earnest seeking, and great faith; if it is not the outcome of such intense yearnings, it must be strengthened continuously by them. Lips and heart must be in full accord in its practice.

In this kind of Nembutsu the mind focusses itself on the name and not on the outward form of the Buddha. His thirty-two physical marks of greatness are not pictured out in the mind of the devotee. The name possesses the entire field of consciousness. So we read in the *Smaller Sukhā-vativyūha*:[1] *amitāyuṣas tathāgatasya nāmadheyam śroṣyati śrutvā ca manasikariṣyati. . . .* (Let him hear the name of the Tathā-gata Amitāyus and, having heard it, keep it in mind. . . .)

The Chinese translator has *chih-ch'ih* for *manasikṛi*, meaning 'to hold an object of thought fixedly in mind'. The name itself is held at the centre of attention, not mere lip

[1] *Anecdota Oxoniensia*, Aryan series, Vol. I, Part II, p. 96.

repetition but an utterance of the heart. There is no doubt that this kind of Nembutsu is a great help to concentration. The calling-up of the form of the Buddha is pregnant with many psychological dangers or evils, and the devotee may become an incurable victim of hallucinations. The vocalization is a great step forward to the attainment of a true religious Samādhi.

The object of the Nembutsu, we see clearly, has gone through modifications. In the beginning it was remembering the Buddha, longing to see him again as he had lived among his followers—a desire entirely human and natural. Later, it came to mean the coming into the presence of an idealized Buddha, eternally living in the Land of Purity and Happiness. And, finally, by holding the name firmly in mind the explicit object became a desire to turn the gracious attention of the Buddha towards the sinful devotee. This modification is thus interpreted by masters of the Pure Land school to be in full accord with the teaching of the Buddha as expounded in the various sūtras belonging to that school.

But the question that arises here is: Is there no psychological background which elicits this gradual modification? Has the vocal Nembutsu no implicit object? Has it no other object than to direct the devotee to the Pure Land of Amida? The masters might not have been conscious of the fact, but was there not a psychological experience on their part which made them teach the simple vocal Nembutsu instead of other religious deeds, such as sūtra-reading, meditating on the Buddha, making bows to him, or singing hymns of praise?

If moral or spiritual enhancement is to be achieved, the mere uttering of the name, even though it be the name of the Holiest One, does not seem to elevate the mind so much as meditating on him and reading his sermons. The Pure Land teachers honestly believed in the sutras when the vocal Nembutsu was recommended. But as far as the sūtras are concerned they teach many other things also, and, if the teachers so desired, they could therein develop some other teachings than the Nembutsu. For a sūtra or in fact any religious literature generally lends itself, according to the reader's personal experience, to varities of interpretation.

The development of the vocal Nembutsu, therefore, must be said to have its psychological ground, as well as its philosophical and religious ones. It was, of course, the philosophical side that chiefly and therefore consciously governed the religious consciousness of the teachers.

It would be against reason to assert that the psychology of the vocal Nembutsu is all that constitutes the foundation of the Pure Land teachings. For such conceptions as sin, the reality of suffering, and the all-embracing love of Amida, are also essential factors, but my present study is solely to analyse the psychological aspect of it.

To give a name is to discriminate; to discriminate is to recognize the reality of an individual object, and to make it accessible to the human understanding as well as to the human heart. Therefore, when the name is pronounced, we feel that the object itself is with us, and it was a most natural process of development that thinking of the Buddha gradually turned into pronouncing his name. But what we wish to examine now is that the name of the Buddha continued to retain its original Sanskrit form, or rather its transliteration, throughout its long history in China and Japan.

Why was not the Buddha addressed by the Chinese or Japanese equivalent instead of by the original or modified Sanskrit? *Namu amida butsu* and *Nan wu o mi to fo* are the Japanese and the Chinese way of reading *namo 'mitābhāya buddhāya*. *Namo* or *namas* means 'adoration' or 'salutation', and *amitābhāya buddhāya* means 'to the Buddha of Infinite Light', which in Chinese is *kuei i wu liang kuang fo*. Why did they not say 'Adoration to the Buddha of Infinite Light', instead of 'Namu Amida Butsu' or 'Nan-wu O-mi-to Fo'?

These transliterations give no sense ordinarily to the Japanese or Chinese mind, as they are modified Sanskrit sounds and apparently carry no meaning. It is to them a sort of Dhāraṇī or Mantram which is to be pronounced as it stands with no translation; for when translated a Dhāraṇī conveys no intelligent thought, being no more than a stream of jargon. What was the reason of this—intelligence giving way to non-intelligence, sense to non-sense, clearness to obscurity, discrimination to non-discrimination? Why, all the time, Namu Amida Butsu, Namu Amida Butsu?

In my view, the reason is to be sought not in the magical effect of the name itself, but in the psychological effect of its repetition. Wherever there is an intelligent meaning, it suggests an endless train of ideas and feelings attached thereto; the mind then either becomes engaged in working a logical loom, or becomes inextricably involved in the meshes of imagination and association. When meaningless sounds are repeated, the mind stops there, not having chances to wander about. Images and hallucinations are less apt to invade it. To use Buddhist terminology, the external dust of discrimination covers the original bright surface of the inner mirror of enlightenment.

To avoid this tragedy, it is necessary that sounds intended for the vocal Nembutsu should be devoid of intelligible meaning. When the reflective and the meditative Nembutsu developed into the vocal Nembutsu, there must have been some such psychological experience on the part of the masters who wanted to concentrate their minds on Buddhahood itself and not on the personality of the Buddha. The thought of the personality of the Buddha, as they saw it, demands a higher process of mentality and yet does not always yield genuine results.

The Jōdo masters are always quite emphatic on the triple attitude of mind which should always accompany the vocal Nembutsu: 1. Sincerity of heart; 2. Inwardness of faith; and 3. The desire for the Land of Amida. Without these subjective factors, indeed, no amount of Nembutsu will be of use to the devotee in gaining the object of his desire. But the masters in their apparently too earnest desire to propagate the so-called easy method of salvation, and to bring out in the strongest possible light the necessity of the vocal Nembutsu, seem sometimes to set aside the importance of these subjective conditions. As a result the students of the Pure Land schools are often attracted too irresistibly to the vocal Nembutsu at the expense of the right subjective conditions.

This is not right, but one may wonder whether there is not something in the attitude of the masters which will justify this erroneous assumption. Are they not emphasizing the importance of the subjective factors in order to make the vocal Nembutsu effective to its utmost extent? If a man had all these inner requirements fulfilled, it does not seem, as far as ordinary logic goes, to matter very much whether he was a devotee of sūtra-reading, or of bowings, or of the vocal Nembutsu. But the masters, especially of the Jōdo school of Genku and Hōnen, are unmistakably insistent on uttering the name of the Buddha in the form of 'Namu Amida Butsu' as the most essential practice, relegating all other devotional exercises to a secondary category. According to them, therefore, the 'Namu Amida Butsu' is what finally guarantees one's rebirth in the Land of Bliss.

How can this be so unless the vocal Nembutsu works in some mysterious manner in the consciousness of the devotee? When a certain state of consciousness is induced by repeatedly pronouncing the Buddha-name it is likely that the Buddha himself comes to take possession of the mind, whereby the devotee is assured of his future destiny. Was this psychology what was aimed at by Shan-tao, Hōnen, and other teachers of the Jōdo school?

When such great Jōdo teachers as Shan-tao, Tao-ch'o, and Huai-kan give two ways of rebirth in the Pure Land, (1) saying the Nembutsu and (2) practising other meritorious deeds, and prefer the first to the second as being more in accord with the teachings of the sūtras, and further when they identify 'thinking of' or 'meditating on' (*nien* in Chinese, *anusmṛiti* in Sanskrit) with 'voicing' or 'uttering' (*shêng*), saying that to think of Buddha is to utter his name, do they find this reason for identification in logic or in psychology? Logically, to think intensely of an object does not necessarily mean uttering its name; the thinking is independent of the uttering of its name; the thinking is independent of the uttering especially when the mind meditatively dwells on an object of devotion and reverence. But as a matter of psychological fact, the thinking of abstract ideas is greatly helped by looking at some graphical representations, letters, or diagrams, and also by pronouncing names mentally or audibly. Grounded on this psychological fact, they must have come to the conclusion that thinking of the Buddha is uttering his name, that the thinking and the uttering are identical.

And again, according to Huai-kan's commentary[1] on the noted passage in the *Tai-chi yüeh-tsang Ching*:[2] 'By great thinking (*nien*) one sees great Buddha, and by small thinking, small Buddha. Great thinking means calling out the Buddha [-name] at a high pitch; small thinking at a low pitch.' While I am not quite sure as to what is exactly meant by 'seeing great Buddha and small Buddha', it is readily seen that the teachers are here making much of saying the Nembutsu loudly. The more muscular effort we make in uttering the name of the Buddha the higher degree of concentration will be attained, and thus the holding in mind of 'Namu Amida Butsu' will be the more effective.

Whatever doctrinal interpretations were given to the fact, the teachers must have had some psychological experience before they confirmed the identification of thinking (*nien*) and uttering (*shêng*). Do we not see here something of Zen psychology in which ' "Wu", "*Wu*", all day today, and "*Wu*", "*Wu*", over again all day tomorrow',[3] is practised? Hence their exhortation to say the Nembutsu all day, or every day regularly, or so many times a day—ten thousand times, fifty thousand, and even up to a hundred thousand times a day. There is a Jōdo temple in Kyoto, the

---

[1] Quoted by Hōnen in his *Senjaku-shu*, Fas. I.
[2] *Candra-garbha*, translated into Chinese by Narendrayaśas, A.D. 550-577.
[3] In one of Kung-ku Lung's letters.

name of which is 'One Million Times', referring to the number of the vocal Nembutsu to be repeated. The mental fact that vocalization helps concentration is the basis of the doctrine of the vocal Nembutsu (*shōmyō*, or *shêng-ming*).

When the Buddha-name is so frequently repeated as ten or twenty thousand times at a stretch, the practice grows mechanical with no conscious effort, therefore with no conscious realization of the three factors of devotion. Is this mechanization to be considered the effective means of the rebirth? Is there no need of the devotee's making a determined effort to grow up in his belief and devotion? Does this constant muttering or uttering of meaningless sounds produce in the consciousness of the devotee a definite sense of assurance whereby he cherishes no doubt as to his rebirth in the Pure Land, or as to his salvation through the grace of Amida?

When the Nembutsu is turned into pronouncing a Dhāraṇī without any conscious reference to its meaning, literary and devotional, its psychological effect will be to create a state of unconsciousness in which ideas and feelings superficially floating are wiped off. Morally speaking, this is a condition of innocence as there is no discrimination of good and bad, and in this way the Jōdo teachers state that the Nembutsu wipes off all the sins accumulated during one's lives in countless past ages.

The perpetual reiteration of 'Namu Amida Butsu'[1] has its parallel in Sufism whose followers repeat the name 'Allah', as has been observed by R. A. Nicholson in his *Studies in Islam Mysticism*, 'as a method practised by Moslem mystics for bringing about *fana*, i.e. the passing away from self, or in Pascals' phrase, "*oubli du monde et de tout hormis Dieu*".'[2]

We cannot think that the mere repetition of 'Namu Amida Butsu' assures the devotee of his rebirth in the Pure Land in spite of all the guarantee that is given in the sutras

[1] In the practical recitation, this is pronounced something like *nam man da bu, nam man da bu, . . .*
[2] Pp. 7-9.

and by the teachers of that school, unless the reiteration produces a certain mental effect wherein he attains the realization by himself. And is not this realization what is known as the Samādhi of Nembutsu or the Samādhi of Oneness (*ekavyūha*)?

In the *Anrakushu* (*An-lê-chi*, Part II) by Tao-ch'o, the passages bearing on this Samādhi are quoted from various sūtras. The author's intention here is to prove the Samādhi to be the efficient means of bringing the devotee into the presence of all the Buddhas of the past, present, and future. But, from the point of view of salvation (or enlightenment), what is the use of seeing the Buddhas unless their assurance of salvation evokes the sense of its truth in the consciousness of the devotee? The seeing of the Buddha objectively must be in correspondence with the inner realization and, as far as psychology is concerned, inner realization is the more important topic of consideration.

There is a sūtra entitled *Bosatsu Nembutsu Sammai* (*samādhi*) *Kyo*, first translated by Dharmagupta of Sui, in which all the necessary instructions concerning the practice of the Nembutsu Samādhi are given in detail. According to this work, the chief merit accruing from the Samādhi seems to be the realization of supreme enlightenment. Evidently the coming into the presence of all the Buddhas is not to see them in their company as spiritually enlightened beings, to be in communion with them in a world transcending all forms of corporeality. The devotee is persuaded to practise the Nembutsu in order to see the Buddhas, but when he actually enters into a Samādhi he sees them in a way quite different from what he might have expected in the beginning.[1]

Hōnen quotes in his *Senjakushu*, Part II, a passage from *Lives of the Pious Followers of the Pure Land School*, in which reference is made to Shan-tao's attainment of the Samādhi. According to this account, the Samādhi among other things seems to give one a prophetic insight into the spiritual condition of others; for the account reveals that Shan-tao

[1] Cf. Hakuin's story of the two Jōdo devotees told below, p. 195.

could tell about the past lives of his own teacher, Tao-ch'o, and also about the rebirth of the latter in the Land of Amida.

By the fact that the Samādhi could not go any farther than the attainment of these miraculous powers, we may say that it has not much to do with one's spiritual enhancement and assurance of emancipation. There must be something more in the Samādhi acquired by means of the Nembutsu. The teachers of the Pure Land school have been too eager to advance their religious views regarding rebirth after death, ignoring the psychological effect which is sure to follow the constant reiteration of 'Namu Amida Butsu'. They have been too busy reminding us of this degenerate age in which the pure form of Buddhism is too difficult to maintain itself, and, therefore, that the uttering of the Buddha-name is the best, easiest, and surest for beings of this degenerate age to come into the presence of the Buddhas and to be embraced in the arms of their infinite love.

In this respect, Shinran pushed this idea to its utmost logical end; for he states in connection with one's rebirth in the Pure Land by uttering the name of the Buddha only ten times that 'this does not mean to specifically and quietly meditate on the Buddha, or to think of him intensely, but merely to pronounce the name'. With all their expostulations about the Nembutsu, about saying it once or up to ten times, which will surely be heard by the Buddha, I cannot imagine that the teachers were utterly unconscious of the psychology of the Nembutsu, as has already been referred to.

### 5. *What is the Object of the Nembutsu Exercise?*

One may ask in this connection: Whatever the content of the Samādhi, which is the real object of the Nembutsu, rebirth in the Pure Land or the Samādhi itself? Or is the Samādhi a kind of foretaste of the rebirth? No teachers of the Jōdo as far as I can learn make this point thoroughly clear for us. But if we can so view the matter, the Samādhi may be regarded as the subjective and psychological aspect of the Nembutsu exercise, and the rebirth as the objective and ontological aspect.

In this case, the Samādhi and the rebirth are only the same thing described in two ways, but as the Samādhi is attainable in this life while rebirth is an affair taking place after death, the Samādhi must be said to be identical with the rebirth in a most specific sense; that is, the rebirth is not to be judged as an objective and temporal event, but as a form of subjective assurance of a thing that is surely to take place. If so, the rebirth means a spiritual regeneration and as such it can be regarded as identical with the Samādhi.

This view of the Samādhi is supported in the *Anjin Ketsujōshō* by an unknown author, which is, however, one of the most significant books on the teaching of the Jōdo school. In this the author states that the faith is to be firmly established by the realization of the Samādhi—the faith in the original vow of Amida whereby the devotee is assured of his future destiny. For the Samādhi obtains when the mind of the devotee is so perfectly identified with the mind of Amida that the consciousness of the dualism is altogether effaced from it. This conclusion, not only in logic but from the factual point of view, is inevitable seeing that the entire structure of Buddhist philosophy is based on an idealistic monism, and no exception is to be made about the realistic Jōdo. Read this from the *Meditation Sūtra*:

'The Buddha said to Ānanda and Vaidehī: After you have seen these, you should think of the Buddha. You may ask, How? Every Buddha-Tathāgata has his body in the spiritual world (*dharmadhātu*) and enters into the mind of every sentient being. Therefore, when you think of the Buddha, your mind itself becomes endowed with the thirty-two marks of greatness and also with the eighty secondary marks of excellence. This mind is transformed into Buddhahood, this mind is no other than the Buddha himself. The ocean of true all-knowledge possessed by the Buddhas grows out of your own mind and thought. For this reason, you should apply yourselves with singleness of thought to meditation on the Buddha-Tathāgata, who is an Arhat and a Fully-enlightened One.'

In the *Pratyutpannasamādhi Sūtra*,[1] which is thought by the Jōdo teachers to be one of the sources of their teachings, we have this:

'And again, Bhadrapāla, when a young man of fine mien wishes to see his own features, ugly or handsome, he takes up a vessel of refined oil or of clean water, or he brings out a crystal or a mirror. When either one of these four objects reflects his image in it, he definitely knows how he looks, ugly or handsome. Bhadrapāla, do you think that what the young man sees in these four objects has been already in existence there?

'Answered Bhadrapāla, O no, Blessed One.

'Is it to be regarded altogether as a non-entity?

'O no, Blessed One.

'Is it to be regarded as being within them?

'O no, Blessed One.

'Is it to be regarded as outside them?

'O no, Blessed One. As the oil and water and crystal and mirror are clear, transparent, and free from muddiness and dust, the image is reflected in them when a person stands before them. The image does not come out of the object, nor does it get into them from the outside, nor is it there by itself, nor is it artificially constructed. The image comes from nowhere, vanishes away to nowhere; it is not subject to birth and death; it has no fixed abode.

'When Bhadrapāla finished thus answering, the Buddha said:

'Bhadrapāla, so it is, indeed, as you say. When the

---

[1] Translated into Chinese for the first time by Chih Lou-chia-ch'ien, who came to China in the latter half of the second century, during the latter Han dynasty. The English translation is drawn from Jñānagupta's Chinese translation (A.D. 586), instead of from Chih Lou-chai-ch'ien (A.D. 179); for Jñānagupta's is more intelligible, though Chih Lou-chia-ch'ien is better known to students of the Pure Land school. The Taisho Tripitaka, Nos. 416–419.

objects are pure and clean, the image is reflected in them without much trouble. So is it with the Bodhisattva. When he meditates on the Buddhas with singleness of thought, he sees them; having appeared to him they stay with him; staying with him, they explain things to him that he wishes to understand. Being thus enlightened by them he is delighted; he now reflects: Whence do these Buddhas come? And whither does this body of mine vanish? When he thus reflects he sees that all the Tathāgatas come from nowhere and go out nowhere. So it is with my own body; it has no definite path by which it comes, and how can there be any returning to anywhere?

'He reflects again: This triple world exists only because of the mind. According to one's own thought, one sees oneself in one's own mind. My now seeing the Buddha is after my own mind; my mind becomes the Buddha; my mind itself is the Buddha; my mind itself is the Tathāgata. My mind is my body, my mind sees the Buddha; the mind does not know itself, the mind does not see itself. When thoughts are stirred, there is Nirvāṇa. All things have no reality in themselves, they take their rise owing to thought and laws of origination. When that which is thought vanishes, the thinking one himself vanishes. Bhadrapāla, you should know that all the Bodhisattvas by means of this Samādhi attained great enlightenment.'

Viewing the Samādhi of Nembutsu from this absolute idealistic point of view—the Samādhi that is realized by constant reiteration of 'Namu Amida Butsu'—we can state that the Samādhi, and the establishment of faith in the Buddha, and the assurance of rebirth in his Land of Purity, describe one and the same psychological fact which constitutes the foundation of the Jōdo (Pure Land) doctrine.

Hōnen says in his commentary on the *Meditation Sūtra* that the devotee should be like a man who has lost his senses, or like a deaf and dumb person, or like an idiot, when he devotes himself exclusively to the practice of the Nembutsu, pronouncing the name of the Buddha day and night, whether sitting or standing, lying down or walking, and for any length of time, one day, two days, a week, a month, a year, or even two or three years. When the practice is carried on in such wise, the devotee will surely some day attain the Samādhi and have his Dharma-eye opened, and he will view a world that is altogether beyond thought and imagination. This is 'a mysterious realm where all thoughts cease and all imaginings are swept away, being in full correspondence with a state of Samādhi'.

In this Samādhi where the devotee is fully confirmed in the faith, according to the author of the *Anjin Ketsujōshō*, 'The body becomes "Namu Amida Butsu", and the mind becomes "Namu Amida Butsu".' If so, is this not a mystic state of consciousness corresponding to that which is realized by the koan exercise?

The explicit claim made by the Jōdo teachers, that the repetition of the Nembutsu is the easiest method of salvation for all beings, is of course based on the original vow of Amida, in which the Buddha assures his followers of their rebirth in his Land of Bliss, if they only pronounce his name as showing their good faith and willingness to be thus saved.

To re-enforce or strengthen their teaching, they describe, on the one hand, in glowing terms the beauties of the Pure Land, while, on the other hand, they are never tired of picturing the miseries and horrors of this world, and the sinfulness and the helpless ignorance of the beings therein. Therefore, those who wish to be helped by this doctrine will have to be earnest devotees of 'Namu Amida Butsu' and be pronouncing and reciting the phrase all the time. But when they are doing this, their ultimate object of being members of the Pure Land community may gradually give way to the immediate daily practice itself of the Nembutsu. And even when their deliberate attention is focussed upon it, the psychology of the unconscious may begin to function by itself independently of the ultimate aim, which is supposed to take place at the end of this life; for the nearer happenings always claim the more intimate and intense concentration of mind.

Let this concentration be brought up to the highest pitch and there will be the intuition of such mystical truths as these: Rebirth is no-birth; to think of Buddha is not to have any thought; every moment is the last; this mind is no other than the Tathāgata himself; while the body belongs to this world, the mind is enjoying itself in the Pure Land; this body, as it is, is of the same order as Maitreya Bodhisattva, etc. Such statements seem to be not so typically Jōdo; in fact they go much against its generally realistic tendency, but we cannot altogether ignore this mysticism entering into the structural foundations of practical Jōdo, and there is no doubt that this comes from the psychology of the Nembutsu.

The Shin Branch of the Pure Land sect emphasizes faith as the only condition of rebirth in the land of Amida. Absolute trust is placed in the wisdom of the Buddha which goes altogether beyond human conception. Put, therefore, your faith in this wonder-working wisdom of Amida and you will straightway be taken up by him; there is no need for your waiting for the last moment when a band of welcoming Buddhas comes down from above; nor need you entertain any anxious fears about your destiny after death, thinking whether or not you are after all bound for Naraka (hell). All that is required of you is to abandon all thoughts regarding yourself and to put your unconditioned trust in the Buddha who knows best how to look after your welfare.[1] You need not worry at all about the last hour when you have to bid farewell to this life on earth. If, while living, you had been instructed by a wise adviser and had awakened one thought of trust in the Buddha, that moment of awakening was for you the last moment on earth. When trusting the original vow of Amida 'Namu Amida Butsu' is once pronounced, you are assured of rebirth in his Land; for this believing heart is the rebirth.[2]

But how can one really have this believing heart which

[1] *Shūji-shō.*
[2] From *Yui-shin Shō Mon-i.*

raises the owner at once to the order of the fully-enlightened One, bringing him up to the company even of Maitreya?[1] Mere listening to the teachers will not do it. Nor will the mere saying of the Nembutsu. How does one come to have this absolute faith—the faith which is evidently the same in substance as enlightenment? How can we be sure of our rebirth? How do we come to entertain no doubts as to our future destiny?

A certain state of consciousness must be awakened within us whereby we can be confirmed in our faith. Reasoning, or reading the sūtras, or listening to the discourses of the wise and enlightened will not induce this consciousness. As the history of religions tells us, there must be an intuitive insight into the truth, which is the abandoning of the self into the original vow of Amida. And is not this the moment when 'Namu Amida Butsu' gushes out of one's inmost heart (adhyāśaya)? Is this not what the Shin teachers mean when they say, 'Utter the Name once, and you are saved'?

### 6. *Mysticism of the Nembutsu, and the Uttering of the Name*

When we thus interpret the Nembutsu, we are able to understand the discourse of Ippen:[2] 'The rebirth means the first awakening of thought, and this assumes an existence, i.e. one in whom a thought is awakened. The "Namu Amida Butsu" itself is the rebirth, and the rebirth is no-birth. When this realization takes place, I call it provisionally the first awakening of thought. When one is absorbed in the Buddha-name that is above time, there is the rebirth that knows no beginning, no end.

'Sometimes the distinction is made between the last moment of life and everyday life, but this is a teaching that is based on confused thought. In the "Namu Amida Butsu"

[1] Op. cit.
[2] The founder of the Ji sect of the Pure Land school, 1229–1289. His *Sayings* is full of mystic thoughts.

itself there is no last moment, no everyday life; it is a reality abiding through all periods of time. As regards human life, it is a series of moments lasting only between an in-breath and an out-breath, and therefore the very moment of thought is the last moment of life. If so, every thought-moment is the last moment and every moment is a rebirth.'

The meaning of this mystical utterance by Ippen will become more transparent when the following quotations are gone through. 'When one's mind (or consciousness) is all annulled by saying "Namu Amida Butsu", this is the right thought for the last moment.' 'There is the Buddha-name only, and beyond it there is neither the one who says it, nor the one to whom it is addressed. There is the Buddha-name only, and beyond it there is no rebirth. All things existent are virtues included within the body of the Buddha-name itself. If so, when you attain the perception of all things as unborn, where all traces of a conscious mind vanish, saying "Namu Amida Butsu", a first thought then awakened is called the right thought of one's last moment; for this is no other than the thought of enlightenment, which is "Namu Amida Butsu".'

'Rather be possessed by the name than be possessing the name. All things are of one mind, but this mind is not manifested by itself. The eye cannot see itself, the wood cannot burn itself though it is by nature combustible. But hold a mirror before yourself and the eye can see itself—this is the virtue of the mirror. And the mirror is the one owned by every one of us and is known as the Great Mirror of Enlightenment; it is the name already realized by all the Buddhas. This being so, see your own original features in the Mirror of Enlightenment. Do we not read in the *Meditation Sūtra* that it is like seeing one's own face in the mirror?

'Again, wood will be burned when ignited by fire—the fire that burns is identical with the fire that is latent in the wood. It is thus through the concordance of causes inner and outer that all things are brought into actual existence. Though we are all endowed with the Buddha-nature, this of itself does not burn up the passions unless it be enkindled by the fire of transcendental wisdom which is the name (*nāmadheya*). The Jōdo school teaches that to take hold of an object one has to get away from it. The injunction is to be called to mind in this connection.'

Literally, 'Namu Amida Butsu' is not the name (*nāmadheya*) itself; it contains more than that, because *namu* (*namas* in Sanskrit) means 'adoration' or 'salutation'; but generally the whole phrase, 'Namu Amida Butsu', is regarded as the name, and its mysterious working is extolled. The masters of the Pure Land school exhausted their philosophical ingenuity on the subject, but strangely they keep quiet about the psychological aspect of the experience. Perhaps this silence comes from their conception of Amida, which is fundamentally ontological. But when it is asserted that the name alone exists and thus in it vanishes the dualistic contrast of the one who reiterates it and the one to whom it is addressed, this is the statement of a mystical experience and not of metaphysical reflection. The experience arising from the utterance of the name is of the same nature as that which ensues from the koan exercise. When the objective aspect of the experience is metaphysically interpreted, the name is objectified and Amida is absolute 'other-power'; but, on the other hand, let the devotee be a follower of Zen, and his understanding of it will be thoroughly idealistic.

The author of the *Anjin Ketsujōshō* may also, like Ippen, be considered an emphatic upholder of the name, for he says: 'As there is not a moment's separation between the devotee who says "Namu" and Amida-butsu himself, every thought cherished by him is "Namu Amida Butsu". This being so, every breath of his has never even for a moment been separated from the virtues of the Buddha; his whole being, indeed, is the substance of "Namu Amida Butsu". . . . When there is an understanding as to the meaning of the Nembutsu-Samādhi, both his body and his mind are "Namu Amida Butsu".

'For that reason, when all beings of the past, present, and future raise one thought of faith [in the original vow of Amida], the very thought goes back to the one thought of Enlightenment [which was originally awakened in the Buddha]; and the minds of all sentient beings in the ten quarters, when they utter the name, also go back to the one thought of Enlightenment. No thought, no utterance ever issuing from the devotees remains with them [they all go back to the source whence comes Enlightenment]. As the original vow is an act in which the name and essence are synthesized, the name contains in itself the whole essence of Enlightenment, and as it is thus the essence of Enlightenment, it is rebirth on the part of all beings in the ten quarters.'

Whether the masters of the Jōdo school, including the Shin, are conscious of the fact or not, there is something distinctly psychological in their metaphysical conclusions, or in their theology if that term could be used in Buddhism. Psychology cannot be said to be everything in religion, though it constitutes the groundwork of it. Thus even in Shin, where faith is made the chief principle of its teachings, there are many statements of Shinran, its founder, which are unintelligible unless his mystical experience is taken into consideration.

For instance, when he teaches the identity of the name and the original vow in their going beyond human understanding, he bases it on the Buddha's teaching itself. The explanation is simple enough, but how do we get confirmed in our belief? Especially when the masters of Shin all exhort us to abandon learning and reasoning, how can we accept everything that is poured into our heads rather mechanically; that is, on what authority? Some psychological state must come to us, even to the most unlogical minds, that leads us to say 'yes' to all that is told us to believe. Why is the name to be pronounced in addition to believing in the vow? It may be that the pronouncing is the believing and *vice versa*, but this identification, too, must be an outcome of experience and not a logical inference.

'The vow and the name are not two separate things, for there is no name apart from the vow, nor is there any vow apart from the name. Even making this statement involves human understanding. When, believing in the vow as beyond the understanding and also in the name as beyond the understanding, you utter the name in oneness of thought, why should you exercise your own understanding?'[1]

The believing alone seems to be sufficient to guarantee a man's rebirth in the Pure Land, or in Enlightenment, and why should this uttering the name be considered essential too? There is no uttering the name, it is declared, separate from the faith, and also there is no believing thought disjoined from the name; but why such importance given to the name? Why is 'Namu Amida Butsu' so essential to the confirmation of faith?

The name, whose meaning consists in having no meaning as it transcends the relativity of human knowledge, must be once demonstrated in experience before one realizes that it is really so. 'Namu Amida Butsu', from the Zen point of view, is a koan given to followers of the Pure Land school. One day the mystery of the name is realized as it is uttered, and this is the moment when the key is delivered into the hand of the devotee, to whom the entire treasure of religious consciousness is now safely entrusted.

'The original vow of Amida is to welcome anybody to his Land of Bliss who should utter his name in absolute confidence; being so, blessed are those who utter the name. A man may have the faith, but if he utters not the name, his faith will be of no avail. Another may utter the name singlemindedly, but if his faith is not deep enough his rebirth will not take place. He, however, who firmly believes in the rebirth as the outcome of the Nembutsu and utters the name, will doubtless be reborn in the Land of Recompense.'[2]

It can readily be understood that without faith rebirth

---

[1] *Mattōsho*. This is a collection of Shinran's letters, twenty-three in all.
[2] *The Mattōsho.*

is impossible, but why the uttering of the name? To comprehend this mystery, which constitutes the transcendental wisdom of all the Buddhas, the depths of our own being must be penetrated, and there is no doubt, according to the Jōdo, that it is the 'Namu Amida Butsu' which fathoms these depths.

## 7. *Experience and Theorization*

All religion is built upon the foundation of mystical experience, without which all its metaphysical or theological superstructure collapses. This is where religion differs from philosophy. All the philosophical systems may some day be found in ruins, but the religious life will for ever go on experiencing its deep mysteries. The Jōdo and the Zen cannot separate themselves from these mysteries. The Jōdo bases its theory on the Nembutsu and the Zen bases theirs on the koan exercise. As far as their theoretical edifices are concerned they seem very dissimilar to each other.

The Jōdo wants to see its followers reborn in the Land of Bliss and there attain their enlightenment. To do this they are taught about their sinfulness, about their intellectual inabilities to grasp the higher truths of Buddhism, and also about their being too heavily laden by their past karma to shake themselves free of their shackles by their own limited efforts. Amida is now held up before them, whose original vow is to give them a helping hand for crossing the stream of birth and death. But this helping hand cannot be reached unless they utter the name of their saviour with singleness of thought (*ekacitta*).

To awaken this state of singlemindedness, that is, 'one thought of faith', as it is technically termed, is the great problem of the Jōdo teaching. The vow, the name, the 'one thought of faith', the uttering of the name, the rebirth— these are the links making up the chain of the Pure Land doctrine. When any one of these links is held fast the entire chain will be in your hand, and the masters of the Jōdo have set up the uttering of the name in the most prominent position. In this the Jōdo experience is the counterpart of the Zen experience. The vocal Nembutsu and the koan exercise are here standing on a common ground.

Psychologically considered, the aim of the vocal Nembutsu is to do away with the fundamental dualism which is a condition of our empirical consciousness. By achieving this the devotee rides over the theoretical difficulties and contradictions that have troubled him before. With all intensity of thought and will (*adhyāśana*) he has thrown himself into the deeps of his own being. He is not, however, a mere wanderer without anything to guide him, for he has the name with him. He walks along with it, he goes down to the abyss with it; though he finds himself frequently divorced from it, he always remembers it and keeps in its company.

One day, without knowing how, he is no more himself, nor is he with the name. The name alone there is, and he is the name, the name is he. Suddenly even this disappears, which is not a state of mental blankness or of total unconsciousness. All these psychological designations fail to describe the state of mind in which he now is. But he stays not even here, for he awakes from it as suddenly as before. As he awakes, he awakes with a thought, which is the name and the faith in the original vow of Amida and the rebirth. This emerging from a state of absolute identity is marked with the utterance of 'Namu Amida Butsu', because he comes to this awakening through the teaching of his school.

Religion is fundamentally a personal experience, but the intellect enters into every fibre of the faith thus realized. For when the experience receives its name, that is, when it comes to be designated as faith, it has already gone through the baptism of intellection. Though the latter in itself is powerless, it gains authority as soon as it is combined with the experience. Thus we find almost all religious controversies centering about the philosophy of the experience; in other words, about theological subtleties and not about the experience itself. How to interpret the experience thus becomes frequently the cause of a most irreligious persecution or the bloodiest warfare.

However this may be, the religious experience always remains the sustaining and driving energy of its metaphysical system. This explains the diversity of intellectual interpretations even within one body of Buddhism, the one as Zen and the other as Jōdo, while their experience remains as far as psychology is concerned fundamentally the same.

This also explains the historical connection that came to exist between Zen and Jōdo. Superficially or intellectually observed, take for instance one of the numerous Zen koans and compare it with the 'Namu Amida Butsu'. How utterly unrelated they appear! 'What is it that stands for ever companionless?' 'I'll tell you when you have swallowed up in one draught all the waves of the Hsi!' 'What was Bodhidharma's idea in coming from the West?' 'The eastern mountains move over the waves.'

Between these koans and 'Namu Amida Butsu' there is no possible relationship as far as their appeal to the intellect is concerned. 'Namu Amida Butsu', as literally meaning 'Adoration to Amitābha Buddha', is intelligible enough; but as to the mountains moving over the waves, or one swallowing a whole river in one draught, there is no intelligible sense; all we can say about them is 'nonsense!' How can these nonsensical utterances be related to the Nembutsu?

As was explained above, however, the Nembutsu ceased to mean 'meditating on the Buddha' and came to be identified with the name (*ming-hao*), or rather with 'uttering the name' (*ch'êng-ming*). Meditation, or 'coming into the presence of the Buddha', thus gave way to the constant reiteration of the phrase as not always or necessarily referring to any definite objective reality, but merely as a name somehow beyond comprehension, or rather as a symbol standing for something indescribable, unpredictable, altogether transcending the intellect, and therefore suggesting a meaning beyond meaning.

When the Nembutsu comes to this, the name closely approaches the koan. Hitherto the Nembutsu and the koan exercise have been walking down their different routes of historical development, but now they find themselves near each other, and, as they look at each other, each most unexpectedly recognizes himself in the other.

Zen wants to clear one's consciousness of all its intellectual sediments so that it can receive the first awakening of thought in its purity, in its unaffected simplicity; for this purpose the koan, which is devoid of sense as ordinarily understood, is given to its followers. The idea is to go back to the original blankness in which there was as yet no functioning consciousness. This is a state of no-birth. Zen starts from it and so does the Jōdo.

## 8. *Hakuin's View on Koan and Nembutsu*

By way of conclusion, let me quote the following, which is a part of a letter[1] written by Hakuin to one of his noblemen followers, and in which he discusses the relative merit of the Nembutsu and the koan as instrumental in bringing about the state of satori. Hakuin does not slight the value of Nembutsu or Shōmyō, which is practically the same in the minds of the Pure Land followers, but he thinks the koan exercise is far more effective in that it intensely awakens the spirit of inquiry in the Zen Yogin's mind, and it is this spirit that finally rises up to the Zen experience. The Nembutsu may also achieve this, but only accidentally and in some exceptional cases; for there is nothing inherent in Nembutsu which would stir up the spirit of inquiry.

Hakuin also cites examples of some Nembutsu devotees who attained thereby a satori. Let us begin with this citation:

During the Genroku period (1688–1703) there were two such Buddhists, the one was called Yenjo and the other Yengu. After the realization Yenjo saw Dokutan, the Zen master, who asked, 'Where is your native land?'

---

[1] From a booklet known as the *Orategama* which is a collection of some of his letters. The work is read very much by his followers.

'Yamashiro,' was the answer.

'What is your faith?'

'The Pure Land.'

'What is the age of Amida?'

'Of the same age as myself.'

'What is yours?'

'Same as that of Amida.'

'Where is he now?' Dokutan demanded.

Yenjo closed the left hand a little and raised it.

Dokutan was surprised to see this and said, 'You are a real follower of the Nembutsu.'[1]

Later on, Yengu also attained realization.

There was another man about the same time who was called Sokuwo, also a Nembutsu devotee. By virtue of his singleminded practice, he was also enabled to realize the truth of Buddhism. Hakuin writes that he himself has recorded these facts elsewhere.

Hakuin was, we can thus see, by no means an exclusive upholder of the Zen exercise, but he did not wish to see his Zen followers diverted from their regular discipline. The letter further reads:

'When I say that the "*Mu*" (*wu*) and the Myōgō (*nāmadheya*, or Buddha-name, or Nembutsu) are of the same order, I must not forget to mention that there is some difference between the two as regards the time of final experience and the depth of intuition. For those Zen students of the highest capacity who wish to stop up the leakage of dualistic imaginations and to remove the cataract of ignorance, nothing compares to the effectiveness of the "*Mu*". So we read in the verse of Fa-yen of Wu-tsu Shan:

' "Chao-chou's sword blade is out of its scabbard,
How cold like frost, how blazing like a flame!
If one attempts to ask 'How so?'
A division at once sets in—this and that."

[1] Shuo-shan Shih-chieh was asked by a general, 'What is the age of Shuo-shan?' 'Same as vacuity of space.' 'What is the age of space?' 'Same as Shuo-shan.' *The Transmission of the Lamp*, XI. (Here Hakuin describes the psychological state of the Zen Yogin who practises the '*Mu*' exercise. This was already quoted on p. 140.)

'At this supreme moment [of Zen experience], Nirvāṇa and Saṁsāra are like a dream of yesterday, and the ocean of worlds in the great chiliocosm appears like a bubble, and even all the holy ones of the past, present, and future are like the flashes of great lightning. This is the great moment of satori known as the occasion of *ho ti i hsia* (exclaiming "*Họ!*").[1]

'The experience is beyond description, and can never be transmitted to others. It is those who have actually drunk water that know whether it is cold or warm. The ten quarters are melted into the spot of your presence; the past, present, and future are concentrated in this moment of your consciousness. Even among the celestial beings no joy is ever comparable to this, much less among humankind. Such advancement in one's spiritual life can be acquired even in a few days, if only the Yogins are devoted enough to the exercise.

'How is it possible to stimulate a spirit of inquiry to a state of great fixation?

'Not necessarily avoiding moments of activity, nor specially favouring places of quietude, inquire into the meaning of the "*Mu*", saying to yourself that "This body of mine is the '*Mu*' itself, and what does it all mean?" Throw away all thoughts and imaginations, exclusively applying yourself to the "*Mu*"—what does it mean? What sense is there in it? When you go on like that with singleness of purpose, the moment will surely come to all of you when finally a state of great fixation prevails.

'When you hear of this state of absolute unification, you are apt to harbour a feeling of uneasiness mixed with fright, but you must remember that you are by this exercise going to experience the inner realization attained by all the Buddhas because the frontier gate of eternal transmigration is thereby successfully broken down. Some hardships are bound to accompany the attainment.

[1] See also p. 126 where similar expressions are quoted. They all point to the abruptness of the Zen experience as advocated by Hui-nêng and his followers.

'As I think of the matter, there have been an innumerable number of the Zen Yogins who have experienced a great joy after going through the state of great fixation and of "great death"; but as to those followers of the Nembutsu who, by means of the Myōgō (*nāmadheya* = "Namu Amida Butsu"), have come even to a fraction of realization, I have heard of only a few of such. It was quite possible for the master of Yeshin In with his virtue, spiritual strength, and sincerity of faith to gain an insight into the truth of Buddhism say in a month or two or at the longest within a year, and find out that he himself was an embodiment of Suchness, if only he could have applied himself to the study of the "*Mu*" or the "three *chin* of flax". It was a great pity that he had to devote himself with wonderful persistency to the recitation of the "Namu Amida Butsu" for forty long years. This is all due to the absence of a great spirit of inquiry even in the most earnest devotee of the Nembutsu. This spirit is surely the highway to final realization.

'Another instance may be seen in the person of Hōnen Shōnin whose morality, humanity, industry, and spiritual virility were phenomenal, and who is said to have been able to read the sūtras in the dark with the light issuing from his own eyes. A soul so highly endowed could easily attain the highest enlightenment if only a spirit of inquiry were present in him. There was no chance indeed for him to complain about the rope being too short to sound the depth of the spring.

'On the other hand, how was it that such masters of great abilities as Yang-ch'i, Huang-lung, Chên-ching, Hsi-kêng, Fo-chien, and Miao-hsi (Tai-hui), who must have known hundreds of thousands of Buddha-names as well as hundreds of thousands of Mantrams or Dhāraṇīs which might be given to their disciples as objects of meditation, should have chosen the "*Mu*" as the means of reaching the goal of an exercise? They would not have done this unless there was something especially recommendable in the "*Mu*". What is this? It is no other than this that the "*Mu*" is apt to awaken a spirit of inquiry in the mind of a Zen Yogin whereas this is difficult with the reciting of the Myōgō—"Namu Amida Butsu".

'The reason, however, why even among Zen followers the Nembutsu or the Shōmyō has been entertained and the rebirth in the Land of Purity desired, is owing to the historical fact that the spirit of Zen was on the wane at the time [that is, in Yüan and especially in Ming], when the Jōdo idea came to be countenanced. While Zen was still in its heyday, not only in China but in India, the masters were strict and strongly conscious of the mission of Zen. Their only fear was that if Zen were allowed to degenerate, its spirit should soon totter to its fall; they never dreamed of referring to the Nembutsu or to the rebirth. But alas, as time went on, there was a lame master towards the end of Ming whose name was Chu-hung of Yün-hsi; his training in Zen was short of finality, his Zen insight did not go deep enough; he found himself wandering about in midway between Nirvāna and Samsāra. And it was natural for such a soul to abandon the true spirit of Zen discipline and to seek salvation in the echoes of the White Lotus Society, anciently led by Hui-yüan.

'Calling himself the teacher of the Lotus Pond, he wrote commentaries on the sūtras of the Pure Land school to instruct his disciples. Yüan-hsien of Ku-shan, known as Yung-chiao the Teacher, joined forces with Chu-hung by writing a book on the doctrine of the Pure Land (Ch'ing-t'zŭ yao-yü). Since then the purity of the Zen spirit became contaminated beyond repair not only in China itself but in Japan. Even with the master hands of Lin-chi, Tê-shan, Fên-yang, T'zŭ-ming, Huang-lung, Chên-ching, Hsi-kêng, Miao-hsi, and others, it is difficult to push back this tempestuous tide from the field of Zen proper.

'When I say this, I may seem to be unnecessarily hard on the teaching of the Pure Land school and slighting the practice of the Nembutsu. But in truth it is not so. What I blame most is the habit of those Zen followers who, claiming to be training themselves in Zen, are lazy, weak-minded, and while being so slack in the discipline they begin to take fright as they grow older in the thought of an approaching end and start anew with the practice of the Nembutsu, telling people that the Nembutsu is the best method of salvation and most suited for beings of these latter days. They look pious enough, but really they are revilers of Zen, pretending to be its faithful devotees. They are like those insects which, growing from the wooden post, feed upon it and finally tear it down. They deserve therefore a severe criticism.

'Since Ming these Nembutsu followers, disguising themselves to be those of Zen, have been very great in number. They are all worthless muddy-headed students of Zen. I heard, now about fifty years ago, a Zen master complaining of the way things were going on then in the world of Zen: "Alas! What would be the state of affairs three hundred years after this? The whole Zen world might turn into the Nembutsu hall where the wooden bell is heard all the time in accompaniment with the Nembutsu." This is indeed not an unfounded pessimism as far as I can see. Here is the last word of kindness an old man like myself can now offer for your perusal, which is: Do not regard this as a mere form of "*Kwats!*" nor take it for a Dhāraṇī, much less swallow it down as a sort of bitter pill. What is the kindest word of Zen? A monk asked Chao-chou, "Is the dog in possession of the Buddha-nature?" Chou said, "*Mu!*" '[1]

---

[1] While this was in the press, Mr. Kōson Goto of the Myōshinji monastery, Kyoto, informed me of the existence of a letter of Hakuin, still unpublished, in which he says that 'lately he has come to give the koan of "One Hand" to his students, instead of "*Mu*", because the "One Hand" awakens a spirit of inquiry much more readily than the "*Mu*".' Since then the 'One Hand' has become quite a favourite koan with all the descendants of Hakuin down to this day. The koan is, 'Hear the sound of one hand.' A sound issues when two hands are clapped, and there is no way of its issuing from one single hand. Hakuin now demands his pupils to hear it. One can say that this koan is more intellectual than the '*Mu*'. That Hakuin, who is a great upholder of the inquiring spirit against the mechanical method of the Nembutsu exercise, has now come to use the 'One Hand' as a first eye-opener, is full of signification in the history of Zen consciousness. When I write the history of Zen Buddhism in China, I wish to treat of the subject from a point somewhat different from what has been presented in this Essay.

# APPENDICES[1]

## I

'Oh, this one rare occurrence,
For which would I not be glad to give ten thousand pieces of
  gold!
A hat is on my head, a bundle around my loins;
And on my staff the refreshing breeze and the full moon I
  carry!'

According to the Second Part of the *Transmission of the Lamp*,[2] this was given out by the monk Hui-yüan who came to a realization when he accidentally stumbled while walking in the courtyard. The same is, however, quoted in another place as uttered by Chêng-wu Hsiung-yung.

## 2

Hui-t'ang Tsu-hsin[3] (1025-1100) studied Zen under Hui-nan of Huang-po for several years, but without success. One day he was going over the history of Zen, in which he read this:

A monk came to To-fu and asked, 'How is the bamboo grove of To-fu?'

[1] This section contains some of the 'Tōki-no-ge' (see First Series of *Zen Essays*, p. 248) uttered by the Zen masters, and the circumstances that led them to a state of satori, in the hope that they will help students of the psychology of religion to have a glimpse into the mind of the Zen Yogin, which is being matured for the final experience. When these are studied in connection with the technique of the koan exercise, much light will be shed on the nature of Zen Buddhism.

[2] *Hsü chuan têng lu*, afterwards abbreviated *Hsü-chuan*, consisting of thirty-six volumes, contains records of the Zen masters between the latter part of the tenth and the fourteenth centuries. The work is the continuation of the *Chuan têng lu*. The account of Hui-yüan is found in Vol. XX, and that of Hsiung-yung in Vol. XIV. Vol.=Fas.

[3] *Hsü-chuan*, XV.

'One or two of the bamboos are slanting.'

'I do not understand.'

'Three or four of them are crooked.'

This 'Mondō' opened Tsu-hsin's eyes. He came up to the master Hui-nan, and when he was about to make bows after spreading out his *tso-chü*, the master smiled and said, 'You have now entered into my room.' Tsu-hsin was very pleased and said, 'If the truth of Zen is such as I have now, why do you make us take up the old stories[1] and exhaust our efforts by striving how to get at their meaning?' Said the master, 'If I did not thus make you strive in every possible way to get at the meaning and make you finally come to a state of non-striving or effortlessness when you see with your own eye and nod to yourself, I am sure you would lose all chance to discover yourself.'

3

'The murmuring mountain stream is the Buddha's broad, long
    tongue;
The mountain itself in its ever-varying hues—is this not his
    Pure Body?
Eighty-four thousand gāthās were recited during the night,
But how may I some day hold them up before others?'

This comes from the pen of Su Tung-po the poet.[2] He was one of the greatest literary stars illuminating the cultural world of Sung. When he was in Ching-nan, he heard of a Zen master called Hao residing at Yü-ch'üan who was noted for his trenchant repartee. Tung-po was also great in this. Wishing to silence the Zen master, one day the poet called on him in disguise. The master asked, 'What is your name?' 'My name is Ch'êng (scale). It scales all the masters of the world.' Hao burst out in a

[1] Hua-t'ou is, in short, a Zen interview recorded of the masters. When it is used for training the Zen Yogins, it is a koan.
[2] *Hsü-chuan*, XX.

'*Kwatz!*' and said, 'How much does it weigh?' The conceited poet made no answer; he had to take his hat off to his superior.

### 4

When I-hai[1] came to Ch'i of Yün-chü, Ch'i asked, 'What is it that thus comes to me?' This opened Hai's mind to a state of satori, and the result was this verse:

> ' "What's that?" comes from Yün-chü;
> Asked thus, one is stupefied:
> Even when you nod right away saying, "That's it,"
> You cannot yet help being buried alive.'

### 5

> 'For twenty years I've pilgrimaged
> All the way from east to west:
> And now, finding myself at Ch'i-hsien,
> Not a step have I ever put forward.'

This comes from Chih-jou,[2] of Ch'i-hsien monastery at Lu-shan, who had a satori under Yüan-t'ung.

### 6

When Yang-shan was studying Zen under Pai-chang he had such a flowing tongue that to Pai-chang's one word he had ten words to answer. Chang said, 'After me, there will be somebody else who will take care of you.' Yang later went to Wei-shan. Wei asked, 'I am told that while you were under Pai-chang you had ten words to his one;

[1] *Hsü-chuan*, XI.
[2] *Hsü-chuan*, XII.

is that so?' Yang said, 'Yes, that is what they say.' Wei asked, 'What do you have to state about the ultimate truth of Buddhism?' Yang was about to open his mouth when the master shouted '*Kwatz!*' The question was repeated three times; the mouth vainly opened three times, and the '*Kwatz!*' was uttered three times. Yang finally broke down; drooping his head and with tears in his eyes, he said, 'My late master prophesied that I should do better with someone else, and today I have this very one.'

Determining to experience the truth of Zen in himself, he spent three years of intense spiritual discipline. One day Wei-shan saw him sitting under a tree. Approaching, he touched him on the back with the staff he carried. Yang-shan turned round, and Wei said, 'O Chi [which was Yang's name], can you say a word now, or not?' Yang replied, 'No, not a word, nor would I borrow one from others.' Wei said, 'O Chi, you understand.'[1]

7

To understand the story of Tao-yüan which is told below, the knowledge of Pai-chang and his old fox is needed. Hence the following:

Whenever Pai-chang had his sermon on Zen, there was an old man in the audience listening to him. One day the old man did not depart with the rest of the congregation. Pai-chang then asked him who he was. Answered the old man: 'At the time of the Buddha Kāśyapa I used to live in this mountain. One day a monk asked if a Yogin who went through great spiritual training should be subject to the law of causation, and I told him, "No, he is not subject to it."[2] On account of this, I have fallen into the animal path of existence and have been a fox ever since the time of the Buddha Kāśyapa. My wish is that you will kindly give me a statement which will save me from transmigration.'

[1] Quoted by Shih-wu Ch'ing-hung (1272–1352) in his *Sayings*.
[2] *Pu lao yin kuo*, literally, 'not to fall into cause and effect'.

Pai-chang said, 'Then you ask.'

The old man asked, 'Is a Yogin who went through great spiritual training subject to the law of causation, or not?'

Pai-chang replied, 'He does not obscure the law.'[1]

He had scarcely finished when the old man came to an insight as to the working of the law of causation. When leaving Pai-chang, he said: 'I am now freed from the animal path of existence. I used to live at the back of this mountain, and you will be good enough to cremate my body after the funeral rite accorded to a monk.'

Pai-chang made his secretary issue the proclamation that after the midday meal a funeral ceremony for a dead monk would take place and that all the Brotherhood was expected to attend it. The Brotherhood did not know what the proclamation meant, because they knew of no death among them. Pai-chang, however, at the head of the whole party went around to the other side of the mountain, and from a rock-cave he picked out a dead fox. The remains were cremated and, as requested by the strange old man, buried according to the proper rite given to a monk.

This question of *pu lao yin kuo* or *pu mei yin kuo* is a great one not only for Buddhists of all schools but for philosophers and religiously minded people. In other words, it is the question of freedom of the will, it is the question of divine grace, it is the question of transcending karma, it is the question of logic and spirit, of science and religion, of nature and super-nature, of moral discipline and faith. Indeed, it is the most fundamental of all religious questions. If *pu lao yin kuo*, this jeopardizes the whole plan of the universe; for it is *yin-kuo*, the law of causation, that binds existence together, and without the reality of moral responsibility the very basis of society is pulled down.

What then is the difference between *pu-lao* (not falling) and *pu-mei* (not obscuring)? 'Not to fall' is a moral deed, and 'not to obscure' is an intellectual attitude. The former makes one stand altogether outside the realm of causation, which is this world of particulars and where we have our

[1] *Pu mei yin kuo*, literally, 'not to obscure cause and effect'.

204

being. This is a contradiction—to be in it and yet to be out of it. In the case of *pu-mei*, 'not to obscure', what happens is the shifting of our mental attitude towards a world above cause and effect. And because of this shifting the whole outlook of life assumes a new tone which may be called spiritual *pu lao yin kuo*.

With this introductory note the following will be intelligible.

Tao-yüan,[1] who was studying Zen under Hui-nan (1002-1069), one day heard two monks engaged in discussion regarding the koan of Pai-chang and the fox. The one said, 'Even when you say *pu mei yin kuo*, this won't make you free from the fox form of existence.' The other immediately responded, 'That is *pu mei yin kuo*, and who had ever fallen into the fox form of existence?' Listening to this, Tao-yüan's inquiring spirit was aroused in an unusual manner, and, without realizing how, he found himself walking up to the mountain; and when he was about to cross the stream, his mind suddenly opened to the truth contained in the koan. As he was later telling the incident to Hui-nan, tears streaked down his cheeks. Nan ordered him to have a rest in his attendant's chair. From a sound sleep he abruptly awoke and uttered this:

'Cause and effect—not falling? not obscuring?
Whether monk or layman, there is nothing for him to shun.
Here's the man whose sovereign will is peerless,
Him no bag can hold, no wrappage hide;
Swinging his staff right and left as he will,
Straight into a troop of golden-haired lions jumps he, the
    master fox.'

8

I-huai of T'ien-i,[2] who flourished in the latter half of the eleventh century, was the son of a fisherman. Some years

[1] *Hsü-chuan*, XVI.
[2] *Hsü-chuan*, VI.

after he joined the Brotherhood, he came to Ming-chiao to study more of Zen.

Chiao asked, 'What is your name?'

'My name is I-huai.'

'Why don't you have it changed into Huai-i?'

'It was so given to me at the time.'

'Who got the name for you?'

'It is already ten years since I was ordained.'

'How many pairs of sandals did you wear out in your pilgrimage?'

'O master, pray do not crack a joke.'

Chiao asked now: 'I have committed a countless number of errors, so have you. And what say you to this?'

Huai made no reply.

Thereupon Chiao gave him a slap, saying, 'O this idle talker, get out of here!'

When I-huai saw the master another time, the latter said, 'Affirmation obtains not, nor does negation, nor does affirmation-negation; what do you say?'

Huai hesitated, whereupon the master ejected him with a blow. This was repeated four times.

Huai was now made to look after the water supply of the monastery. While he was carrying water, the pole suddenly broke, and the incident gave him the chance to become conscious of the truth hitherto hidden to him. The poem he composed to express the feeling he then had runs as follows:

'One, two, three, four, five, six, seven—
  Yes, many thousand feet high is the mountain peak, and lo,
    some one stands there on one leg;
  He has carried away the gem from the dragon's jaws,
  And Vimalakīrti's[1] secrets he holds in one word.'

Chiao the master, striking his desk confirmed this view.

[1] *Hsü-chuan*, V.

9

The monk Ling-t'ao[1] was a disciple of Lê-t'an Huai-têng. When the master asked him what was the idea of the Patriarch, who, coming from the West, is said to have transmitted one single mind-seal, which, pointing directly to the human nature, makes one attain Buddhahood, Ling-t'ao confessed ignorance.

T'an said, 'What were you before you became a monk?'

'I used to be a cowherd.'

'How do you look after the cattle?'

'I go out with them early in the morning and come home when it grows dark.'

'Splendid is your ignorance,' remarked the master.

This remark at once brought Ling-t'ao's mind to a state of satori which was expressed thus:

'Throwing up the tether I am a homeless monk,
  The head is shaved, so is the face, and the body wrapped in
      the chia-sha (kāśaya):
  If some one asks, What is the Patriarch's idea of coming
      from the West?
  Carrying the staff crosswise I sing out, La-li-la!'


10

When Yün-fêng Wên-yüeh[2] came to T'ai-yü Shou-chih for study, he heard the master discoursing to this effect: 'O monks, you are gathered here and consuming so many vegetables each day. But if you call them a mere bunch of vegetables, you go to hell as straight as an arrow flies'; and without further remark, the master left the pulpit. Wên-yüeh was astonished, not knowing what all this meant. In the evening he went up to the master's room, and the master asked, 'What is it that you are seeking?' Yüeh said, 'I am

[1] Hsü-chuan, V.
[2] Hsü-chuan, IX.

# KWANNON, MONKEYS, AND A STORK

## By Mu-Ch'i
### (*Early XIIIth Century*)

This well-known triptych deserves much attention in more ways than one. From the Zen point of view, what impresses us strongly is that the triptych expresses artistically in the most fitting manner the spirit breathing through the entire structure of Zen Buddhism. By this I mean that the unity of nature, including sentient and non-sentient beings, is harmoniously represented here. Is not the mother-monkey with the baby under her arm happy in the thought of enlightenment, which they both will finally attain through Kwannon's all-embracing love? Is not the stork elated in the feeling that it too is destined for enlightenment by becoming a member in the community of transcendental wisdom as realised by Kwannon? Not only, indeed, the monkeys and the stork, but the bamboos, the trees, the rock, the water, the meanest grass in the crannies, and the vines overhanging the crags—are they not, each in its way, the so many vyuhas embellishing the Dharmadhatu in which the Bodhisattva has his abode?

The artist probably got the idea of this triptych from Chia-shan Shan-hui's (A.D. 801–881) answer to "What are the sights of Chia-shan?"

> "A monkey holding her suckling in her arms comes back
>     to their home on the bluish hill;
> A bird carrying the flowers in its bill drops them by the
>     greenish crag."[1]

---

[1] *Chuan-téng Lu*, XV. There is no doubt that this couplet is derived from that of Ch'ung-hui (died, A.D. 779) which is quoted on p. 204. Most Zen maters are in one sense nature-mystics.

# YÜEH-SHAN AND LI-AO

By Ma Kung-Hsien
(*XIIth Century*)

Yüeh-shan (or Yao-shan, A.D. 751–834), one of the great Zen masters of the T'ang, was frequently invited by Li-ao, governor of Lang, to come to his district, but the invitation was persistently refused. One day, Li-ao himself came to the mountain where Yüeh-shan resided. Shan was reading the sutra at the time and paid no attention whatever. The attendant-monk said, "The governor is here, master." Li-ao was a short-tempered man and expressed himself at once, "Seeing the face is not like hearing the name." By this he meant that Yüeh-shan's personal presence was not so inspiring as he expected from his reputation. The master called out, "O Governor!" Li replied, "Yes, master." "How is it that you value the ear more than the eye?" Ao bowed respectfully and apologised; and then asked, "What is the Tao?" Yüeh-shan pointed up and down with his hand, and said, "Do you understand?" Li-ao confessed his ignorance. Thereupon Shan said, "A cloud is in the sky and water is in the pitcher." The governor once more bowed respectfully. He then composed the following verse:

> "The body, escetically trained, looks like a
>     stork;
> In the wood of one thousand pines, two sacred
>     scrolls are on the table;
> I come and ask him about the Tao, but no words
>     are wasted,
> Except 'a cloud in the blue sky and water in the
>     pitcher'."

after the truth of the mind.' But the master was not so ready to teach him, for he said: 'Before the wheel of the Dharma (truth) is set moving, the wheel of the staff of life must move. You are yet young and strong; why not go around and beg food for the Brotherhood? My time is all taken up in bearing hunger, and how can I talk of Zen for your sake?' Yüeh meekly obeyed the order and spent his time seeing that the larder of the Brotherhood was properly supplied.

Before long, however, T'ai-yü moved to T'sui-yen and Wên-yüeh followed him. When he asked the master to instruct him in Zen, the master said: 'Buddhism does not mind being covered with too many blisters. For this cold and snowy winter, get a good supply of charcoal for the Brotherhood.' Yüeh obeyed and carried out the master's order faithfully. When he came back, the master again asked him to take up an office in the monastery as there was a vacancy and none was available to fill it. Yüeh did not like this, for he was always ordered about doing things which he thought were not in direct connection with Zen teaching itself; he was sorry to see the master so cross-grained towards him.

While he was working in the back part of the building, perhaps with his mind filled with all sorts of feelings and generally in an intensely strained state of consciousness, the hoops of the wooden cask upon which he was sitting unexpectedly gave way, and he fell from it. This incident was the opportunity to shed an abundance of light into the dark chamber of his hitherto tightly closed mind, and he at once perceived the secret way in which his master's mind had been functioning all the time. He hastily put on his upper robe and came up to see Shou-chih the master. The master greeted him smilingly and said, 'O Wei-na,[1] so pleased to see you realize it!' Twice Yüeh reverentially bowed and went off without a comment.

---

[1] *Karmādāna* in Sanskrit. An office in the Zen monastery, corresponding sometimes to that of master of ceremony, and sometimes to that of general manager or overseer.

II

Yü of Tu-ling,[1] a disciple of Yang-chi (died 1049), used to feed Zen monks on pilgrimage, who passed by his temple. One day he entertained a monk from Yang-chi and asked what his master's teaching of Zen was. The monk said: 'My master would usually ask his pupils the following: A monk once came to Fa-têng and asked, "How should one advance a step when he comes to the end of a pole one hundred feet long?" Fa-têng said, "Oh!" '

When Yü was told of this, it made him think a great deal. The allusion here is to a stanza by Chang-sha Ching-ch'ên,[2] which runs thus:

'A man immovable at the end of a pole one hundred feet long—
He has indeed entered upon the path, but not quite a genuine one is he:
Let him yet move forward at the end of a pole one hundred feet long,
For then the entire universe extending in the ten quarters is his own body.'

The man is already at the end of a pole, and how can he take further steps ahead? But a saltus here is needed to experience the truth of Zen.

One day being invited out, Yü rode on a lame donkey, and when he was crossing over a bridge the donkey got one of its legs caught in a hole, and this at once overthrew the rider on the ground. He loudly exclaimed 'Oh!', and evidently the exclamation waked up his hidden consciousness to a state of satori. The verse gives vent to his experience:

'I have one jewel shining bright,
Long buried it was underneath worldly worries;
This morning the dusty veil is off, and restored its lustre,
Illumining the blue mountains in endless undulations.'[3]

[1] *Hsü-chuan*, XIII.
[2] *Transmission of the Lamp*, X.
[3] Quoted also in my *Essays*, Series I, p. 250.

12

The one bright gem discovered by Yü of Tu-ling helped to illumine the mind of Shou-tuan of Pai-yün.[1] Yang-chi who was also his master one day asked him who ordained him as a Zen monk. Tuan answered, 'Yü of Tu-ling.' Whereupon Chi said: 'I understand that Yü had a fall from a lame donkey, which led him to satori. Do you know by heart the verse he then composed?' Tuan proceeded to recite the whole verse beginning with 'I have one jewel shining bright. . . .'

When he finished the whole verse, Yang-chi gave a hearty laugh and quickly left his seat.

Shou-tuan was astonished, and no sleep had he that night. With the first blush of the day he appeared before the master and inquired of him what was the meaning of his laugh. It happened to be the end of the year. So asked the master, 'Did you see yesterday those devil-chasers going about in the streets?'

'Yes, master,' Tuan replied.

'Compared with them you are somewhat at a disadvantage, are you not?'

This remark was another case of astonishment on the part of Shou-tuan, who asked: 'What does that mean, master? Pray tell me.'

Chi said, 'They love to be laughed at whereas you are afraid of being laughed at.'

Tuan got his satori.

13

Tsu-yin Chü-nê[2] of Shu district, who flourished in the middle part of the eleventh century, was a great scholar versed in the *Puṇḍarīka* and other schools of Buddhist

[1] *Hsü-chuan*, XIII.
[2] *Hsü-chuan*, XIII.

philosophy, and even elderly scholars were willing to study under him. Evidently he did not know anything of Zen. One day he had a caller who was acquainted with the doings of Zen in the South. He said that the entire Buddhist world of China was then taken up by the teaching of Bodhidharma, and that Ma-tsu, one of his ablest descendants, who appeared to fulfil the prophecy of Prajñātala, had exercised great influence over the Buddhist scholars of the country, so that even men of learning and understanding who were renowned throughout the province of Shu, such as Liang and Chien, either gave up their own pupils or burned their library of the commentaries, in order to master the teaching of Zen.

Chü-nê was very much impressed with the report of his Zen friend. Advised strongly by him to go out into the world and see the state of affairs by himself, Chü-nê left his native province and wandered about some years in Ching and Ch'u but without seeing any result. He then moved further west and stayed in Hsiang-chou for ten years under Yung of Tung-shan. One day he was reading a treatise on the *Avataṁsaka* and was deeply impressed by the following passage, which opened finally his mind to the truth of Zen:

'Mount Sumeru towers in the great ocean attaining the altitude of 84,000 yojanas, and its summit is not to be scaled by means of hands and legs. This illustrates that the mountain of 84,000 human woes is rising from the great ocean of passions. When beings attain the state of consciousness in which they cherish no thoughts [of relativity] and from which all strivings vanish, even when confronting this world of multiplicities, their passions will naturally be drained off. All the worldly woes now turn into the mountain of all-knowledge and the passions into the ocean of all-knowledge. On the contrary, when the mind is filled with thoughts and reflections of relativity, there are attachments. Then the greater grow worldly woes and the deeper the passions, and a man is barred from reaching the summit of knowledge which makes up the essence of Buddhahood.'

Chü-nê then observed: 'According to Shih-kuang, "Not

a cue to get hold of," and according to Ma-tsu, "Ignorance since the beginningless past has melted away today." These are indeed no lies!'

14

Ch'ing-yüan Fo-yen of Lung-mên[1] who died in 1120 was first a student of the Vinaya; later, reading the *Puṇḍarīka* he came across the passage, 'This Dharma is something that goes beyond the realm of thought and discrimination.' This impressed him, so he came to his teacher and asked what was this Dharma transcending intelligence. The teacher failed to enlighten him, who then saw that mere learning and scholarship could not solve the ultimate problem of this existence subject to birth and death.

Fo-yen now travelled south in order to see Fa-yen of Tai-p'ing. While begging through the county of Lu, he stumbled and fell on the ground. While suffering pain, he overheard two men railing at each other, when a third one who interceded remarked, 'So I see the passions still cherished by both of you.' He then had a kind of satori.

But to whatever questions he asked of Fa-yen, the answer was, 'I cannot surpass you; the thing is to understand all by yourself.' Sometimes Yen said, 'I do not understand myself, and I cannot surpass you.' This kind of remark incited Ch'ing-yüan's desire all the more to know Zen. He decided to get the matter settled by his senior monk Yüan-li, but Li pulled him by the ear and going around the fire-place kept on saying, 'The best thing is to understand all by yourself.' Ch'ing-yüan insisted: 'If there is really such a thing as Zen, why not uncover the secret for me? Otherwise, I shall say it is all a trick.' Li, however, told him: 'Some day you will come to realize all that has been going on today between you and me.'

When Fa-yen moved away from Tai-p'ing, Ch'ing-yüan left him, and spent the summer at Ching-shan,

[1] *Hsü-chuan*, XXV.

where he got very well acquainted with Ling-yüan. Ch'ing-yüan now asked his advice, saying, 'Lately, I have come to know of a master in the city whose sayings seem to suit my intelligence much better.' But Ling-yüan persuaded him to go to Fa-yen who was the best of the Zen masters of the day, adding that those whose words he seemed to understand best were merely teachers of philosophy and not real Zen masters.

Ch'ing-yüan followed his friend's advice, and came back to his former master. One cold night he was sitting alone and tried to clear away the ashes in the fire-place to see if there were any piece of live charcoal left. One tiny piece as large as a pea happened to be discovered way down in the ashes. He then reflected that the truth of Zen would also reveal itself as one dug down to the rock-bed of consciousness. He took up the history of Zen known as the *Transmission of the Lamp* from his desk, and his eye fell upon the story of the P'o-tsao-to ('broken range'),[1] which unexpectedly opened his mind to a state of satori. The following is the stanza he then composed extempore:

'The birds are too-tooing in the woods,
With the garment covered up I sit alone all night.
A tiny piece of live charcoal deeply buried in the ashes tells
    the secret of life:
The cooking range is broken to pieces when the spirit knows
    where to return.
Revealed everywhere shines the truth, but men see it not,
    confused is the mind;
Simple though the melody is, who can appreciate it?
Thinking of it, long will its memory abide with me;
Wide open is the gate, but how lonely the scene!'

The story of the P'o-tsao-to alluded to in the text is as follows: The P'o-tsao-to is the name given by Hui-an to one of his disciples at Sung-yüeh. It literally means, 'a broken range fallen to pieces', which illustrates an incident in the life of a nameless Zen master, whereby he became

[1] For the story, see below.

215

notorious. There was a shrine in one of the Sung-yüeh villages where a lonely range was kept. This was the object of worship for the country people far and near, who here roasted alive many victims for sacrifice.

The nameless one one day appeared in the shrine accompanied by his attendants. He struck the range three times with his staff, and said: 'Tut! O you an old range, are you not a mere composite of brick and clay? Whence your holiness? Whence your spirituality? And yet you demand so many victims roasted alive for sacrifice!' So saying, the master struck the range for another three times. The range then tipped by itself, and falling on the ground broke in pieces.

After a while there suddenly appeared a man in blue dress with a high headgear, and approaching the master bowed reverentially to him. The master asked who he was, and he answered: 'I am the spirit of the range enshrined here. I have been here for a long time owing to my previous karma. But listening to your sermon on the doctrine of no-birth, I am now released from the bondage and born in the heavens. To offer my special thanks to you I have come.' Said the master: 'No-birth is the original nature of your being. No sermonizing of mine was needed.' The heavenly being bowed again and vanished.

Later on the attendant-monks and others asked the master: 'We have been with you for ever so long, but we have never been permitted to listen to your personal discourses on the Dharma. What effective teaching did the range-spirit get from you which enabled him to be born immediately in the heavens?'

The master said, 'What I told him was simply that he was a composite of brick and clay; I had no further teaching specially meant for him.'

The attendant-monks and others stood quietly without saying a word.

The master remarked, 'Do you understand?'

The chief secretary of the monastery said, 'No, we do not.'

The master continued, 'The original nature of all beings
—why do you not understand it?'

The monks all made bows to the master, whereupon
exclaimed the master: 'It's fallen, it's fallen! It's broken to
pieces, it's broken to pieces!'[1]

15

Wên-chun of Lê-t'an (1061–1115)[2] devoted himself
while young to the mastery of Buddhist philosophy but
later abandoned it, saying that he did not care very much
for it. He then began to study Zen, and going south stayed
with Chên-ju of Wei-shan for many years. However, he
made no progress. He came to Chên-ching of Chiu-fêng,
who was another great Zen master of the time.

Ching asked, 'Where is your native town?'

'Hsing-yüan Fu.'

'Where do you come from now?'

'Tai-yang.'

'Where did you pass your summer?'

'At Wei-shan.'

Ching now produced his hand, saying, 'How is it that my
hand so resembles the Buddha's?'

Chun was dumbfounded and unable to make any
answer.

Ching scolded: 'So far you have been fluent enough in
answering all my questions naturally and in a most splendid
manner. As soon as the subject turned to the Buddha's
hand, you halt. Where is the trouble?'

Chun confessed ignorance.

Ching said, 'Everything lies open in full revelation right
before you; and whom would you get to teach you?'

For ten years Chun stayed with his master Chên-ching
and went about wherever he moved. Ching was a silent
teacher and gave out no special instruction to anybody

[1] *Transmission of the Lamp*, IV.
[2] *Hsü-chuan*, XXII.

although his pupils grew considerably in number. When a monk entered his room for advice he would close his eyes and sit up on his knees and say nothing. If he saw somebody coming to him, he would rise, go out into the garden, and join the gardeners in hoeing. This was his usual way of dealing with his disciples. Wên-chun used to say to his friend Kung: 'Has the master no intention whatever to teach his followers in the Dharma? It is hard to know him.'

One day Wên-chun removed the dam with a stick, and while washing his clothes his mind suddenly woke to a state of satori. He ran to the master and reported to him all that happened to him. But the master coldly blamed him, saying, 'Why have you to be so unmannerly in this?'

16

K'ê-ch'in Fo-kuo[1] who died in A.D. 1135 was born in a Confucian family. While young, he was a great devourer of the classics. One day he went to a Buddhist monastery where he happened to read Buddhist books, and felt as if he were recalling his old memories. 'I must have been a monk in my previous life,' he thought.

Later he was ordained as a Buddhist priest, and devoted himself diligently to the mastery of Buddhist philosophy. He fell ill and when almost at the point of death he reflected: 'The right way to the attainment of Nirvāṇa as taught by the Buddhas is not to be found in words and mere ratiocination. I have been seeking it in sounds and forms and no doubt I deserve death.' When he recovered, he quitted his old method, and came to a Zen master called Chên-chüeh Shêng. Shêng's instruction consisted in making his own arm bleed by sticking a knife into it and remarking that each drop of the blood came from T'sao-ch'i. T'sao-ch'i is where Hui-nêng, the sixth patriarch of

---

[1] *Hsü-chuan*, XXV. He is best known as the author of the *Pi-yen-lu*. His honorary title is 'Yüan-wu Ch'an-shih' (Zen master of Perfect Enlightenment).

Chinese Zen, founded his school, and the remark meant that Zen demanded one's life for its mastery.

Thus inspired, Fo-kuo visited many Zen masters. They were all very well impressed with his attainment, and some even thought that it was he who would establish a new original school in the teaching of Rinzai (Lin-chi). Finally, Kuo came to Fa-yen of Wu-tsu monastery, who, however, refused to confirm Kuo's view of Zen. Kuo thought Fay-en was deliberately contradicting him. Giving vent to his dissatisfaction in some disrespectful terms, Kuo was about to leave Fa-yen, who simply said, 'Wait until you become seriously ill one day when you will have to remember me.'

While at Chin-shan, Fo-kuo contracted a fever from which he suffered terribly. He tried to cope with it with all his Zen experiences heretofore attained, but to no purpose whatever. He then remembered Fa-yen's prophetic admonition. As soon as he felt better, therefore, he went back to the Wu-tsu monastery. Fa-yen was pleased to have his repentant pupil back. Before long Yen had a visitor whose official business being over was to go back to the capital. Being asked by him as to the teaching of Zen, Fa-yen said: 'Do you know a romantic poem whose last two lines somewhat reminds us of Zen? The lines run:

'For the maid she calls—why so often, when there's no
   special work to do?
Only this—perchance her voice is overheard by her lover.'

When this was recited, the young officer said, 'Yes, yes, master.' But he was told not to take it too easily.

Fo-kuo heard of this interview when he came back from outside, and asked: 'I am told you recited the romantic poem for the young visitor while I was away. Did he understand?'

Fa-yen replied, 'He recognizes the voice.'

Fo-kuo said, 'As long as the line says, "The thing is to have the lover overhear her voice", and if the officer heard this voice, what is wrong with him?'

Without directly answering the question, the master abruptly said: 'What is the Patriarch's idea of coming from the West? The cypress-tree in the court-yard. How is this?' This at once opened Fo-kuo's eye to the truth of Zen. He rushed out of the room when he happened to see a cock on the railing give a cry, fluttering its wings. He said, 'Is this not the voice?' The verse he then composed was:[1]

'The golden duck behind the brocade screens has ceased
    sending out its odorous smoke;
Amidst flute playing and singing, he retired, thoroughly in
    liquor and supported by others:
The happy event in the life of a romantic youth,
It is his sweetheart alone that is allowed to know.'

To this Fa-yen the master added: 'The great affair of life that has caused the Buddhas and patriarchs to appear among us is not meant for small characters and inferior vessels. I am glad that I have been a help to your delight.'

17

Hui-ch'in Fo-chien[2] of Tai-ping studied Zen for many years under different masters and thought he was fully accomplished in it. But Fa-yen of Wu-tsu Shan refused to sanction his view, which offended him greatly. He left the master, as did his friend Fo-kuo. But the latter returned to Wu-tsu and attained full realization under him. Fo-chien also came back after a while, but his real intention was to go somewhere else. Fo-kuo, however, advised him to stay with the master, saying, 'We have been separated from each other more than a month, but what do you think of me now since I saw you last?' 'This is what puzzles me,' was his reply.

The signification of this conversation is that Fo-kuo,

[1] This was already cited in the First Series, p. 249.
[2] *Hsü-chuan*, XXV.

as was already recorded under him, had his satori soon after he came back to his former master. This fact, occurring during the month's separation from his friend, had caused such a change in Kuo's spiritual life that Chien wondered what was the cause and meaning of this transformation.

Fo-chien decided to stay at Wu-tsu Shan with his old master Fa-yen and his good friend Fo-kuo. One day Fa-yen referred to the 'mondō' between Chao-chou and a monk:

'The monk asked, "What is your way of teaching?"

'Chao-chou said, "I am deaf; speak louder, please."

'The monk repeated the question.

'Then Chao-chou said, "You ask me about my way of teaching, and I have already found out yours." '

This 'mondō' served to open Fo-chien's mind to satori. He now asked the master, 'Pray point out for me what is the ultimate truth of Zen.' The master answered, 'A world of multiplicities is all stamped with the One.' Chien bowed and retired.

Later when Fo-kuo and Fo-chien were talking on Zen, mention was made of Tung-szŭ's asking Yang-shan about the bright gem from the sea of Chen.[1] When the talk turned to 'no reasoning to advance', Fo-kuo demanded, 'When it is said that the gem is already in hand, why this statement again that there are no words for reply, nor is there any reasoning to advance?' Fo-chien did not know what reply to make. On the following day, however, he

---

[1] The story of the gem is this: Yang-shan came to Hui of Tung-szŭ (A.D. 742–823) for a Zen interview. Hui asked, 'Where is your native place?'

'I come from Kuang-nan.'

'I am told that there is a bright-shining gem in the sea of Chên, of Kuang-nan; is this right?'

'Yes, that's right.'

'What is the shape of the gem?'

'While the moon is shining, it is revealed.'

'Did you bring it along?'

'Yes, I did.'

'Why do you not get it out for your old master?'

'I saw Wei-shan yesterday, and he also wanted to see the gem; but there were no words in which to frame my reply, nor was there any reasoning I could advance.'

said, 'Tung-szǔ wanted the gem and nothing else, but what Yang-shan produced was just an old wicker work.' Fo-kuo confirmed the view, but told him to go and see the master personally.

One day when Fo-chien came to the master's room and was at the point of addressing him, the master rebuked him terribly. Poor Chien had to retire in a most awkward manner. Back in his own quarters, he shut himself up in the room while his heart was in rebellion against the master.

Fo-kuo found this out quietly, and came to his friend's room and knocked at the door. Chien called out, 'Who is it?' Finding that it was his dear friend Kuo, he told Kuo to come in. Kuo innocently asked: 'Did you see the master? How was the interview?' Chien now reproached him saying: 'It was according to your advice that I have stayed here, and what is the outcome of the trick? I have been terribly rebuked by that old master of ours.' Kuo burst out into a hearty laugh and said, 'Do you remember what you told me the other day?' 'What do you mean?' retorted the discontented Chien. Kuo then added, 'Did you say that while Tung-szǔ wanted the gem and nothing else, what Yang-shan produced was just an old wicker work?'

When his own statement was repeated now by his friend, Chien at once saw the point. Thereupon both Kuo and Chien called on the master, who, seeing them approach, abruptly remarked, 'O Brother Ch'ien, this time you surely have it!'

18

Fo-têng Shou-hsün (1079–1134)[1] began to study Zen under Kuang-chien Ying. He came later to Tai-p'ing, where Fo-chien resided, but was at a loss how to take hold of Zen. He put a seal on his bedding and made this vow: 'If I do not attain the experience of Zen in this life, this will never be spread to rest my body in.' He sat in meditation

[1] *Hsü-chuan*, XXIX.

222

during the day, but the night was passed standing up. He applied himself to the mastery of Zen most assiduously as if he had lost his parents. Seven weeks thus elapsed, when Fo-chien gave a sermon saying, 'A world of multiplicities is all stamped with the One.' This opened the eye of Shou-hsün. Fo-chien said, 'What a pity that the lustrous gem has been carried away by this lunatic!'

He then said to Hsün: 'According to Ling-yün, "Since I once saw the peach bloom, I have never again cherished a doubt." What is this when no doubts are ever cherished by anybody?'

Hsün answered, 'Don't say that Ling-yün never cherishes a doubt; it is in fact impossible for any doubt to be cherished anywhere even now.'

Chien said: 'Hsüan-sha criticized Ling-yün, saying, "You are all right as far as you go, but you have not yet really penetrated." Now tell me where is this unpenetrated spot.'

Hsün replied, 'Most deeply I appreciate your grand-motherly kindness.'

Chien gave his approval to this remark. Thereupon, Hsün produced the following stanza:

'All day he has been looking at the sky yet without lifting his head,
Seeing the peach in full bloom he has for the first time raised his eyebrows:
Mind you, however, there's still a world-enveloping net;
Only when the last barrier-gate is broken through, there is complete rest.'

Yüan-wu Fo-kuo who heard of this had some misgiving about Shou-hsün's attainment. He thought he would give it a test and see for himself how genuine Hsün was. He called him in and had a walk with him in the mountain. When they came to a deep pool, Kuo rudely pushed his companion into the water. No sooner he did this than he asked:

# THE SIXTH PATRIARCH TEARING THE SCROLL

## By Liang-Kai

There is no reference to this incident in any of the known history of the "Sixth Patriarch," by whom I presume Hui-nêng of the *Platform Sutra* is meant here. This may be regarded as a symbolic representation of the spirit of Zen Buddhism, which claims to transmit the inner secrets of the Buddhist life. To live the spirit and not to be bound by the letter is the message of Zen. The traditional attitude of the Zen master has thus been to take the sutras and śatras for no more than a bundle of waste paper, and their literary teaching for mere conceptualism which has no vital bearing on life itself.

The picture suggests a "lunatic," whose absolute disregard of decency and conventionalism in whatever sense, is here strongly depicted. He seems to deny the whole world of appearances, which, to the Zen master, is one abstractly constructed. To come in touch, therefore, with the living facts of experience, the student of Zen must once become a lunatic. By this I mean that he has to abandon everything he has "gained" in the way of learning and reasoning. Lao-tzu teaches: Learning gains while the Tao loses. The philosophy of loss in the philosophy of Zen.

古寺天寒夜一宵不敢風冷雪堆堆欲
無筆我何事特上取堂中木佛燒

# TAN-HSIA BURNING THE WOODEN BUDDHA

### By INDRA
#### (*Yüan Dynasty*)

The inscription by Chu-shih (1296–1370) reads:

"One cold winter eve at an old deserted temple he
stayed,

The wind was piercing, snow in flurry—how could
he stand it?

'When no material benefit is forthcoming, what
miracle can [the wooden Buddha] perform?' [the
monk reasoned.]

In the meantime might he not be allowed to take
down the wooden Buddha from the shrine and
commit it to the fire?"

*Chu-Shih*

It is not known who Indra the painter was, an Indian or a Chinese.
He must have been an artist of the first rank in those days, while Chu-shih was a great Zen master towards the end of the Yüan dynasty.
The picture is not to be judged by the ordinary standard of asthetics, for Oriental paintings, especially of the kind here represented, demand special laws of appreciation.

The tearing of the scroll by the "sixth patriarch," and the burning of a Buddha by Tan-hsia,[1] and other deeds of similar nature practised by Zen masters, together with the pictures known as *Suiboku* ("ink-sketches") by such masters as Indra, Mu-ch'i, Shuai-wên, etc., clearly show where the spirit of Zen Buddhism tends.

[1] First Series of *Zen Essays*, p. 330; *Chuan-téng Lu*, XIV.

'How about Niu-t'ou before he saw the Fourth Patriarch?'[1]

'Deep is the pool, many are the fish.'

'How afterwards?'

'The high tree invites a breeze.'

'How when he is seen and not seen?'

'The legs stretched are the legs bent.'

The test fully satisfied Fo-kuo, who was by the way Shou-hsün's uncle in faith.

---

[1] For the interview of Niu-t'ou and Tao-hsin (the fourth patriarch of Zen in China), see my *Essays*, First Series, pp. 201–202. This interview has frequently been made a subject of Zen 'mondō'.

# THE SECRET MESSAGE OF
# BODHIDHARMA[1]

## OR THE CONTENT OF ZEN
## EXPERIENCE

'What is the meaning of Bodhidharma's coming from
the West?' This is one of the questions frequently asked by
Zen masters, and forms one of the most important subjects
in the study of Zen. As an historical event, the question,
however, is not at all concerned with the coming of Bodhidharma to China, that is, with the historical signification
of Bodhidharma in Chinese Buddhism.

His landing on the southern shore of China is recorded
as taking place in the first year of P'u-t'ung (A.D. 520).
But the question has nothing to do with these things. Zen
is above space-time relations, and naturally even above
historical facts. Its followers are a singular set of transcen-
dentalists. When they ask about the first coming of Bodhidharma to China, their idea is to get into the inner meaning,
if there were any, of his special teaching, which is thought
to be spiritually transmitted to his successors. For there
had been so many foreign Buddhist teachers and scholars
who came to China before Bodhidharma, and they were all
learned and pious and translated many Buddhist texts into

[1] The historicity of Bodhidharma is sometimes discussed, but as far as
Zen is concerned the question has no significance. Zen is satisfied with
these historical considerations that there was the beginning of Zen in
China, that it started with some Buddhist teacher from India who had a
special message for the Chinese Buddhists of those days, and that this
message was not an ordinary one which could be transmitted in words or
writings. All that is told or recorded of Bodhidharma in the histories of
Zen and general Buddhism may or may not have been actual facts, and
these can be left to the historians to investigate according to their own
methods of study; but what concerns students of Zen is, 'What is the
message of the first teacher of Zen?' Hence this essay.

the Chinese language; some of them were even great adepts in meditation, and performed wonderful deeds moving the affections of unseen spiritual beings who used to live all over China in those ancient days. Were it not for some well-defined purpose characteristically distinguishing him from his numerous predecessors, there was perhaps no special need for Bodhidharma to appear among them. What was his message, then? What mission did he have for the people of the Far East?

As to that, Bodhidharma did not make any open declaration; he simply vanished from the world, for nine long years as tradition has it, keeping himself in complete retirement at Sung-shan in the dominion of Wei. If he had any message to give to Chinese Buddhists concerning the truth of Buddhism, it must have been something quite unique and out of the way. What was his reason to keep himself in absolute seclusion? What is the signification of his silent teaching?

Perhaps when this is mastered, Buddhism may yet open up some hidden treasure which cannot be described in words and reasoned out logically. The question, therefore, 'What is the meaning of Bodhidharma's coming from the West?' points directly to the presence of some truth innerly and mystically lying in the system of Buddhism. It amounts to this: 'What is the essence of Buddhism as understood by the First Patriarch of Zen Buddhism?' Is there anything in Buddhism which cannot be expressed and explained in the canonical writings classified into the Three Baskets (*tripitaka*) and arranged in the Nine or Twelve Divisions? Shortly, what is the truth of Zen? All the answers, therefore, given to this all-important question are so many different ways of pointing to the ultimate truth.

As far as it is recorded in history still in existence, the question seems to have been first raised in the latter half of the seventh century, that is, about one hundred and fifty years after the coming of Bodhidharma, but the idea for some time before must have been in a state of brewing. When Hui-nêng, the sixth patriarch, established what may

be called the native Chinese school of Zen in contradistinction to the Indian Zen of the First Patriarch, Chinese
Buddhists must have come to realize the significance of
the spiritual message of the Zen patriarchs. Since then the
question 'What is the meaning of the First Patriarch's
coming from the West?' naturally came to be one of the
most meaningful subjects to be discussed among the Zen
followers.

The first questioners as to the meaning of Dharma's
coming to China were Tan-jan and Huai-jang, according
to *The Transmission of the Lamp*, who in the latter half of the
seventh century came to Hui-an, the national teacher, and
asked:

'What is the meaning of the First Patriarch's coming
from the West?'

'Why don't you ask about your own mind?' the teacher
answered.

'What is our own mind, sir?'

'You should contemplate the secret working.'

'What is the secret working, sir?'

The teacher merely opened and closed his eyes, instead
of giving any verbal explanation.

Perhaps the next questioner on record was a certain
monk who came to Hsüan-su of Hao-lin, very early in the
eighth century, and asked the question to which the master
answered, 'When you understand, it is not understood;
when you doubt, it is not doubted.' Another time his answer
was, 'It is that which is neither understood nor doubted,
again neither doubted nor understood.'

As in other cases the masters' answers to the question
show such an endless variety as to bewilder the uninitiated,
making them wonder how they could ever expect to see
into its essence through this labyrinth of thought. And the
worst thing is that the variety of answers increases in proportion with the frequency of the question asked, for no
masters will ever give the same answer as far as wording
goes; indeed, if they did there would have been no Zen
long before this. The originality and individuality, how-

ever, thus shown by the masters, instead of clearing up the matter, complicates it to the utmost.

But when one goes carefully over the answers, it is not so difficult to handle them under a certain number of headings. Of course, this classifying does not mean that the unintelligibility grows thereby less unintelligible, only that it may help the student to a certain extent, however tentatively, to find some clues to the orientation of the Zen message. The following is thus my imperfect attempt to erect a few signposts for the guidance of the student.

1. Cases where an object near by is made use of in answering the question. The master when questioned may happen to be engaged in some work, or looking out of the window, or sitting quietly in meditation, and then his response may contain some allusion to the objects thus connected with his doing at the time. Whatever he may say, therefore, on such occasions is not an abstract assertion on an object deliberately chosen for the illustration of his point.

Wei-shan, for instance, questioned by Yang-shan, answered, 'What a fine lantern this!' Probably he was looking at a lantern at the moment, or it stood nearest to them and came in most convenient for the master to be utilized for his immediate purpose. On another occasion his answer to the same question may not be the same; he is sure to find it more desirable and appropriate to demonstrate Zen in some other way. This is where Zen differs from the conceptual arguments of the philosopher.

Chao-chou's answer was, 'The cypress-tree in the court'; and Fên-yang Shan-chao's 'How cool this blue silk fan is!' The connection between the Zen patriarch's visit to China and all those objects such as the lantern, cypress-tree, or silk fan may seem to be the remotest possible one, and these answers charge our imaginative faculty to do its utmost. But this is what the Zen student is asked to find; for according to these masters, when the cypress-tree in the court is understood, the reason of Zen Buddhism is understood, and when the reason of Zen Buddhism is understood, everything else will be understood, that is, all the variety of answers to be given below will be more or less thoroughly understood. One string passes through the one hundred and eight beads of a rosary.

2. Cases where definite judgments are given concerning the question itself or the position of the questioner.

Tai-mei Fa-ch'ang's answer was quite decisive. 'There is no meaning in his coming from the West.'

Mu-chou Tsung: 'I have no answer to give.'

Liang-shan Yüan-kuan: 'Don't talk nonsense.'

Chiu-fêng P'u-man: 'What is the use of asking others?'

Pao-ming Tao-ch'êng: 'I have never been to the Western world.'

Nan-yüeh Szŭ: 'Here goes another one walking the same old way.'

Pên-chüeh Shou-i: 'It is like selling water by the riverside.'

Pao-ning Jên-yung: 'It is like adding frost to snow.'

Lung-ya Chü-tun: 'This is the hardest question to answer.'

Shih-t'ou Hsi-ch'ien: 'Ask the post standing there.' When this was not comprehended by the inquiring monk, the master said, 'My ignorance is worse than yours.'

Ching-shan Tao-ch'in: 'Your question is not to the point.'

The monk asked, 'How shall I get it to the point?'

'I will tell you when I am dead,' was the master's way to get it to the point.

I cannot help quoting Lin-chi here, who was singularly 'reasonable' with regard to this question although he was notorious for his 'rough' treatment of the monks and for his exclamation 'Kwatz!' When he was asked about the meaning of the patriarchal arrival from the West, he said:

'If there were any meaning, no one could save even himself.'

'If there were no meaning here, what truth is it that the second patriarch is said to have attained under Bodhidharma?'

'What is called "attained",' said the master, 'is really "not-attained".'

'If that is the case, what is the meaning of "not-attained"?'

Lin-chi explained: 'Just because your mind is ever running after every object that comes before it and knows not where to restrain itself, it is declared by a patriarch that you are the foolish seeker of another head over your own. If you turn your light within yourself as you are told to do, without delay, and reflect, and stop seeking things external, you will realize that your own mind and those of the Buddhas and patriarchs do not differ from one another. When you thus come to a state of doing nothing, you are said to have attained the truth.'

3. Cases where the masters appeal to 'direct action'. This has not taken place frequently with regard to the present question, though appealing to direct action is quite an ordinary proceeding in the demonstration of Zen Buddhism since the time of Ma-tsu, whose case is related here. He was one of the greatest masters in the history of Zen, and in fact it was due to his masterly way of handling Zen that it came to be recognized as a great spiritual force in China.

When Shui-liao asked Ma-tsu as to the meaning of Dharma's coming from the West, Ma-tsu at once gave the questioner a kick over the chest which sent him down to the ground. This, however, awakened Shui-liao to the realization of the truth of Buddhism, for when he stood up again on his feet he declared this, clapping his hands and laughing loudly:

'How very strange! how very strange! All the Samādhis without number and all the religious truths unfathomable —I know them all now through and through even as they are revealed at the tip of one single hair.'

He then made a bow and quietly retired.

4. Cases in which some kind of movement is involved either on the part of the master or on the part of the monk. This is the most favourite method with the master,

and we can readily see why it is so. Inasmuch as Zen is not to be explained in words, an acting or a gesture[1] must be resorted to in order to bring its truth nearer home to the student. Since Zen is the truth of life, something more intimate and immediate than words is to be made use of, and this can be found in some kind of movement symbolizing life as it moves on. Words may be used too, but in this case they are not meant to convey ideas, but merely as expressive of something living and doing works. This also explains why cries or exclamations or ejaculations serve as answers.

When Hsüeh-fêng and Hsüan-sha were mending a fence, Sha asked, 'What is the meaning of Dharma's coming from the West?' Fêng shook the fence.

Sha said, 'What is the use of making so much ado?'

'How with you then!'

'Kindly pass me the *mieh-t'ou*,'[2] said Hsüan-sha.

When T'ou-tzŭ Ta-t'ung met T'sui-wei in the Dharma Hall, he asked the master about the meaning of the patriarchal visit from India. T'sui-wei the master kept on looking back for a while. Ta-t'ung wanted some express instruction, whereupon T'sui-wei said, 'Do you want another dipperful of dirt over your head?' This meant that the questioner had already been once bathed in dirt and did not know the fact. When T'sui-wei turned back, there was an answer to the question, and if Ta-'ung had his eye already opened he could have seen into the meaning without further asking for special wordy instruction. But he failed; hence the master's reproach, which, however, ought not to be understood as implying any feeling of slight or unkindness on the part of the master.

---

[1] To say that this acting or gesture explains, is not quite correct, for it is not designed to convey a meaning outside the gesture itself. In case it is so designed, the latter is words uttered by the whole body, though not by certain portions of it, and conveys an idea. In the Zen acting there is no such intention on the part of the master, and whatever perception or understanding there is in the mind of the pupil, it is the meaning of the latter's own inner experience, and not of any outsider's.

[2] An instrument used for mending or making a fence.

In all Zen 'mondō' or transactions, absolute sincerity and confidence exists between master and disciple. Wording may be quite frequently strong and impatient, but this is the way with the Zen master, who only wants to attract such souls as do not break down under his training staff. Zen is by no means a democratic religion. It is in essence meant for the *élite*.

A monk came from Wei-shan to Hsiang-yen when the latter asked the monk: 'There was once a monk who asked Wei-shan concerning the Patriarch's idea of coming to China, and Wei-shan in answer held up his *hossu*. Now how do you understand the meaning of Wei-shan's action?'

Replied the monk, 'The master's idea is to elucidate mind along with matter, to reveal truth by means of an objective reality.'

'Your understanding,' the master said, 'is all right as far as it goes. But what is the use of hurrying so to theorize?'

The monk now turned round and asked, 'What will be your understanding?'

Hsiang-yen held up his *hossu* like the other master.

Another time when Hsiang-yen was asked as to Bodhidharma's idea of coming to China, he put his hand into his pocket, and when he got it out it was formed into a fist, which he opened as if handing the contents over to the questioner. The latter kneeled down and extended both hands in the attitude of receiving. Said Hsiang-yen, 'What is this?' The monk made no reply.

It was again this same Hsiang-yen who proposed the well-known koan of a man in a tree. The koan runs thus: 'It is like a man over a precipice one thousand feet high; he is hanging there by himself with a branch of a tree between his teeth, his feet off the ground, and with his hands not taking hold of anything. Suppose now someone comes to him and asks him the question, "What is the meaning of the First Patriarch coming from the West?" If this man should open his mouth to answer, he is sure to fall and lose his life: but if he should make no answer, he must be said to ignore the questioner. At this critical moment what ought he to do?'

A monk asked Lê-p'u about Dharma's coming, and the master, striking his straw-chair with the *hossu*, said, 'Do you understand?'

The monk confessed his inability to understand, and the master gave this to him, 'A sudden thundering up in the sky and the whole world is taken aback, but a frog 'way down in the well has not even raised its head.'

Was the inquisitive monk the frog in the old well? The master's tongue was sharp and sarcastic. Basho, the great Japanese *Haiku*[1] poet, has the following verse:

> ' 'Tis an ancient pond,
>    A frog leaps in—
>    Oh, the sound of water!'

It was this sound that awakened him to the truth of Zen Buddhism. The experience itself could not be expressed in any other way; hence the *Haiku*, merely descriptive of the occasion with no sentiment, with no comment. The frog frequently figures in Japanese literature and has many poetical associations suggestive of peace and loneliness.

5. Cases where things impossible in this relative world of causation are referred to.

Lung-ya Chü-tun said, 'Wait until the dark stone turtle begins to talk, when I'll tell you what is the meaning of the Patriarch's visit here.'

Tung-shan's answer to Lung-ya was of the same impossible order when the latter wished to know the meaning of this historical event, for he said, 'Wait until the River Tung flows backwards, when this will be told you.' The strange thing was that the river did run backwards and Lung-ya understood the meaning of this remark.

Ma-tsu, who, as I repeatedly said, figures most prominently in the history of Zen, proposed a similar condition to P'ang-yün, the lay Buddhist disciple, in his answer

---

[1] A short epigrammatic verse consisting of seventeen syllables.

to the question at issue, 'When you drink up in one draught all the waters in the River Hsi, I will tell you the meaning of the patriarchal adventure.'

All these are impossibilities so long as space-time relations remain what they are to our final consciousness; they will only be intelligible when we are ushered into a realm beyond our relative experience. But as the Zen masters abhor all abstractions and theorizations, their propositions sound outrageously incoherent and nonsensical. Notice how the following answers, too, harp on the same string of transcendentalism:

Pei-yüan T'ung answered 'A dead pine-tree is hung over the wall, and the bees are busily sucking the flowers.'

Shih-men Tsung answered, 'See the ships sailing over the mountains of Chiu-li.'

A monk came to a master called Shih-shuang Hsing-k'ung to be enlightened on the subject of the patriarchal visit, and the master said, 'Suppose a man is down at the bottom of a well one thousand feet deep; if you could get him out without using a bit of rope, I would give you the answer as to the meaning of our patriarchal visit here.'

The monk did not evidently take this very seriously, for he said, 'Lately, the venerable Ch'ang of Hu-nan was given a monastery to preside over, and he is also giving us all kinds of instruction on the subject.'

Hsing-k'ung called a boy-attendant and ordered him 'to take this lifeless fellow out'.

The boy-attendant, who later came to be known as Yang-shan, one of the most masterful minds in Zen, afterwards asked Tan-yüan how to get out the man in the well, when the master exclaimed, 'Why, this fool, who is in the well?'

The boy-attendant still later asked Wei-shan as to the means of getting the man out of the bottom of the well. Wei-shan called out 'O Hui-chi!', as this was the name of the young monk.

Hui-chi responded, 'Yes, master!'

'There, he is out!' said the master.

When the monk later became a fully qualified adept in Zen and took charge of the monastery at Yuan-shan, he referred to these adventures of his, saying, 'Under Tanyüan, I got the name, while under Wei-shan I got the substance.' May we substitute here philosophy for 'name' and experience for 'substance'?

6. Cases where a truism is asserted. This is just the opposite of the foregoing. Yün-mên said: 'O monks, you go around the world trying to see into the meaning of the Patriarch's coming from the West, but this is known better by the pillar standing in front of you. Do you want to know how it is that the pillar understands the meaning of the patriarchal visit to this country?' This seems so far to go against truism, but after proposing this question Yün-mên proceeds to answer it himself, saying, 'Nine times nine are eighty-one.'

The Zen master has here turned into a mathematician. Evidently he thinks that the multiplication table explains the truth of Buddhism. His allusion to the pillar appears to complicate his position, but this is his artful device (*upāya-kauśalya*); when 'nine times nine are eighty-one' is grasped, the whole procedure gives up its secrets, if there are any.

The Zen student is now asked how to establish an inherent relationship between the impossible statements mentioned above and the truism asserted by Yün-mên. Are they at all reconcilable? They must be. Otherwise, the masters would not be giving the irreconcilables as solutions of the same problem. If there is such a thing as Zen, there must be some way in which all contradictions are to be synthesized. This is indeed where all the masters of Zen Buddhism exhaust their genius, and, as they are not philosophers but pragmatists, they appeal to an experience and not to verbalism—an experience which is so fundamental as to dissolve all doubts into a harmonious unification. All the matter-of-fact-ness as well as the impossibility of the master's statements must thus be regarded as issuing directly from their inmost unified experience.

T'ien-mu Man said, 'Once in three years there is a leap year.' This was a truism when the lunar calendar was in vogue. Everybody knew it, but what connection has it to the patriarchal visit?

The inquiring monk said, 'What are you talking about?'

'The chrysanthemum festival takes place on the ninth day of the ninth month.'

The chrysanthemum festival has been celebrated by the Chinese as well as by the Japanese when the chrysanthemum is at the height of its season. The number nine is a lucky number with the Chinese, and when it is doubled it is doubly lucky, hence the celebration. But does this explain the meaning of Dharma's coming over to China early in the sixth century?

Fo-chien Hui-ch'in's answer was, 'When you taste vinegar you know it is sour; when you taste salt you know it is salty.'

A monk asked San-shêng Hui-jên as to the meaning of the Patriarch's coming from the West, and the master answered, 'Tainted meat collects flies.'

The monk reported this to Hsing-hua who, however, expressed his disagreement. Whereupon the monk asked, 'What is the meaning of the Patriarch's arrival here?'

Hsing-hua replied, 'On the back of a broken-down donkey there are enough flies.'

In what point does Hsing-hua differ from San-shêng, as he claims he does? As far as flies go, does it make much difference to them whether they are upon tainted meat or on a donkey about to die?

7. Cases of silence are not many—I quote one. When Ling-shu Ju-min was approached with the question of Dharma's visit, he kept silent. Later when he died, his disciples wanted to erect a stone monument recording his life and sayings; among the latter there was this incident of silence. At the time Yün-mên was head-monk and they asked him how they should proceed to write out this silence on the part of the master. Yün-mên simply said, 'Master!'

Yün-mên was famous for his one-word answers; he was

no waster of words. Indeed, if one had to say something and this to the utmost limit of bare necessity, a single word, no more and no less, must be pressed to answer the purpose. The one character, 'master', here implies many things, as we can readily observe; and which of those implications was in Yün-mên's mind when he uttered it will be a problem indeed for the Zen student to unravel. Does it really clarify the meaning of the silence which was to be engraved on the monumental stone? Pai-yün Shou-tuan later wrote a Zen poem on this:

'Like a mountain, one character, "master", stands majesti-
    cally;
On it alone is the standard established for all rights and
    wrongs in the world:
All the waters ultimately flow towards the ocean and pour
    themselves into it;
Clouds, massy and overhanging, finally get back to the
    mountains and find their home there.'

8. Cases where the masters make meaningless remarks which are perfectly incomprehensible to the rational mind. While most Zen statements are apparently meaningless and unapproachable, the answers grouped here have by no manner of means any relation whatever to the main issue, except that the uninitiated are hereby led further and further astray. For instance, consider this: A monk came to Shih-shuang Ch'ing-chu and asked him concerning the patriarchal visit, to which the master's reply was, 'A solitary stone in the air!'

When the monk made a bow, probably thanking him for the uninstructive instruction, the master asked, 'Do you understand?'

'No, sir.'

'It is fortunate,' said the master, 'that you do not under-stand; if you did your head would surely be smashed to pieces.'

Nan-tai Ch'in's answer was, 'A tortoise's hair an inch long weighs seven pounds.'

Yen-chiao Ta-shih's was, 'Today, and tomorrow.'

Yün-mên T'ao-hsin said, 'A graveyard snake one thousand years old has today grown a pair of horns on its head.'

'Is this not your habitual way of teaching?'

'He who interprets loses life,' replied the master.

Does the Zen-understanding snake bite such a self-complacent monk as this? It is hard to make sense out of these remarks if we are mere literary interpreters. The Zen experience so-called must then be such as to annihilate all space-time relations in which we find ourselves living and working and reasoning. It is only when we once pass through this baptism that a single hair of the tortoise begins to weigh seven pounds and an event of one thousand years ago becomes a living experience of this very moment.

9. Cases in which the masters make some conventional remarks which are not exactly truisms, nor entirely meaningless statements as in the preceding cases, but such as people make in their daily life. As far as our rationality goes, such conventionalism has not the remotest relation to the meaning of the question here at issue. But no doubt the masters here as elsewhere are in earnest and the truth-seekers are frequently awakened to the inner sense of the remarks so casually dropped from the master's lips. It is therefore for us to try to see underneath the superficial verbalism.

Yüeh-ting Tao-lun gave this answer: 'How refreshingly cool! The breeze has driven the heat away from the porch.'

The following three masters' reference to natural phenomena may be said to belong to the same order:

Pao-hua Hsien said, 'The frost-bearing wind causes the forest leaves to fall.'

'What is the meaning of this?' the monk asked.

'When the spring comes they bud out again,' was the reply.

When Kuang-fu T'an-chang was asked about the patriarchal visit to China, he said, 'When the spring comes, all plants bloom.'

The monk expressed as usual his inability to comprehend,

and the master continued, 'When the autumn comes, the leaves fall.'

Pao-ch'an P'u's answer was also concerned with the season and vegetation. He said, 'As to the tree-peony, we look for its flowers in spring.'

The monk failed to get into the meaning of this, and the master helped him by this further comment on botany, 'As to the yellow chrysanthemum, it blooms in the auspicious ninth month of the year.'

The monk, who apparently liked to talk, said, 'If so, you are exerting yourself for the edification of others.'

The master's final dictum was, 'Mistaken!'

The statements grouped here are more intelligible than those concerning the tortoise's hair weighing seven pounds or the river swallowed up in one draught, but the intelligibility does not go very far; for when we consider how they are to explain the meaning of Bodhidharma's arrival in China we realize an irrelevancy here, our imagination fails to penetrate the veil of mystery hanging over the entire field. As to making reference to natural events in the interpretation of Zen problems, the literature gives many instances and we are almost led to think that all the masters are naïve realists who have no higher idealistic aspirations.

10. Cases where the immediate surroundings are poetically depicted. The masters are generally poets. More than anything else, their way of viewing the world and life is synthetical and imaginative. They do not criticize, they appreciate; they do not keep themselves away from nature, they are merged in it. Therefore, when they sing, their 'ego' does not stand out prominently, it is rather seen among others as one of them, as naturally belonging to their order and doing their work in their co-partnership. That is to say, the 'ego' turns into a blade of grass when the poet walks in the field; it stands as one of the cloud-kissing peaks when he is among the Himalayas; it murmurs in a mountain stream; it roars in the ocean; it sways with the bamboo-grove; it jumps into an old well and croaks as a frog under the moonlight. When the Zen masters take to the natural

course of events in the world, their poetic spirit seems to roam among them freely, serenely, and worshippingly.

A monk asked Ta-t'ung Chi, 'What is the meaning of the Patriarch's coming from the West?'

The master replied:

> 'The bamboo grove in the front court-yard,
> How freshly green it is, even after the frost!'

When the monk wanted to know what was the ultimate signification of the remark, the master went on in the same strain:

> 'I listen to the wind rustling through the grove,
> And realize how many thousands of bamboos are swaying
>       there.'

Yang-shan Yung's way of describing the pagoda, perhaps in his own monastery grounds among the mountains, was quite poetic, though the English rendering altogether misses the poetic ring contained in each of the five Chinese ideograms: 'A solitary spire which penetrates the wintry sky!'

T'ien-i Hui-t'ung was another Zen poet who beautifully describes a lonely mountain path which meanders along a purling stream; like so many others his monastery too must have been situated in a mountainous district far away from human habitation. When asked about the patriarchal visit he said:

> 'Hanging over a lone unfrequented path,
>   The pine-trees, ever green, cast their shadows.'

The monk did not understand and the master added this:

> 'Through a green bamboo grove, in refreshing rustle,
> There flows the mountain stream, murmuring and dancing.'

'Following this instruction of yours, we shall all be freed from doubt,' the monk thanked.

'Take your time, don't be too premature,' he was cautioned by the master.

T'ien-chu Ch'ung-hui who died towards the end of the eighth century gave out many poetic Zen statements, and his answer to this question on the patriarchal visit is widely known:

'A grey coloured monkey with her children in arms comes
    down from the verdant peaks,
While the bees and butterflies busily suck the flowers
    among the green leaves.'

In all this I wish to call the special attention of the reader to the fact that while other Zen masters are altogether too objective and apparently so coolly above the affectional side of life, Ch'ung-hui has a fine touch of emotion in his reference to the motherly monkey and the industrial insects. Out of his view of the patriarchal visit to China, something tenderly human gleams.

11. We now come to a group of singular cases, the like of which can probably not be found anywhere in the history of religion or philosophy. The method adopted by the Zen master in the following cases is altogether unique and makes us wonder how the master ever came to conceive it, except in his earnest desire to impart the knowledge of Zen Buddhism to his disciples.

A monk came to Ma-tsu and asked, 'Transcending the four propositions and one hundred negations, please tell me directly what is the meaning of the patriarchal visit to this country.'

In the master's answer there was nothing 'direct', for he excused himself by saying, 'I am tired today and unable to tell you anything about it; you had better go to Chih-t'sang and ask.'

The monk went to Chih-t'sang as directed, and proposed the question:

'What is the idea of the Patriarch's coming from the West?'

'Why do you not ask the master about it?'

'It was the master himself who told me to come to you.'

T'sang, however, made the following excuse: 'I have a headache today and do not feel like explaining the matter to you. You had better go to our brother Hai.'

The monk now came to Hai and asked him to be enlightened.

'When it comes to this, I don't know anything,' said Hai.

When the monk reported the whole affair to the master, the latter made this proclamation, 'T'sang's head is white while Hai's is black.'

Whatever Zen truth is concealed here, is it not the most astounding story to find an earnest truth-seeker sent away from one teacher to another, who evidently pretends to be too sick to elucidate the point to him? But is it possible that Zen is cunningly conveyed in this triviality itself?

Fêng-chou Wu-yeh asked Ma-tsu, 'What secret spiritual seal did the Patriarch transmit when he came from the West?' As this is differently worded, it may seem to differ from the question under consideration, but its ultimate sense comes to the same. In this case too, Ma-tsu, the teacher of more than eighty fully qualified masters, resorted almost to the same method as the one just related. For Ma-tsu excused himself again from answering the inquirer by saying thus, 'I am busy just now, O venerable monk; come some other time.'

When Wu-yeh was about to leave, the master called out, 'O venerable monk!' and the monk turned back.

'What is this?' said the master.

Wu-yeh at once understood the meaning and made bows, when another remark came from the master, 'What is the use of bowing, O you block-headed fellow?'

T'sing-ping Ling-tsun asked T'sui-wei Wu-hsiao, 'What is the meaning of the Patriarch's coming from the West?'

'Wait till there is nobody about us. I will tell you then.'

After a while Tsun asked again, 'Nobody is here now.'

Instead of answering this, Wei took the monk with him

to a bamboo grove. Seeing the master still in silence, Tsun the monk reminded the master of the question and of there being nobody about them. Wei then pointed at the bamboos and announced, 'What a long bamboo this! and what a short one that!' This awakened Tsun's mind to the realization of Zen truth. When later he came to preside over a monastery, he told his monks how kind-heartedly his late master exercised himself for the sake of others, and how since then he did not know what was good and what was not.

This last case reminds one of Kuei-sung T'ao-ch'üan's observation about stones. When the monk asked the master if there were any Buddhism in the mountains of Chiu-fêng Shan where he resided, the master answered, 'Yes.' The monk's further inquiry brought this from the master, 'Bigger stones are big, and smaller ones small.'

12. Cases where the master makes the questioner perform an act. This method has not been resorted to so very much in the present case as in some other cases. I have just one or two examples to offer here. When Lung-ya Chü-tun first saw T'sui-wei, he asked, 'What is the meaning of the Patriarch's coming from the West?' T'sui-wei said, 'Kindly pass me the *ch'an-pan* over there.' When this was handed to T'sui-wei, the latter took it and struck Lung-ya therewith.

Lung-ya later went to Lin-chi and asked him the same question. Lin-chi ordered him to perform a similar act as if they were in consultation beforehand. Lin-chi said, 'Please pass me the cushion over there.' When this was done, Lin-chi struck him with it just as T'sui-wei did with his *ch'an-pan*. In both cases, however, Lung-ya refused to accept the treatment as proper, for he said, 'As to striking, they may do so as much as they please; but as to the meaning of the patriarchal visit, there is none whatever in this.'

The following case may not be classed exactly as belonging to this group; there is something in it which reminds us of the cases mentioned under (11). When Lê-tan Fa-hui asked Ma-tsu about the patriarchal visit, Ma-tsu said, 'Softly, come nearer.'

The questioner approached, and was boxed by Ma-tsu who said, 'Six ears are out of harmony today, you'd better come tomorrow.'

The following day Hui came into the Hall of the Dharma, and accosting the master implored to be edified on the subject.

Ma-tsu said, 'Wait till I get up on the platform when I will testify for you.'

This proved to be the eye-opener to the monk, who then declared, 'I thank you for the testimony of the whole congregation.'

So saying, he went around the Hall once and left.

A monk asked Mu-chou Tsung about the Patriarch's coming from the West, and the master answered, 'Why doesn't that monk come nearer?'

The monk approached, and the master wondered, 'I called upon the one from the east of the Chê and what has the one from the west of the Chê to do with me?'

13. Cases in which answers are merely indicated with no definite settling of the point raised in the question. This is generally the case with most answers given by the Zen masters, and in this respect their answers so-called are no answers at all in the logical sense of the word. Mere poetical descriptions of objects one sees about, or suggestions to perform a certain act, are not at all satisfactory to those who have been educated to look for conceptual interpretations in everything they encounter. The cases enumerated here thus partake of the general characteristic of all the Zen statements. The reason why they are grouped here as one special class is chiefly that they do not properly fall in with any of the other cases already mentioned. The reader will understand this when actual examples are given.

A monk approached Chu-an Kuei with the inevitable question about the Patriarch, and the master answered, 'While the eastern house is lighted, the western house sits in the dark.'

Failing to understand this, the monk asked for further enlightenment. The master added, 'In the case of a horse we saddle it, but in the case of a donkey we let it turn a millstone.'

T'ien-t'ung Huai-ch'ing's answer was, 'Don't get sand into your eyes.' When asked how to take the statement, the master said, 'Don't get water into your ears.'

T'ao-yüan Hsi-lang's rejoinder was a grim one, for he declared, 'If there is any meaning in it, cut my head off.' When asked why, he reasoned, 'Don't you know the teaching, "Give your life for the Dharma"?'

Yün-kai Chih-yung's reference to an old stone monument gives one some hope to get into the idea he had of the patriarchal visit: 'The inscription on an old monastery stone is hard to read.' Does this refer to the difficulty of explaining to an average mind the matter in any intelligible way? For he added, when requested for further comment, 'Readers all wrinkle their foreheads.'

As I remarked elsewhere, Chinese is the language of Zen Buddhism *par excellence*. As its grammatical connections are very loose, much is often wholly left to the reader's imagination and judgment, and for this very reason an apparently indifferent expression from the mouth of the master may grow laden with meaning. For instance, when Ch'êng-hsin T'sung answered, 'The foot-passenger thinks of his journey,' was he thinking of the Patriarch's journey to China? Or did he intend to liken the monk's attempt to understand Zen unto the hardships of a traveller on foot, over the stormy roads for which China is notorious? Or did he want the questioner, perhaps in travelling attire, to think of his own doings?

The text has nothing explicit about all these possibilities except the bare saying itself of the master. When he was asked to say something further to make the sense clearer, he simply remarked, 'Tighten the sandals well.' No more, no less.

To give another example: Chao-ming Tsê said, 'A refreshing breeze is stirred in the azure heavens.' Does it refer to Dharma's subjective mind in which all the egotistic impulses are dead like unto the vastness of the sky? Or does it refer to the stirring of the wind, the whence and whither of which one is absolutely ignorant? The master's further statement leaves the question in no better light: 'The full moon is reflected in the Yang-tzŭ-chiang.'

Does this mean to say that while the moon has no idea to see its reflection in the water, it does so just because there is water which reflects it and will continue to do so whenever there is a moon and wherever there is water, even a dirty puddle of water on the roadside? Was Dharma's coming from the West like the lunar reflection in the Yang-tzŭ-chiang river? A thought was awakened to him to come to China just as the moon comes out of the clouds when they are dispersed, and he came and taught and died—even as the moon sheds its silvery rays over the waves of the Yang-tzŭ-chiang.

Hei-shui Chêng-ching's idea, which is quoted below, has something grander and more energetic than the last-mentioned, which excels in serenity and aloofness. According to Hei-shui, the meaning of Dharma's coming to China was this:

> 'How vastly, broadly, infinitely it expands all over the
>     universe!
> Look at the illumining Buddha-sun as the murky fog
>     rises and dissipates itself!'

When he was further questioned about the functioning of the Buddha-sun, he said, 'Even the great earth could not hide it, and it is manifesting itself this very moment!'

14. We now come to the last group, which, however, may not be the last if we more closely examine all the answers given to the question under consideration, 'What is the meaning of Dharma's coming from the West?' For some more cases may be found in Zen literature, which cannot very well be classified under any of the fourteen groups I have here enumerated. But I believe the above have almost exhausted all the varieties sufficiently to give the reader a general idea as regards what Zen statements are, concerning

at least one particular theme. This therefore may fairly be regarded as the last group of answers given to the patriarchal visit to China.

This will include cases where the master's answers are more or less directly concerned with the person. of the Patriarch himself. So far the answers had nothing to do with the principal figure in the question; but they now begin to take him up and assertions are made about his doings. Still, the answers do not touch the central point of the questions: that is, the meaning of the patriarchal visit to China is not explained in any way that we of plain minds would like. In this respect the cases mentioned here are just as far off the mark as the other cases already mentioned.

Hsiang-lin Ch'ên-yüan's answer was, 'A long tiresome sitting for him!' Did the nine years' sitting make Dharma all tired out? Or is this just a general assertion concerning sitting in meditation, including the master's own case? Or is it an apologetic remark for having kept him sitting so long?

One may find it hard to decide which. This is where Zen is difficult to understand by the ordinary way of thinking. Mere words are insufficient to convey the meaning, but as rational beings we cannot avoid making statements. And these statements are at once puzzling and illuminating according to our own insight. But in the case of Chang-pei Shan the reference is obvious, for he said, 'He came from the Western kingdom and disappeared in the land of T'ang.' The next one is concerned with the second patriarch and not with the first. According to Fu-ch'ing Wei, 'It was not very hard to be standing in snow; the mark was hit when the arms were cut off.'

Evidently in his view the second patriarch's self-mutilation was the meaning of Dharma's coming overseas. Or did he mean that the meaning in question was to be realized only after the severest spiritual training? If so, this was not at all an answer to the question, but, one may remark, only pointing at the way to its final solution.

Yüeh-hua's answer was, 'The Emperor of the Liang

dynasty did not know him.' Requested to be further enlightened, he said, 'He went home carrying one shoe with
him.' This is simply a narration of the life of Bodhidharma,
with which Huang-shan Lin's remark is of the same order,
when he says, 'At the palace of Liang nothing was achieved,
and in the kingdom of Wei he was most profoundly absorbed
in meditation.'

With these two masters Shang-ch'üan Ku keeps company, as is to be observed in the following, 'He never
appeared at the Liang palace; after Wei he went home
westward with one shoe in his hand.'

Ching-fu Jih-yü's reply also falls in with these masters.
'Nobody knew him when he spent nine years gazing at the
wall, but he was heard all over when he returned west with
one shoe in his hand.' To further enlighten the questioner,
the master added, 'If one wants to know about the event in
the remote era of P'u-tung, it is not necessary to get an intelligence on the T'sung-ling range.'

The T'sung-ling is a range of mountains dividing China
from central Asia, which Bodhidharma, the first patriarch
of Zen Buddhism in China, is reported to have crossed on
his way back to India. He was then bare-footed and
carried one of his shoes in his hand while the other was
found in his grave, which was opened when the report
of his return over the T'sung-ling range got widely known
among his Chinese followers.

As we can see plainly now, all these remarks have really
no connection with the question at issue, which wants to
know the meaning or reason of the Patriarch's coming from
the West; that is to say, the truth of Zen Buddhism as distinguishing itself from the philosophical teaching of the
other Buddhist schools. While the statements touch the life
of the Patriarch, the masters are not evidently willing to dis-
close the meaning of Zen in any more intelligible manner
than others.

After enumerating all these varieties of Zen answers
given to one single question, there is at least one conclusion

which we can draw out of them as a most legitimate one. It is this: the truth of Zen Buddhism as symbolized in the coming of the first patriarch to China is something demonstrable by every possible means of expression under human control, but at the same time incommunicable to others when the latter are not mentally prepared for it.

The truth can be expressed in words, and also interpreted by action, though it is not quite proper to say that it is thus explained or interpreted or demonstrated. For what the Zen master aims at in giving out those impossible propositions or nonsensical phrases or in performing mysterious movements is merely to let his disciples perceive by themselves wherein lies the truth which is to be grasped. They are all so many indicators and have in fact nothing with interpretation or definition or any other such terms as are used in our so-called scientific parlance. If we seek the latter in the Zen answers we shall be altogether off the track. And for this very reason all the contradictions and absurdities which we have seen are made to serve the purpose of the master. When they are understood to be indicators pointing at the one truth, we shall inevitably be led to look where all these divers hands converge. At the points where they all converge there sits the master quite at home with himself and with the world.

It is like so many rays radiating from one central luminary. The rays are innumerable, and as long as we stand at the end of each ray we do not know how to reconcile one ray with another. Here is a range of mountains towering high, there is a sheet of water extending far out to the horizon, and how can we make mountains out of the foam and foam out of the mountains as long as we but see the foam-end or mountain-end of the ray? With Zen irrationality alone is considered, it remains forever as such, and there is no way to see it merged with rationality. The contradiction will ever keep us awake at night.

The point is to walk along with a ray of absurdity and see with one's own eyes into the very origin where it shoots out. The origin of the luminary itself once in view, we know how to travel out into another ray at the end of which we may find another order of things. Most of us stand at the periphery and attempt to survey the whole; this position the Zen master wants us to change; he who sits at the centre of eternal harmony knows well where we are bound, while we at the furthest end remain bewildered, perplexed, and quite at a loss how and where to proceed. If this were not the case, how could the master be so miraculously re-sourceful as to produce one absurdity or inconsistency after another and remain so comfortably self-complacent?

This is, however, the way we logic-ridden minds want to read into the answers given by the Zen master. As to the master himself, things may appear quite in another light. He may say that there is no periphery besides the centre, for centre is periphery and periphery is centre. To think that there are two things distinguishable the one from the other and to talk about travelling along the ray-end to-wards the luminary itself is due to a false discrimination (parikalpa). 'When one dog barks at a shadow, ten thou-sand dogs turn it into a reality'—so runs the Chinese saying. Beware therefore of the first bark, the master will advise.

When Lo-han Jên was asked as to the meaning of the patriarchal visit, he asked back, 'What is it that you call the meaning?'

'If so, there is no meaning in this coming from the West?' concluded the inquiring monk.

'It comes from the tip of your own tongue,' said the master.

It may all be due to our subjective discrimination based on a false conception of reality, but, our good Zen master, without this discrimininating faculty, false or true, how can we ever so conceive of you? The master is a master because we are what we are. Discrimination has to start somewhere. It is quite true that gold dust, however valuable in itself, injures the eye when it gets into it. The thing will then be to keep the eye open clear, and use the gold dust in the way it ought to be used.

After reviewing all these propositions, suggestions, or

expressions as given by the masters, if someone comes to me and proposes the question, 'What is after all the meaning of Bodhidharma's coming from the West?', what shall I say to him? But as I am not an adept in Zen I know not how to answer from the standpoint of Zen transcendentalism; my answer will be that of a plain-minded person, for I will say 'Inevitable!' How does this 'inevitable' start? Nobody knows how and where and why; because it is just so and not otherwise. 'That which abides nowhere' comes from nowhere and departs nowhere.

> 'For nine years he had been sitting and no one knew
>     him;
> Carrying a shoe in his hand he went home quietly,
>     without ceremony.'[1]

---

[1] Most quotations in this essay are taken from the work entitled *Ch'an lin lei chü* in twenty fasciculi compiled in the year 1307. The title means 'Zen materials (literally, woods) classified and collected'. The book is now very rare.

# TWO ZEN TEXT-BOOKS:

## PI-YEN-CHI AND WU-MÊN-KUAN

### I

#### THE PI-YEN-CHI

The *Pi-yen-chi* or *Pi-yen-lu*[1] is one of the most valued books in the Rinzai (*lin-chi*) school of Zen Buddhism, especially in Japan. It consists of Hsüeh-tou's poetical comments on one hundred 'cases'[2] mostly selected from the history of Zen masters, called *The Transmission of the Lamp*, and of *Yüan-wu's* additional notes. Hsüeh-tou was a great master of the Yün-mên school and flourished early in the Sung dynasty (980–1052). He was noted for his literary ability, and when his poetical comments on the one hundred cases were made public, they at once created universal applause in the literary circles of the time.

While Yüan-wu (1063–1135) was residing in the capital of Shu, he took up, in response to the request of his pupils, Hsüeh-tou's work as the text-book for his discourses on Zen. When he later came to Ling-chüan Yüan at Chia-shan, in Li-chou, during the Chêng-hua period (1111–1118) he was again asked to discourse on the work. The notes taken by his disciples came to be compiled into a regular book. Each case was preceded by an introductory remark, and the case itself was annotated and criticized in a way peculiar to Zen, and finally Hsüeh-tou's poems were treated in a similar manner.

[1] *Hekiganshu*, or *hekiganroku*, in Japanese. *Pi-yen* means 'Green Rock', *chi* is 'collection', and *lu* 'record'. The Green Rock was the name of Yüan-wu's study.

[2] 'Case' may not be a very good term for *Tsê*, by which each example in the *Pi-yen* is usually known. *Tsê* means 'a standard', or 'an item', or 'a clause' in enumeration.

As Yüan-wu was indifferent about collating and revising these notes taken by his various disciples, the notes began to circulate in an unfinished and confused form among his followers. Fearing that some day the text might get irretrievably muddled, Kuan-yu Wu-tang, one of Yüan-wu's pupils, decided to have an authorized *editio princeps* of it and thus to put a stop to all possible variations that might follow from promiscuous copyings. The book came out in print late in the spring of 1125, which was twenty years after a third lecture had been given by the master on the text. Neither the editor, Kuan-yu Wu-tang, nor the preface-writer, P'u-chao, however, makes any reference to the text having been gone through by the author personally before it was published in printed form.

Later, Tai-hui, the most brilliant and most gifted disciple of Yüan-wu, burned the *Pi-yen-chi*, seeing that it was not doing any good to the truthful understanding of Zen. While it is not quite clear what he actually did, the book apparently stopped circulating. It was not until about two hundred years later (1302) that Chang Ming-yüan, of Yü-chung, found a good copy of the *Pi-yen-chi* at Chêng-tu, in Shu. He collated this with other copies obtained in the South, and the result was the current copy we have now.

Dōgen, the founder of the Sōtō school of Zen in Japan, it is reported, was the first who brought the *Pi-yen-chi* from China in the third year of Karoku (1227) about eighty years prior to the Chang edition. It is not definitely known when the latter was imported to Japan, but as there was much intercourse between the Japanese and the Chinese Zen masters in those days, the book must have come to this shore through some of the Japanese monks who went to China to study Buddhism. Early in the fifteenth century we have already a Japanese edition of the *Pi-yen-chi*.

The constitution of the book is generally in the following order: Each case is preceded by Yüan-wu's introductory note (1); the case itself is interpolated with critical sentences (2); then comes an expository comment on the case (3); which is followed by Hsüeh-tou's poetical appreciation or criticism, which is also interposed with Yüan-wu's remarks (4); and finally we have explanatory notes to the poem (5).

The following is an English translation of the Case LV faithfully rendered to the extent admissible by the construction of the original, which in itself is almost altogether unintelligible to those who are not acquainted with Zen literature. This will be realized by the reader even when perusing my translation, which is far from being literal.

## II

### THE CASE LV—TAO-WU AND CHIEN-YÜAN VISIT A FAMILY TO MOURN THE DEAD[1]

#### a. Introductory Note

[The perfect master of Zen] quietly within himself asserts the whole truth and testifies it at every turn;

[1] Tao-wu, whose personal name was Yüan-chih, was a disciple of Yüeh-shan, and died in 835, of the T'ang dynasty, at the age of sixty-seven. When he was once in attendance with his brother-monk Yün-yen on their master Yüeh-shan, the latter said to Yüan-chih: 'Where the intellect fails to fathom, beware of giving utterance to it; if you utter a word, horns will grow on your forehead. What would you say to this?' Yüan-chih, without making any reply, went out of the room. Yün-yen now asked the master, 'How is it that my senior brother-monk does not give you any answer?' Said the master, 'My back aches today; you'd better go to Yüan-chih himself, as he understands.' Yün-yen came to his brother-monk, Yüan-chih, and said: 'Why did you not answer our master a while ago? Please tell me the reason, Brother.' 'You'd better ask our master himself,'—this was Yüan-chih's enigmatic suggestion.

Shih-shuang was a disciple of Tao-wu Yüan-chih. He once asked the master, 'If someone after your passing happens to ask me about the ultimate thing, what shall I say to him?' The master, Yüan-chih, did not answer the question, but simply called to his attendant-boy who at once came forward in response. Said the master, 'You fill the pitcher now with fresh water.' After remaining silent for a little while, the master now turned towards Shih-shuang and asked, 'What did you want to know a while ago?' Shih-shuang repeated his first question, whereupon the master rose from his seat and left the room. This leaving the room was evidently a favourite way with Tao-wu Yüan-chih when he wished to demonstrate the truth of Zen.

His other sayings and doings are recorded in *The Transmission of the Lamp*, XXIV.

wading through the cross-currents he controls the circumstances and directly sees into the identity of things. As in the sparks struck from flint or as in the flash of lightning, so instantaneously he makes away with intricacies and complications; while taking hold of the tiger's head he lets not the tail slip off his hands; he is like unto a rugged precipice one thousand feet high. But we will not speak of such [achievements as these on the part of the master]; let us see if there is not an approachable way in which he manifests the truth for the sake of others. Here is a case for our consideration.

### b. The Illustrative Case

Tao-wu and Chien-yüan visited a family to mourn the dead. Chien-yüan knocked at the coffin and said, 'Living or dead?'—What do you say?—Well, you are not at all alive.—This fellow still wanders between two paths.

'Living? I tell you not; dead? I tell you not.'—When a dragon sings fog is formed: when a tiger roars the wind rises.—That hat fits the head.—A grandmotherly kindness!

'Why not tell?'—Gone wrong!—Sure enough, a blunder's committed!

'I say I tell you not.'—Filthy water is poured right over your head!—The first arrow was rather light, but the second goes deeper.

On their way home,—quite lively!

Chien-yüan said, 'O my master, be pleased to tell me about it; if you do not, I will knock you down.'—This is something.—We rarely meet wise men, most of them are fools.—One so full of irrationalities ought to go to Hell faster than an arrow.

'As to your striking it is your own pleasure; as to telling I have nothing to tell.'—Repetition is necessary for serious affairs. —He is not aware even of being robbed.—This old man's tenderness knows no bounds.—The first idea is still asserted.

Chien-yüan struck the master.—Well done!—Tell me what is the use of striking him thus.—Sometimes one has to suffer an unreasonable treatment.

Later when Tao-wu died, Chien-yüan went to Shih-shuang[1] and told him about the aforementioned incident. —Knowingly trespassed!—I wonder if this were right, or not.—If right, how marvellous!

'Living—I tell you not; dead? I tell you not!'—How very refreshing!—Even an everyday meal is relished by some!

'Why not tell me?'—The same wording, and no difference in sense either.—Tell me if this is the same question as the first.

'I say I tell you not,' said Shih-shuang.—Heaven above, earth below!—When the waves are surging like this at Tsao-chi, how many common mortals are drowned on land!

This instantly awakened Chien-yüan to an understanding.—O this purblind fellow!—I am not to be deceived!

One day Chien-yüan came out into the Dharma Hall with a spade, and walked up and down from east to west, from west to east.—The dead resuscitated!—Good! This showing himself off in behalf of the late master!—Don't ask of others.—Behold how this fellow is disgracing himself!

'What are you doing?' asked Shih-shuang.—Blindly treading in the steps of another!

'I am seeking the sacred bones of the late master.'—Too late, like hanging a medicine bag behind the hearse carriage.—Too bad that he missed the first step.—What do you say?

'The huge waves are rolling far and near, the foaming seas are flooding the sky, and what sacred bones of the late master should you seek here?' said Shih-shuang.—As to this, let another master see to it.—What is the use of following the masses?

Hsüeh-tou remarks here: 'What a pity! What a pity!' —Too late.—This is like stretching the bow after the burglar is gone. Better have him buried in the same grave.

Said Chien-yüan, 'This is the very moment to be thankful for.'—Say, now, where does all this finally come to?—What did the late master tell you before?—This fellow has never known from beginning till end how to free himself.

Monk Fu of T'ai-yüan remarks here, 'The holy bones of the late master are still here.'—O my disciples, see them?—It is like the stroke of lightning.—What sort of worn-out sandals these!—This is after all worth something.

---

[1] See *supra*.

### c. Commentary Remarks

Tao-wu and Chien-yüan went out one day to see a family in order to mourn the dead. Chien-yüan knocking at the coffin said, 'Living? or dead?' And Tao-wu said: 'Living? I tell you not: dead? I tell you not!' If you gain an insight right here at this remark, you will know then where you are bound for. Just here and nowhere else is the key that will release you from the bondage of birth and death. If you have not yet gained it, you are liable to slip away at every turn. See how earnest those ancient students of Zen were! Whether walking or standing, sitting or lying, their constant thoughts were fixed upon this matter. As soon as they came into a house of mourning, Chien-yüan knocking at the coffin lost no time in asking Tao-wu, 'Living? or dead?' Tao-wu instantly responded: 'Living? I tell you not: dead? I tell you not!' Chien-yüan straight-way slipped over the literary meaning of his master's remarks. Hence his second question, 'Why not tell?' To this Tao-wu answered, 'I say I tell you not!' How full of kindness was his heart! One error succeeds another.

Chien-yüan had not yet come to himself. When they were halfway on their homeward walk, he again accosted his master, saying: 'O master, do please tell me about it. If you don't I will strike you.' This fellow knows not a thing. It is the case of a kindness not being requited. But Tao-wu, who was ever grandmotherly and full of tenderness, responded, 'As to striking, it is your own pleasure; as to telling, I have nothing to tell you.'

Thereupon Chien-yüan struck. While this was unfortunate, he may be regarded as having gained one point over the master. From the very bottom of his heart, Tao-wu did everything to enlighten his disciple, and yet the disciple significantly failed to grasp the meaning at the moment. Being thus struck by his disciple, Tao-wu said: 'It will be better for you to leave our monastery for a while. If our head-monk learns somehow of this incident you may get into trouble.'

Chien-yüan was then quietly sent away. How full of tenderness Tao-wu was! Chien-yüan later came into a small temple where he happened to listen to one of the lay-brothers there reciting the *Kwannon Sūtra* in which he read, 'To those who are to be saved by him assuming the form of a Bhikkhu (monk), Kwannon will preach to them in the form of a Bhikkhu.' When Chien-yüan heard these words, he at once came to a realization and said to himself: 'I was at fault indeed; I knew not at the time what to make of my late master. This matter has really nothing to do with mere words.'

An ancient master remarked, 'Even the extraordinarily wise stumble over words.' Some try to make an intellectual guess at Tao-wu's attitude, saying that when he flatly refused to say a word about the matter, he had really already said something, and that such an attitude on the part of the master was known as playing a backward somersault in order to lead people astray and to make them feel all confused. If this were to be so interpreted, I would say, How could we ever come to enjoy peace of mind? Only when our feet are treading the solid ground of reality we know that the truth is not a hair's breadth away from ourselves.

Observe, when those seven wise ladies of India visited the Forest of Death, one of them asked, pointing at a corpse, 'The dead body is here, but where is the person?' Said the eldest: 'What? What?' Thereupon the entire company is said to have had the *anutpattikadharmakśānti*, realization of the truth that all things are primarily unborn. How many of such do we come across these days? Perhaps only one in a thousand or ten thousand.

Chien-yüan later went to Shih-shuang and asked him to enlighten him on the matter above referred to. But Shih-shuang also repeated Tao-wu and said: 'Living? I tell you not! Dead? I tell you not!' When Chien-yüan demanded, 'Why don't you tell me?' Shih-shuang replied, 'I say I tell you not!' This opened up Chien-yüan's mind.

One day Chien-yüan carried a spade out into the Dharma Hall, where he walked up and down with it. The

idea was to present his view to the master, who as he expected did not fail to inquire and say, 'What are you doing?'
Chien-yüan said, 'I am seeking for the sacred bones of my
late master!' Shih-shuang, trying to cut Chien-yüan's feet
right off from the ground, remarked, 'The huge waves are
rolling far and near, the white foaming seas are flooding
even to the sky: and what sacred bones of your master are
you seeking here?'

Chien-yüan had already expressed his intention to seek his
late master's bones, and what did Shih-shuang mean when
he made this remark? If you understand what is implied in
the words 'Living? I tell you not! Dead? I tell you not!'
you would know that Shih-shuang is behaving himself from
beginning to end with his whole heart and soul opened to
your full observation. But as soon as you begin to reason
about it and hesitate and ponder, the thing will never come
to view.

Chien-yüan's reply, 'That is the very moment to be
thankful for,' shows how different his attitude is, when
compared with his former one while still uninitiated. Tao-
wu's skull is shining in golden colour, and when it is struck
it gives a resonant sound like that of copperware. Hsüeh-
tou's remark: 'What a pity! What a pity!' has a double
signification, while T'ai-yüan's statement, 'The sacred bones
of the late master are still here!' naturally hits the mark and
is well said.

To put the whole matter in one bundle and thrust it
before your eyes, tell me now where lies the most essential
point of this episode? And where is the point at which you
have to be thankful? Don't you know the saying, 'If one
point is broken through, a thousand and even ten thousand other points are broken through'? If you successfully
pass through at the point where Tao-wu says 'I say I tell
you not!' you will be able to shut out every tongue that
wags in the whole world. If you are unable to pass through,
retire into your own room and exert yourself to the utmost
to get into the truth of Zen. Don't idle away your precious
time by doing nothing all day.

### d. Hsüeh-tou's Appreciation in Verse

The hare and the horse have horns:—Cut them off.—How remarkable!—How refreshing!

The cow and the sheep have no horns.—Cut them off.— What a fuss!—Others may be cheated, but not I.

Not a speck of dust, not a particle!—Heaven above, earth below, I alone am the honoured one!—Where do you intend to grope?

[Yet] like the mountains, like the peaks!—Where are they? —This is stirring up waves on dry land.—It is rubbed in hard against your nose.

The sacred bones in golden yellow are still here;—The tongue is cut off and the throat choked.—Put it aside.—I'm afraid nobody knows him.

The white foaming waves are flooding the sky, and where can we seize upon them?—A hold is released a little.— Slipped right over it.—Eyes and ears are filled with it.

Nowhere to seize upon them!—Just as I told you!—This is something after all.—Surely tumbled into an abyss!

With a single shoe [Bodhidharma] went off to the west, and where is his trace now?—When fathers leave things unfinished, their descendants suffer the consequence.—Striking a blow, one should say, 'Why is it here now?'

### e. Commentary Notes

This is Hsüeh-tou's appreciative verse showing how thoroughly he understood the case. As he is a descendant of the Yün-mên school[1] he knows how to put a triple hammering point into the body of one sentence. His verse seizes the most vital portion by giving an affirmation where no affirmation is possible and by opening a passage where no opening is practicable. So he declares:

> 'The hare and the horse have horns;
> The cow and the sheep have no horns.'

[1] One of the five schools of Zen. The five are: Lin-chi, T'sao-tung, Yün-mên, Wei-yang, and Fa-yen.

Let me ask how it is that hares and horses have horns whereas cows and sheep have none. When you understand the aforementioned case, you will then see into the meaning of Hsüeh-tou's statement in which he has a scheme for the benefit of others. There are some who entertain a mistaken view as regards this and say: 'Whether a master affirms or denies, just the same he is affirming something. Negation is after all no more than an affirmation. As hares and horses have no horns, he says that they have horns; and as cows and sheep have horns, he says that they have no horns.'

Such an understanding of the subject-matter has no bearing whatever on it. On the contrary, the ancient master is full of arts and therefore knows how to perform such miracles; and they are all for your benefit so that you are enabled to break up the dark cave of haunting spirits. When you pass through this, it is not after all worth much of anything.

> 'The hare and the horse have horns;
> The cow and the sheep have no horns.
> Not a speck of dust, not a particle!
> [Yet] like the mountains, like the peaks!'

These four lines are like a wish-fulfilling gem which Hsüeh-tou throws out in perfect form to your face. The rest of the verse decides the case according to the affidavit:

> 'The sacred bones in golden yellow are still here;
> The white foaming waves are flooding the sky, and
>     where can we seize upon them?'

This is concerned with the remarks by Shih-shuang and Fu of T'ai-yüan. But why the following lines?

> 'Nowhere to seize upon them!
> With a single shoe [Bodhidharma] went off to the
>     west, and where is his trace now?'

This is like a sacred tortoise leaving its track. And here is where Hsüeh-tou takes a turn in order to do others good.

Says an old master, 'Apply yourself to a living word and
not to a dead one.' If its trace is already lost, why is all
the world vying with one another to get hold of it?


# III

## THE WU-MÊN-KUAN

The *Wu-mên-kuan*[1] is another text-book of Zen Buddhism, on which discourses are frequently held in the
monasteries. It is a simpler book than the preceding one,
*Pi-yen-chi*, for it contains only forty-eight 'cases' and is one
man's work. The composition of it is also simple, containing a case and comments in prose and verse, both
of which are short. Hui-k'ai (1183–1260)[2] is the author who
flourished in the latter part of the Sung (960–1279). The
supplementary part of the *Transmission of the Lamp* mentions
him as a disciple of Wan-shou Ch'ung-kuan. When he
understood the secrets of Zen by the study of the '*Wu*',
he expressed himself in the following verse:

> 'From the blue sky, the sun glowing white—a peal
>       of thunder!
> All living things on earth open their eyes widely,
> Multiplicities endless uniformly bow their heads
>       in respect;
> Lo and behold, Mt. Sumeru is off its base dancing
>       a *San-tai*!'[3]

Hui-k'ai dedicated his *Wu-mên-kuan* ('The Gateless
Frontier Pass') to the Emperor Li-tsung in celebration of
the fourth anniversary (1229) of his coronation. In the
preface, he says:
'In all the teachings of the Buddha the most essential
thing is to grasp the Mind. While there are so many en-
trances leading to it, the most central one is without a gate.

[1] *Mu-mon-kwan* in Japanese.
[2] *Hsü-chuan*, XXXV.
[3] A popular merry dance.

'How do we get them into this gateless entrance?

'Have you not heard this said by an ancient worthy: "Things that come through a gate are worthless, anything obtained by a relative means is bound for final destruction?" Such statements as these look very much like stirring up waves when there is no wind, like pricking a sore on the smooth skin. As to those who seek wisdom in the words, or who attempt to beat the moon with a stick, or who scratch an itching over the shoe, what real concern have they with the truth?

'While I was spending a summer at Lung-hsiang of Eastern China in the first year of Shao-ting (1228), I had to look after a number of student-monks who wished to be instructed in Zen. So, I made use of the ancient masters' koans as a piece of brick which is used for knocking at the gate. The students were thus disciplined each according to his ability. The notes gradually accumulated and finally came to assume a book-form. There is no systematic arrangement in the forty-eight cases herein collected. The general name "*Wu-mên-kuan*" has been given to them.

'If one is really a courageous fellow, he will mind no perils besetting his way but push himself single-handed through the enemy's line. Like Nata with eight arms, his progress is not to be checked by anybody. Even the twenty-eight patriarchs of India and the six of this country will have to beg for their lives before such a dauntless spirit. If one is however hesitating, it will be like watching a horseman through a window; even before your closed eyes are re-opened he will no more be there. Here is my verse:

> 'The great highway has no gates,
> [Yet] how criss-cross the passages!
> Let this frontier pass be crossed,
> And in royal solitude you walk the universe.'

In order to give an idea of what kind of text-book the *Wu-mên-kuan* is and to see how different it is from the *Pi-yen-chi*, the following extract (Case I) is selected:

## Case I. Chao-chou's Wu

A monk came to Chao-chou and asked, 'Is the dog endowed with the Buddha-nature?' Chao-chou said, '*Wu!*'

### Wu-mên's comment

In the study of Zen, what is most needed is to pass
through the frontier-gate erected by the ancient masters.
To experience a satori, all the mental passages are to be cut
off. So long as the frontier-gate is not passed through and
the mental passages are not cut off, you are like spirits
depending on grass-leaves and plants. What then is the
frontier-gate erected by the masters? It is no other than this
'*Wu!*' which is indeed the gate of Zen, and hence the title
of this book '*Wu-mên-kuan*'.

Those who pass through the gate are allowed to see not
only the old master Chao-chou himself but all the masters
who have successively transmitted the truth of Zen. For
then you walk with them hand in hand, you interview
them face to face, what they see and hear you also see and
hear. No joy surpasses this.

Do you wish to pass through the gate?

If so, turn your whole body with its three hundred and
sixty bones and eighty-four thousand hair-holes into one
spirit of inquiry and have it concentrated on this one
character '*Wu!*' Keep it constantly night and day before
your mind. Do not take it in the sense of mere emptiness,
nor in the relative sense of being and non-being. It would
be like swallowing a red-hot iron ball; even if you wanted
to throw it up you could not do so. Let all the evil knowledge and learning you have been in the habit of accumulating so far be ejected. When you are trained in this
exercise for a sufficiently long time, your mind will gradually mature to a state of oneness inside and outside. When
this obtains you will know it by yourself without being told.

It is like a dumb person having a dream. He knows what he has seen, but is unable to let others see it. When the time comes for a final explosion, the result will resemble the whole world being taken in surprise. Again, it is like being supplied unexpectedly with Kuan-yü's big sword, which you can swing as you please. No matter who confronts you, a Buddha or master, you put him out of the way unceremoniously. There is nothing that makes you now feel uneasy or unsteady even when you stand at the critical moment of life and death. Indeed, you are perfect master of yourself, walking through the six paths of existence and the four forms of life.

How, you may ask, to exercise yourself in the 'Wu'? Exhaust all your mental energy you have on the koan, do not allow any intermittence in the exercise, and the time may arrive when another Dharma-lamp is likely to be lighted. Here is my verse:

'The Buddha-nature in the dog? ["*Wu!*"]
The lifting is complete, the command unequivocal;
No sooner you waver between being and non-being,
Than a lifeless corpse you are.'

# PASSIVITY IN THE BUDDHIST LIFE

*Preliminary Note*

'Thy way, not mine, O Lord,
    However dark it be;
Lead me by Thine own hand,
    Choose out the path for me.
Smooth let it be or rough,
    It will be still the best;
Winding or straight, it leads
    Right onward to Thy rest.
Choose Thou for me my friends,
    My sickness or my health;
Choose Thou my cares for me,
    My poverty or wealth.
Not mine, not mine the choice
    In things or great or small;
Be Thou my guide, my strength,
    My wisdom, and my all.[1]

The feeling of passivity in religious experience, so typically given expression here, is universal and natural, seeing that the religious consciousness consists in realizing, on the one hand, the helplessness of a finite being, and, on the other, the dependability of an infinite being, in whatever way this may be conceived. The finite side of our being may protest, saying, 'Why hast thou forsaken me?', but while this protest possesses us there is no religious experience, we are not yet quite saved. For salvation comes only when we can say, 'Father, into thy hands I entrust my spirit,' or 'Lord, though thou slay me, yet will I trust in thee.'

This is resignation or self-surrender, which is a state of passivity, ready to have 'thy will' prevail upon a world of finite beings. This is the characteristic attitude of a religious

[1] Horatius Bonar, 1808–1889.

mind towards life and the world; and we know that all religious experience is psychologically closely connected with the feeling of passivity. The object of the present Essay is to see how this feeling rules and in what forms it expresses itself in the Buddhist life, including that of Zen.


# I

## The Doctrine of Karma

Superficially, passivity does not seem to be compatible with the intellectual tendency of Buddhism, especially of Zen, which strongly emphasizes the spirit of self-reliance as is seen in such passages as 'The Bodhisattva-mahāsattva retiring into a solitude all by himself, should reflect within himself, by means of his own inner intelligence, and not depend upon anybody else;'[1] or as we read in the *Dhammapada*:

> 'By self alone is evil done,
> By self is one disgraced;
> By self is evil undone,
> By self alone is he purified;
> Purity and impurity belong to one;
> No one can purify another.'[2]

Besides the four Noble Truths, the Twelvefold Chain of Origination, the Eightfold Path of Righteousness, etc.—all tend towards enlightenment and emancipation, and not towards absolute dependence or receptivity. 'To see with one's own eyes and be liberated' is the Buddhist motto, and there is apparently no room for passivity. For the latter can

---

[1] *The Laṅkāvatāra*, the author's English translation, p. 115. Bodhisattvo mahāsattva kākī rahogataḥ svapratyātmabuddhyā vicārayaty apara-praṇeyaḥ.
[2] The *Dhammapada*, p. 165. The translation is by A. J. Edmunds.
   Attanā 'va katam pāpam attanā samkilissati,
   Attanā akatam pāpam attanā 'va visujjhati,
   Suddhi asuddhi praccattam nā 'ñño aññam visodhaye.

take place only when one makes oneself a receptacle for an outside power.

The attainment of passivity in Buddhism is especially obstructed by the doctrine of Karma. The doctrine of Karma runs like warp and weft through all the Indian fabrics of thought, and Buddhism as a product of the Indian imagination could not escape taking it into its own texture. The Jātaka Tales, making up the history of the Buddha while he was yet at the stage of Bodhisattvahood and training himself for final supreme enlightenment, are no more than the idea of Karma concretely applied and illustrated in the career of a morally perfected personage. Śākyamuni could not become a Buddha unless he had accumulated his stock of merit (kuśalamūla) throughout his varied lives in the past.

The principle of Karma is 'Whatever a man sows that will he also reap', and this governs the whole life of the Buddhist; for in fact what makes up one's individuality is nothing else than his own Karma. So we read in the *Milindapañha*, 'All beings have their Karma as their portion; they are heirs of their Karma; they are sprung from their Karma; their Karma is their refuge; Karma allots beings to meanness or greatness.'[1] This is confirmed in the *Samyutka-nikāya*:

> 'His good deeds and his wickedness,
> Whate'er a mortal does while here;
> 'Tis this that he can call his own,
> This with him take as he goes hence,
> This is what follows after him,
> And like a shadow ne'er departs.'[2]

According to the *Visuddhimagga*, Chapter XIX, Karma is divisible into several groups as regards the time and order of fruition and its quality: (1) that which bears fruit in the present existence, that which bears fruit in rebirth, that which bears fruit at no fixed time, and bygone Karma;

---

[1] Quoted from Warren's *Buddhism in Translations*, p. 255.
[2] Loc. cit., p. 214.

(2) the weighty Karma, the abundant, the close-at-hand, and the habitual; (3) the productive Karma, the supportive, the counteractive, and the destructive.[1] There is thus a round of Karma and a round of fruit going on all the time. And who is the bearer of Karma and its fruit?

'No doer is there does the deed,
Nor is there one who feels the fruit;
Constituent parts alone roll on;
This view alone is orthodox.

And thus the deed, and thus the fruit
Roll on and on, each from its cause;
As of the round of tree and seed,
No one can tell when they began.

Not in its fruit is found the deed,
Nor in the deed finds one the fruit;
Of each the other is devoid,
Yet there's no fruit without the deed,

Just as no store of fire is found
In jewel, cow-dung, or the sun,
Nor separate from these exists,
Yet short of fuel no fire is known;

Even so we ne'er within the deed
Can retribution's fruit descry.
Not yet in any place without;
Nor can in fruit the deed be found.

Deeds separate from their fruits exist,
And fruits are separate from the deeds;
But consequent upon the deed
Fruit doth into being come.

No god of heaven or Brahma-world
Doth cause the endless round of birth;
Constituent parts alone roll on,
From cause and from material sprung.[2]

---

[1] Loc. cit, pp. 245 *ff*.
[2] Warren, pp. 248-9.

# KUEI-TSUNG CHIH-CH'ANG AND LI-P'O, GOVERNOR OF CHIANG-CHOU

## By INDRA
### (*Yüan Dynasty*)

There is another picture by Indra, with Chu-shih's inscription in verse which reads:

> "Within the cocoa-nut [-like body] are hoarded
> ten thousand books;
> The governor at the time unnecessarily wasted
> apologetic remarks.
> In my hands I hold a stick made of a mountain
> tree;
> Even when the Buddha comes he will not be
> spared."

*Chu-shih*

Kuei-tsung was a disciple of Ma-tsu (died, A.D. 788), who was a most prominent figure in the T'ang history of Zen Buddhism. Li-p'o, governor of Chiang-chou, once visited Kuei-tsung and asked; "According to the sutra, Mount Sumeru contains in it a mustard-seed and a mustard-seed contains in it Mount Sumeru. The first statement I can readily believe, but as to the second, can it be more than a senseless tale?" The master answered: "I am told that your excellency has read ten thousand books; is that true?" Li said, "Yes, master." "But a body not bigger than a cocoa-nut, measuring from head to feet,—how can it take into itself as many books as ten thousand?" Li merely hung down his head.[1]

[1] *Thf Chuan-téng Lu*, VII.

# PU-TAI

This, with Bodhidharma and Fêng-kan, forms a triptych. The verse reads:

"How freely he goes about!
How hurriedly he runs away!
There is no place where he is not to be seen;
But a certain leakage is traceable here and there.
The front court of the Jewel-tower.
Since Sudhana left,
Is covered with a verdant lawn:
Is he recognised there, or not?"

*Yen-ch'i Kuang-wén,*
*Residing at Chin-shan*

Pu-tai, or Hotei in Japanese, is partly a legendary and partly a historical character. According to the *Chuan-téng Lu*, XXVII, he lived in the Latter Liang era, dying in A.D. 916. His figure seems to have been extremely out of proportion. He was a kind of vagabond with no fixed residence. Wherever he went, he carried a bag of monstrous size, in which everything he needed was promiscuously put. When he saw a monk passing by, he gently stroked the back of the unknown friend. When the latter turned back, he begged for a penny. The monk said, "If you can say a word or two [regarding your Zen], I will give you a penny." Pu-tai set the bag on the ground and stood with his hands folded before the chest. In China he is considered a transformation-body of the Bodhisattva Maitreya. When he died, he left among others the following verse:

"O Maitreya, O true Maitreya!
Thou dividest the body into hundreds of
thousands of millions of forms.
Thus manifesting thyself to men of the
world;
But how they are ignorant of thee!"

The story of Sudhana and the Jewel-tower which is Maitreya's residence is told in the *Gandavyūha*. It will be given in the Third Series of my *Zen Essays*, part II.

The working of Karma is apparently quite impersonal, as is explained in these quotations, and it may seem altogether indifferent for anybody whether he did something good or bad. There is no doer of deeds, nor is there any sufferer of their fruit. The five Aggregates or constituent parts (*skandhas*) are combined and dissolved in accordance with the inevitable law of Karma, but as long as there is no personal agent at the back of all this, who really feels the value of Karma, it does not seem to matter what kind of deed is committed and what kind of fruit is brought forth. Still the Buddhists are advised not to practise wickedness:

> 'If a man do wrong,
> Let him not do it repeatedly,
> Let him not take pleasure therein;
> Painful is wrong's accumulation.'[1]

Why painful? Why pleasurable? The Hīnayānist reasoning is logically thoroughgoing, but when it comes to the question of practical psychology, mere reasoning does not avail. Is the feeling no more real than the mere bundling together of the five Aggregates? The combination—that is, unity—seems to be more than the fact of combination. Whatever this is, as I am not going to discuss the doctrine of Karma here in detail, let it suffice to give another quotation from Nāgārjuna's *Mūlamadhyamakakārikās*, Chapter XVII, where the doctrine of Karma appears in a new garment.[2]

'All sentient beings are born according to their Karma: good people are born in the heavens, the wicked in the hells, and those who practise the paths of righteousness realize Nirvāṇa. By disciplining himself in the six virtues of perfection, a man is able to benefit his fellow-beings in various ways, and this is sure in turn to bring blessings upon him, not only in this but also in the next life. Karma may be of

---

[1] *The Dhammapada*, p. 117, translated by A. J. Edmunds.
[2] Edited by Louis de la Vallée Poussin. Pp. 302 *ff*. For a detailed exposition of the theory of Karma, see the *Abhidharmakośa* (translated by the same author), Chapter IV. What follows is an abstract.

two sorts: inner or mental, which is called *cetana* and physical, expressing itself in speech and bodily movement. This is technically known as Karma "after having intended".[1]

'Karma may also be regarded as with or without "intimation".[2] An act with intimation is one the purpose of which is perceptible by others, while an act without intimation is not at all expressed in physical movements; it follows that when a strong act with intimation is performed it awakens the tendency in the mind of the actor to perform again deeds, either good or bad, of a similar nature.

'It is like a seed from which a young plant shoots out and bears fruit by the principle of continuity; apart from the seed there is no continuity; and because of this continuity there is fruition. The seed comes first and then the fruit; between them there is neither discontinuity nor constancy. Since the awakening of a first motive, there follows an uninterrupted series of mental activities, and from this there is fruition. Apart from the first stirring of the mind, there will be no stream of thoughts expressing themselves in action. Thus there is a continuity of Karma and its fruit. Therefore, when the ten deeds of goodness and purity are performed, the agent is sure to enjoy happiness in this life and be born after death among celestial beings.

'There is something in Karma that is never lost even after its performance; this something called *aviprāṇāśa*[3] is like a deed of contract, and Karma, an act, is comparable to debt. A man may use up what he has borrowed, but owing to the document he has some day to pay the debt back to the creditor. This "unlosable" is always left behind even after Karma and is not destroyed by philosophical intuition.[4] If it is thus destructible, Karma will never come to fruition. The only power that counteracts this "un-

---

[1] *Cetayitvā.*
[2] 'Indication', *vijñapti.*
[3] 'Not lost', or 'unlosable', or 'indestructible'.
[4] *Darśanamārga.*

losable" is moral discipline.[1] Every Karma once committed continues to work out its consequence by means of
the "unlosable" until its course is thwarted by the attainment of Arhatship or by death, or when it has finally borne
its fruit. This law of Karma applies equally to good and bad
deeds.' *exhaust*

While Nāgārjuna's idea is to wipe out all such notions
as doer, deed, and sufferer, in other words, the entire
structure of Karma-theory, this introduction of the idea
'unlosable' is instructive and full of suggestions.

Taking all in all, however, there is much obscurity in
the doctrine of Karmaic continuity, especially when its
practical working is to be precisely described; and, theor-
etically too, we are not quite sure of its absolute tenability.
But this we can state of it in a most general way that
Karma tends to emphasize individual freedom, moral
responsibility, and feeling of independence; and further,
from the religious point of view, it does not necessitate
the postulate of a God, or a creator, or a moral judge,
who passes judgments upon human behaviour, good or
bad.

This being the case, the Buddhist conviction that life is
pain will inevitably lead to a systematic teaching of self-
discipline, self-purification, and self-enlightenment, the
moral centre of gravity being always placed on the self,
and not on any outside agent. This is the principle of
Karma applied to the realization of Nirvāṇa. But, we may
ask, What is this 'self'? And again, What is that something
that is never 'lost' in a Karma committed either mentally
or physically? What is the connection between 'self' and
the 'unlosable'? Where does this 'unlosable' lodge itself?

Between the Buddhist doctrine of no-ego-substance and
the postulate that there should be something 'not to be
lost' in the continuation of Karma-force, which makes the
latter safely bear fruit, there is a gap which must be bridged
somehow if Buddhist philosophy is to make further development. To my mind, the conception of the Ālayavijñāna

[1] *Bhāvanamārga.*

('All-conserving soul') where all the Karma-seeds are deposited was an inevitable consequence. But in the meantime let us see what 'self' really stands for.

### The Conception of Self

'Self' is a very complex and elusive idea, and when we say that one is to be responsible for what one does by oneself, we do not exactly know how far this 'self' goes and how much it includes in itself. For individuals are so intimately related to one another not only in one communal life but in the totality of existence—so intimately indeed that there are really no individuals, so to speak, in the absolute sense of the word.

Individuality is merely an aspect of existence; in thought we separate one individual from another and in reality too we all seem to be distinct and separable. But when we reflect on the question more closely we find that individuality is a fiction, for we cannot fix its limits, we cannot ascertain its extents and boundaries, they become mutually merged without leaving any indelible marks between the so-called individuals. A most penetrating state of interrelationship prevails here, and it seems to be more exact to say that individuals do not exist, they are merely so many points of reference, the meaning of which is not at all realizable when each of them is considered by itself and in itself apart from the rest.

Individuals are recognizable only when they are thought of in relation to something not individual; though paradoxical, they are individuals so long as they are not individuals. For when an individual being is singled out as such, it at once ceases to be an individual. The 'individual self' is an illusion.

Thus, the self has no absolute, independent existence. Moral responsibility seems to be a kind of intellectual makeshift. Can the robber be really considered responsible for his deeds? Can this individual be really singled out as the one who has to suffer all the consequences of his anti-social habits? Can he be held really responsible for all that made him such as he is? Is his *svabhāva* all his own make? This is where lies the main crux of the question, 'How far is an individual to be answerable for his action?' In other words, 'How far is this "he" separable from the community of which he is a component part?' Is not society reflected in him? Is he not one of the products created by society?

There are no criminals, no sinful souls in the Pure Land, not necessarily because no such are born there but mainly because all that are born there become pure by virtue of the general atmosphere into which they are brought up. Although environment is not everything, it, especially social environment, has a great deal to do with the shaping of individual characters. If this is the case, where shall we look for the real signification of the doctrine of Karma?

The intellect wants to have a clear-cut, well-delineated figure to which a deed or its 'unlosable' something has to be attached, and Karma become mathematically describable as having its originator, perpetrator, sufferer, etc. But when there are really no individuals and Karma is to be conceived as nowhere originated by any specifically definable agent, what would become of the doctrine of Karma as advocated by Buddhists? Evidently there is an act, either good or bad or indifferent; there is one who actually thrusts a dagger, and there is one who actually lies dead thus stabbed; and yet shall we have to declare that there is no killer, no killing, and none killed? What will then become of moral responsibility? How can there be such a thing as accumulation of merit or attainment of enlightenment? Who is after all a Buddha, and who is an ignorant, confused mortal?

Can we say that society, nay, the whole universe, is responsible for the act of killing if this fact is once established? And that all the causes and conditions leading to it and all the results that are to be connected with it

*Karma is the illusion of self*
*ultimate present*

are to be traced to the universe itself? Or is it that the individual is an ultimate absolute fact and what goes out from him comes back to him without any relation to his fellow-beings and to his environment, social and physical?

In the first case, moral responsibility evaporates into an intangible universality; in the second case, the intangible whole gets crystallized in one individual, and there is indeed moral responsibility, but one stands altogether in isolation as if each of us were like a grain of sand in no relation to its neighbours. Which of these positions is more exactly in conformity with facts of human experience? When this is applied to the Buddhist doctrine of Karma, the question comes to this: Is Buddhist Karma to be understood individualistically or cosmologically?

### Mahāyāna Buddhism on the Theory of Karma

As far as history goes, Buddhism started with the individualistic interpretation of Karma, and when it reached its culminating point of development in the rise of Mahāyāna, the doctrine came to be cosmically understood. But not in the vague, abstract, philosophical way as was before referred to but concretely and spiritually in this wise: the net of the universe spreads out both in time and space from the centre known as 'my self', where it is felt that all the sins of the world are resting on his own shoulders. To atone for them he is determined to subject himself to a system of moral and spiritual training which he considers would cleanse him of all impurities, and by cleansing him cleanse also the whole world of all its demerits.

This is the Mahāyāna position. Indeed, the distinction between the Mahāyāna and the Hīnayāna forms of Buddhism may be said to be due to this difference in the treatment of Karma-conception. The Mahāyāna thus came to emphasize the 'other' or 'whole' aspect of Karma, and, therefore, of universal salvation, while the Hīnayāna adhered to the 'self' aspect. As Karma worked, according to the

279

Hīnayānists, apparently impersonally but in point of fact individualistically, this life of pain and suffering was to be got rid of by self-discipline, by moral asceticism, and self-knowledge. Nobody outside could help the sufferer out of his afflictions; all that the Buddha could do for him was to teach him the way to escape; but if he did not walk this way by himself, he could not be made to go straight ahead even by the power and virtue of the Buddha. 'Be ye a lamp and a refuge to yourselves' (attadīpa-attasarana) was the injunction left by the Buddha to his Hīnayāna followers, for the Buddha could not extend his spiritual virtue and attainment over to his devotees or to his fellow-beings. From the general position of the Hīnayānists, this was inevitable:

> 'Not in the sky,
> Not in the midst of the sea,
> Nor entering a cleft of the mountains,
> Is found that realm on earth
> Where one may stand and be
> From an evil deed absolved.'[1]

But the Mahāyāna was not satisfied with this narrowness of spiritual outlook; the Mahāyāna wanted to extend the function of Karuṇā (love) to the furthest end it could reach. If one's Prajñā (wisdom) could include in itself the widest possible system of universes, why could not Karuṇā too take them all under its protective wings? Why could not the Buddha's wish (praṇidhāna) for the spiritual welfare of all beings also efficiently work towards its realization? The Buddha attained his enlightenment after accumulating so much stock of merit for ever so many countless kalpas (eons). Should we conceive this stock of merit to be available only for his own benefit?

Karma must have its cosmological meaning. In fact, individuals are such in so far as they are thought of in connection with one another and also with the whole system which they compose. One wave good or bad, once stirred, could not help affecting the entire body of water. So with

[1] *The Dhammapada*, p. 127. Translated by Albert J. Edmunds.

the moral discipline and the spiritual attainment of the Buddha, they could not remain with him as an isolated event in the communal life to which he belonged. Therefore, it is said that when he was enlightened the whole universe shared in his wisdom and virtue. The Mahāyāna stands on this fundamental idea of enlightenment, and its doctrine of the Tathāgatagarbha or Ālayavijñāna reflects the cosmological interpretation of Karma.

## II

### *The Development of the Idea of Sin in Buddhism*

As long as Hīnayāna Buddhism restricted the application of Karma to individual deeds, its followers tried to overcome it by self-discipline. Life was pain, and pain was the product of one's former misconduct, and to release oneself from it, it was necessary to move a force counteracting it. Things thus went on quite scientifically with the Hīnayānists, but when the Mahāyānists came to see something in Karma that was more than individual, that would not be kept within the bounds of individuality, their scheme of salvation had to go naturally beyond the individualism of the Hīnayānistic discipline. The 'self-power' was not strong enough to cope with the problem of cosmological Karma, and to rely upon this self as segregated from the totality of sentient beings was not quite right and true.

For the self is not a final fact, and to proceed in one's own religious discipline with the erroneous idea of selfhood will ultimately lead one to an undesirable end and possibly bear no fruit whatever. A new phase was now awakened in the religious consciousness of the Buddhist which had hitherto been only feebly felt by the Hīnayānists; for with the cosmic sense of Karma thus developed there came along the idea of sin.

In Buddhism sin means ignorance, that is, ignorance as to the meaning of the individual or the ultimate destiny of the self. Positively, sin is the affirmation of the self as a final *svabhāva* in deed, thought, and speech. When a man is above these two hindrances, ignorance and self-assertion, he is said to be sinless. How to rise above them, therefore, is now the question with the Mahāyānists.

Calderon, a noted Spanish dramatist, writes, 'For the greatest crime of man is that he ever was born.' This statement is quite true, since sin consists in our ever coming into existence as individuals severed from the wholeness of things. But as long as this fact cannot be denied from one point of view, we must try to nullify its evil effects by veering our course in another direction. And this veering can take place only by identifying ourselves with the cosmos itself, with the totality of existence, with Buddhatā in which we have our being. The inevitability of sin thus becomes the chance of devoting ourselves to a higher plane of existence where a principle other than Karmaic individualism and self-responsibility reigns.

When Karma was conceived to be controllable by the self, the task of releasing oneself from its evil effects was comparatively an easy one, for it concerned after all the self alone; but if it is sin to believe in the ultimate reality of an individual soul and to act accordingly, as if salvation depended only on self-discipline or on self-enlightenment, the Mahāyānist's work is far greater than the Hīnayānist's. As this goes beyond the individual, something more than individual must operate in the Mahāyānist heart to make its work effective. The so-called self must be aided by a power transcending the limitations of the self, which, however, must be immanently related to it; for otherwise there cannot be a very harmonious and really mutually-helping activity between the self and the not-self.

In fact, the idea of sin, and hence the feeling of pain and suffering, is produced from the lack of a harmonious relationship between what is thought to be 'myself' and what is not. The religious experience with the Mahāyānists is to be described in more comprehensive terms than with the Hīnayānists.

282

## A Reality Beyond Self

Buddhatā or Dharmatā is the name given by the Mahā-yānists to that which is not the self and yet which is in the self. By virtue of this, the Mahāyānists came to the consciousness of sin and at the same time to the possibility of enlightenment. Buddhatā is the essence of Buddhahood, without which this is never attained in the world. When the Buddha is conceived impersonally or objectively, it is the Dharma, law, truth, or reality; and Dharmatā is what constitutes the Dharma. Dharmatā and Buddhatā are interchangeable, but the experience of the Mahāyānists is described more in terms of Buddhatā.

With the conception of Buddhatā, the historical Buddha turns into a transcendental Buddha; he ceases to be merely the Muni of the Śākyas; he now is a manifestation of the eternal Buddha, an incarnation of Buddhatā; and as such he is no more an individual person limited in space and time; his spirituality goes out from him, and whatever power it has influences his fellow-beings in their advance or development towards Buddhahood. This will take place in proportion to the intensity of desire and the sincerity of effort they put forward for the attainment of the goal. The goal consists in getting cleansed of sin, and sin consists in believing in the reality of self-substance (*svabhāva*), in asserting its claims as final, and in not growing conscious of the immanency of Buddhatā in oneself.

The cleansing of sin is, therefore, intellectually seeing into the truth that there is something more in what is taken for the self, and conatively in willing and doing the will of that something which transcends the self and yet which works through the self.

This is where lies the difficulty of the Mahāyānist position—to be encased in what we, relative-minded beings, consider the self and yet to go beyond it and to know and will what apparently does not belong to the self. This is almost trying to achieve an impossibility, and yet if we do not achieve this, there will be no peace of mind, no quietude of soul. We have to do it somehow when we once tumble over the question in the course of our religious experience. How is this to be accomplished?

That we are sinful does not mean in Buddhism that we have so many evil impulses, desires, or proclivities, which, when released, are apt to cause the ruination of oneself as well as others; the idea goes deeper and is rooted in our being itself, for it is sin to imagine and act as if individuality were a final fact. As long as we are what we are, we have no way to escape from sin, and this is at the root of all our spiritual tribulations. This is what the followers of Shin Buddhism mean when they say that all works, even when they are generally considered morally good, are contaminated, as long as they are the efforts of 'self-power', and do not lift us from the bondage of Karma. The power of Buddhatā must be added over to the self or must replace it altogether if we desire emancipation. Buddhatā, if it is immanent—and we cannot think it otherwise—must be awakened so that it will do its work for us who are so oppressed under the limitations of individualism.

The awakening and working of Buddhatā in mortal sinful beings is not accomplished by logic and discursive argument, as is attested by the history of religion. In spite of the predominantly intellectual tendency of Buddhism, it teaches us to appeal to something else. The deep consciousness of sin, the intensity of desire to be released from the finality of individual existence, and the earnestness of effort put forward to awaken Buddhatā—these are the chief conditions. The psychological experience resulting therefrom will naturally be connected with the feeling of passivity.

## A New Phase of Buddhism

Buddhism, whose intellectual tendency interpreted the doctrine of Karma individualistically in spite of its teaching of non-ego (*anatta*), has at last come to release us all from the iron fetters of Karma by appealing to the conception of Buddhatā. Finite beings become thus relieved of the logical chain of causation in a world of spirits, but at the same time the notion of sin which is essentially attached to them as limited in time and space has taken possession of their religious consciousness. For sin means finite beings' helplessness of transcending themselves. And if this be the case, to get rid of sin will be to abandon themselves to the care of an infinite being, that is to say, to desist from attempting to save themselves, but to bring about a spiritual state of passiveness whereby the ground for the entrance of a reality greater than themselves is prepared. Thus sings Wordsworth:

> 'Nor less I deem that there are powers
> Which of themselves our minds impress;
> That we can feed this mind of ours
> In a wise passiveness.
>
> Think you, 'mid all this mighty sum
> Of things for ever speaking,
> That nothing of itself will come
> But we must still be seeking.
>
> —Then ask not wherefore, here, alone,
> Conversing as I may,
> I sit upon this old grey stone,
> And dream my time away.'

We can thus say that Karma is understood by the Mahāyānists rather cosmologically, or that the super individualistic aspect of Karma came to assert its importance more than its individualistic aspect. Nāgārjuna's attempt to nullify Karma is the negative side of this evolution which has taken place in the history of Buddhism. As long as Karma was conceived individualistically by Hīnayānists, there was no room for them to entertain a feeling of passivity. But with the Mahāyānist interpretation of Karma a sense of overwhelming oppression came to possess the minds of the Buddhists, because Karma was now understood to have a far deeper, stronger, and wider foundation than hitherto thought of. It grew out of the cosmos itself, against which finite individuals were altogether powerless. This feeling of helplessness naturally turned the Mahāyānists towards a being who could overcome the enormity of Karma-force.

There was another factor in the religious consciousness of the Mahāyānists which made them ever persistent in applying for the super-individualistic powers of Buddhatā. By this I mean the feeling of compassion (*karuṇā*) going beyond individualism. This is an annoying feeling, to say the least; it goes directly against the instinct of self-preservation. But there is no doubt that its roots are deeply laid, and in fact it makes up the very foundation of human nature.

Compassion then walks hand in hand with sorrow, for a compassionate soul is always sorrowful when he observes how ignorant and confused the world is, and grows conscious of something in himself that makes him feel his own participation in universal confusion and iniquity. The sense of sin is the outcome of all this. Perhaps here lies one of the reasons why the practice of asceticism has a strong appeal to the religiously-minded, who feel a shadow of penitence not always realizing exactly why they do. When the overwhelming force of Karma is thus combined with compassion, sorrow, and even sin, the attitude of the Buddhist towards himself assumes an altogether different aspect; he is no more a self-reliant individualist, he now wants to identify himself with a power that holds in itself the whole universe with all its multitudinousness.

# III

## *The Psychology of Passivity*

Passivity is essentially psychological, and to interpret it metaphysically or theologically is another question. The feeling that one has been cleansed of sin is passive as far as the sinner's consciousness is concerned. This subjectivism may be objectively verified or may not. But to say that in this consciousness there is absolutely no other feeling than passivity is not correct.

This feeling, which came upon us indeed quite abruptly or without our being conscious of every step of its progress, is no doubt predominant especially when we know that with the utmost voluntary efforts we could not induce a state of liberation. But when the feeling is analysed and its component factors are determined, we realize that this passivity is made possible only when there is something intensely active within ourselves. Let this active background be all blank, absolutely colourless, and there is not even a shadow of passivity felt there. The very fact that it is felt to be passive proves that there is a power on our side that prepares itself to be in a state of receptiveness. The exclusive 'other-power' theory which is sometimes maintained by advocates of the Shin school of Buddhism as well as by the Christian quietists is not tenable.

While a man is attached to individualism, asserting it consciously or unconsciously, he always has a feeling of oppression which he may interpret as sin; and while the mind is possessed by it, there is no room for the 'other-power' to enter and work, the way is effectively barred. It is quite natural, therefore, for him to imagine that with the removal of the bar he became altogether empty. But the removal of the bar does not mean utter emptiness, absolute nothingness. If this is the case, there will be nothing for the 'other-power' to work on.

The abandoning of the 'self-power' is the occasion for the 'other-power' to appear on the scene; the abandoning and the appearance take place simultaneously; it is not that the abandoning comes first, and the ground remaining empty there is a vacancy, and finally the 'other-power' comes in to claim this vacuity. The facts of experience do not justify this supposition, for nothing can work in a vacuity. On the contrary, there must be a point to which the 'other-power' can fix itself, or a form into which it can, as it were, squeeze

# BODHIDHARMA

By An Unknown Artist [1]

This occupies the centre of the triptych with Fêng-kan and Pu-tai on its either side. The inscription in verse is by T'ien-mu Wên-li (1167–1250):

> "Only with 'I know not' he drummed on his lips
>     and teeth;
> The barbarian's language—how could it be con-
>     founded with the flowery [tongue of the
>     Middle Kingdom]?
> If old Hsiao [the Emperor] had under his skin
>     warm blood running,
> He would, chasing his Dharma, have even gone
>     beyond the Stream of Sand."
>
> *T'ien-mu Wên-li*

The reference to old Hsiao which means the Emperor of Liang is quite a noted story. According to the *Pi-yen Lu*, the Emperor, after the well-known interview with Bodhidharma, asked a monk called Chih-kung who this man was. Chih-kung said, "Do you not know him?" "No, I do not." "He is Kwannon the Mahasattva himself, who has come here to transmit the seal of the Buddha-mind." The Emperor was astonished to learn this, and wanted to send an envoy at once after the fugitive Bodhisattva. Chih-kung, however, declared, "Your Majesty, it is of no use to send for him, for even when all the people of this country run after him, he will not retrace his steps."

---

[1] This is sometimes ascribed to Mên Wu-kuan, but without authority.

# FÊNG-KAN

## (Bu-kan)

This forms the right wing of the Bodhidharma triptych. The verse by Yen-ch'i Kuang-wên (1189–1263) reads:

> "Thou canst only take hold of the tiger's neck,
> But knowest not how to manage its tail;
> That the poor old Lü-ch'i was in trouble,
> Was entirely due to thine own fault."

*Yen-ch'i Kuang-wén, at Chin-shan*

Fêng-kan was another vagrant philosopher of the T'ang dynasty. He frequently visited the Kuo-ching monastery at T'ien-tai, but nobody knew where he came from. He was found sometimes riding on a tiger and chanting hymns, which frightened the monks. When he was asked what was the teaching of the Buddha, he simply answered, "*Sui shih*," which meant "Follow the time." He was a great friend of Han-shan (Kanzan) and Shih-tê (Jittoku), whose pictures are given in the Third Series of *Zen Essays*.

The reference to Lü-ch'i in Kuang-wên's inscription is found in the *Chuan-téng Lu*, XXVII. It was due to Lü-ch'i's interview with Han-shan and Shin-tê that made the two recluse-poets mysteriously vanish in a crevice of the mountain-rocks, and this interview was the outcome of Fêng-kan's advice. Hence the blame "thine own fault."

itself; this self-determination of the 'other-power' is impossible if there is nothing but an absolute emptiness of passivity. The suppression of the self does not mean its utter annihilation, but its perfect readiness to receive a higher power into it. In this receptivity we must not forget that there is a power which receives, which has been made passive. The absolute 'other-power' doctrine is not psychologically valid, nor metaphysically tenable.

## Absolute Passivism and Libertinism

The doctrine of absolute passivity is frequently productive of disastrous consequences in two ways. The one may be called negative as it tends to quietism, laziness, contemplative absorption, or all-annihilating Dhyāna or Nirodha; while the other is decidedly positive, being quite aggressive and self-assertive in its practical functioning as is shown, for instance, by the doctrine and the life of the advocates of the Free Spirit in the fourteenth century. When the 'I' is completely annihilated and altogether replaced by God, it is not then the 'I' that thinks, desires, and moves about, but God himself; he has taken complete possession of this 'I', he works through it, he desires in it. The following[1] is an extract from Ruysbroeck's *The Twelve Beguines*, in which he gives quite clearly the position of the Free Spirit sect in Belgium:

'Without me, God would have neither knowledge nor will nor power, for it is I, with God, who have created my own personality and all things. From my hands are suspended heaven, earth and all creatures. Whatever honour is paid to God, it is to me that it is paid, for in my essential being I am by nature God. For myself, I neither hope nor love, and I have no faith, no confidence in God. I have nothing to pray for, nothing to implore, for I do not render honour to God above myself. For in God there is no distinction, neither Father nor Son nor Holy Spirit . . . since

[1] Quoted in A. Wautier D'Aygalliers' *Ruysbroeck the Admirable*, p. 46.

with this God I am one, and am even that which he is . . .
and which, without me, he is not.'

Another writer quotes the following dialogue[1] between
a Free Spirit brother and his questioner:

'What is freedom of the Spirit?' Conrad Kanner is asked
by Ebernard de Freyenhausen, the inquisitor.

'It exists when all remorse of conscience ceases and man
can no longer sin.'

'Hast thou attained to this stage of perfection?'

'Yes, so much so that I can advance in grace, for I am one
with God and God is one with me.'

'Is a brother of the Free Spirit obliged to obey authority?'

'No, he owes obedience to no man, nor is he bound by
the precepts of the Church. If any one prevents him from
doing as he pleases, he has the right to kill him. He may
follow all the impulses of his nature; he does not sin in
yielding to his desires.'

Antinomianism upholds a life of instinct and intuition,
and it works in either way, good or bad, according to the
fundamental disposition of the agent. All religious life tends
towards antinomianism, especially that of the mystic. It
grows immoral and dangerous when the reason is too weak
to assert itself or is kept in the background in too subordi-
nate a position. This frequently takes place with those
whose sense of passivity and so-called spiritual freedom are
allied with each other as they are apt to be, and the result is
inimical. D'Aygalliers (pp. 46–47) describes the view of
certain followers of the Free Spirit as follows:

'Hence they go so far as to say that so long as man has
a tendency to virtues and desires to do God's very precious
will, he is still imperfect, being preoccupied with the
acquiring of things. . . . Therefore, they think they can
never either believe in virtues, or have additional merit or
commit sins. . . . Consequently, they are able to consent to
every desire of the lower nature, for they have reverted to a
state of innocence, and laws no longer apply to them.

[1] A. Allier, *Les Frères du Libre-Esprit*, quoted by A. Wautier D'Aygalliers in his *Ruysbroeck*, p. 43.

'Hence, if the nature is prone to that which gives it satisfaction, and if, in resisting it, mental idleness must, however slightly, be either checked or distracted, they obey the instincts of nature. They are all forerunners of Antichrist, preparing the way for incredulity of every kind. They claim indeed to be free, outside of commandments and virtues. To say what pleases them and never to be contradicted, to retain their own will and in subjection to no one, that is what they call spiritual freedom. Free in their flesh, they give the body what it desires. . . . To them the highest sanctity for man consists in following without compulsion and in all things his natural instinct, so that he may abandon himself to every impulse in satisfying the demands of the body. . . . They wish to sin and indulge in their impure practices without fear or qualms of conscience.'[1]

[1] Compare this attitude of the Free Spirit follower with that of the Prajñāpāramitā : while the former somewhat savours of gross sensualism, the latter is characterized with deep metaphysical intuitions which go beyond the limits of relativity, being and non-being, desire and desirelessness, ignorance and enlightenment. The following strong passages are quoted from the *Prajñāpāramitā* as taught by Mañjuśrī (*Saptaśatikā-prajñāpāramitā* is the Sanskrit title) :

Sāriputra said, 'O Blessed One, according to the *Prajñāpāramitā* taught by Mañjuśrī, it is beyond the understanding of those Bodhisattvas who have just begun their course of discipline.'

At that moment Mañjuśrī said to Sāriputra : 'What I teach is not only beyond their understanding, but also beyond that of those Arhats who have finished all their disciplinary works. There is in fact no one who can really understand my teaching. Why? Because Bodhi [the truth of enlightenment] is something no empirical consciousness (*vijñāna*) can grasp, no intelligence can perceive (*na sambuddhā*), it transcends seeing, hearing, recollecting, it is neither born nor destroyed, it is not to be described, nor specified. Bodhi being of such nature, we cannot say whether it exists, or it does not. It is not an object of perception, nor that of attainment.'

Sāriputra said, 'O Mañjuśrī, is there no Dharmadhātu to be perceived by the Buddha?'

Mañjuśrī said : 'O Sāriputra, there is no Dharmadhātu to be perceived by the Buddha. Why? Because the Dharmadhātu is the Buddha, and the Buddha is the Dharmadhātu, there is no perceiving of itself. The Dharmadhātu means that all things are empty, and this emptiness of all things is Bodhi. Between the two there is no distinction, no duality. As there is no duality, there is no perception ; as there is no perception, no designation (*adhivacana*) ; no designation being possible, there are no thought-constructions (*vijñaptika*) such as doing and non-doing, being and non-being, there are no objects subjectively constructed. This is the

That when the mystic has the feeling that he is entirely possessed of God, or something greater than himself, he is apt to give himself up to a life of sensuousness, is psychologically explainable; for there is a tendency in all religion to assert instincts or native impulses not controlled by reasoned morality.

When existence is accepted as it is as part of the inconceivable wisdom of the Buddha or God, the acceptance often involves acquiescence in all ills the flesh is heir to. This is why orthodoxy is always reluctant to lend its ear unconditionally to the gospel of passivism. Grave dangers are always lurking here. The Shin teachers' announcement that 'you are saved just as you are', or the doctrine that

nature of all things whose manifestation here and there is no more than our thought-construction.

'O Sāriputra, to commit the offences is to achieve the inconceivables, to achieve the inconceivables is to produce Reality. And Reality is non-dual. [Thus, since the offences, the inconceivables and Reality are not to be separated one from another, there is no agent who commits the offences; for this is to achieve the inconceivables, or to produce Reality—which is an impossibility.] Those beings endowed with the inconceivables can go neither to the heavens, nor to the evil paths, nor to Nirvāṇa. Those who commit the offences are not bound for the hells. Both the offences and the inconceivables are of Reality, and Reality is by nature non-dual, it is neither born nor destroyed, neither coming nor departing, neither cause nor effect, neither good nor bad, bound neither for the evil paths nor for the heavens, neither attaining Nirvāṇa nor transmigrating in birth and death. Why? Because in the real Dharmadhātu there is nothing good or bad, nothing high or low, nothing prior or posterior.

'O Sāriputra, the monk who has committed the grave offences is not destined for the hells; he who has faithfully observed the rules of morality is not born in the heavens. The offender does not go down into the path of birth and death, is not to be despised, slighted, exempted from receiving alms, etc., etc.; while the faithful one does not realize Nirvāṇa, is not to be praised, befriended, the recipient of alms, etc., etc. Why? Because in the real Dharmadhātu the principle of sameness obtains and no discrimination is made between violation and observance.' . . .

Mañjuśrī then said to the Blessed One: 'Bodhi is the five offences, and the five offences are Bodhi. Why? Because both Bodhi and the five offences are non-existent and their real nature is not to be comprehended. There is here neither perception nor perceiver, neither seeing nor seer, neither knowledge nor knower, neither analysis nor analyser. This can be said both of Bodhi and of the five offences. If there is one who regards Bodhi as something attainable, something in which discipline is possible, that one commits self-arrogance.'

Amida's all-embracing love takes in all sinful mortals with their sins and defilements even unwashed, is full of pitfalls unless it is tempered by sound reasoning and strong moral feeling. The injunctions such as 'Take no thought of your life', or 'Take no thought for the morrow, for the morrow shall take thought for the things of itself', are fine, and Buddhists too will wholeheartedly uphold the truth contained in them; but at the same time we must realize that this kind of momentarism is a life essentially at one with that of the fowls of the air and the lilies of the field, and harbour the possibility of sliding headlong into the abyss of libertinism or antinomianism.

True religion, therefore, always shuns absolute subjectivism, and rightly so. Still, we can ill afford to ignore the claims of the mystic so simply and innocently expressed in the following life of a pious Buddhist, where there is nothing of the aggressive assertions of Brothers of the Free Spirit.

Kichibei was a wealthy farmer of Idzumo province, but when his religious consciousness was awakened he could no more rest satisfied with his old conditions. He sold all his estate and with the money thus realized he wandered about from one place to another to get instructed in Shin Buddhism. Later he sold out even his godowns, furniture, and house itself; thus freeing himself from all earthly treasures, he devoted himself to the study of Buddhism, that is, he was never tired of travelling far and near listening to the religious discourses of Shin teachers.

Many, many years passed like that and his neighbours used to remark, 'Kichibei goes around in sandals made of gold,' meaning that all his money and property had gone into his religion. He did not at all mind his poverty, saying, 'Enough is the living for the day.' At seventy he was still peddling fish to get his daily livelihood, though his earning was no more than a few *tōbyaku* (pennies). When a neighbouring child brought him one day a bunch of flowers, he was very grateful. 'By the grace of Amida I live this day to make him this flower-offering'; he went up to the altar. The child was rewarded with two pieces of *tōbyaku*, the whole earning of the day.[1]

Is not such a Buddhist a good follower of Jesus too? He had no thought for the morrow, and in these modern days of economic stress how would he have fared? In spite of all this, there is something most captivating in a life like Kichibei's. Rolle speaks of 'a contemplative man [who] is turned towards the unseen light with so great a longing that men often consider him a fool or mad, because his heart is so on fire with the love of Christ. Even his bodily appearance is changed, and is so far removed from other men that it seems as if God's child were a lunatic.'[2] 'God's fool' or 'God's lunatic' are expressive terms. Kichibei was surely changed in his appearance and had become a splendid lunatic. Jesus Freak

## The Passive Life Described

The psychological state of such religious belief can be explained in the language of Madame Guyon as follows:[3]

'I speak to you, my dear brother, without reserve. And, in the first place, my soul, as it seems to me, is united to God in such a manner that my own will is entirely lost in the Divine Will. I live, therefore, as well as I can express it, out of myself and all other creatures, in union with God, because in union with His will. . . . It is thus that God, by His sanctifying grace, has come to me All in All. The self which once troubled me is taken away, and I find it no more. And thus God, being made known in things and events, which is the only way in which the I AM, or Infinite Existence, can be made known, everything becomes in a certain sense God to me. I find God in everything

---

[1] *Anjin Shōwa*, XVIII.
[2] *The Amending of Life*, edited by H. L. Hubbard (1922), p. 91.
[3] A letter to her brother Gregory as quoted in Thomas C. Upham's *Life and Experience of Madam Guyon*, p. 305 et seq.

which is, and in everything which comes to pass. The creature is nothing; God is ALL.'

Thomas C. Upham further gives, according to Madame Guyon's autobiography and other literary material, his own version of the conversation which took place between her and Bossuet, Bishop of Meaux, at this time confessedly the 'leader of the French Church'. The conversation is quite illuminating as regards the quietist point of view of religious experience, and I allow myself to quote the following:

'*Bossuet :* I notice that the terms and phrases which you employ sometimes differ from those with which I frequently meet in theological writings. And perhaps the reason which you have already suggested explains it in part. But still they are liable to be misunderstood and to lead into error: and hence it is necessary to ascertain precisely what is meant. You sometimes describe what you consider the highest state of religious experience as a state of *passivity*; and at other times as *passively active*. I confess, Madame, that I am afraid of expressions which I do not fully understand, and have the appearance at least of being somewhat at variance with man's moral agency and accountability.

'*Madam Guyon :* I am not surprised, sir, at your reference to these expressions; and still I hardly know what other expressions to employ. I will endeavour to explain. In the early periods of man's religious experience, he is in what may be called *a mixed life*; sometimes acting from God, but more frequently, until he has made considerable advancement, acting from himself. His inward movement, until it becomes corrected by Divine grace, is self-originated and is characterized by that perversion which belongs to everything coming from that source. But when the soul, in the possession of pure or perfect love, is fully converted, and everything in it is subordinated to God, then its state is always either passive or passively active.

'But I am willing to concede, which will perhaps meet your objection, that there are some reasons for preferring the term *passively active*; because the sanctified soul, although it no longer has a will of its own, is never strictly inert. Under all circumstances and in all cases, there is really a distinct act on the part of the soul, namely *an act of co-operation* with God; although in some cases it is a simple co-operation with what *now is*, and constitutes the religious state of submissive acquiescence and patience; while in others it is a co-operation with reference to what *is to be*, and implies future results, and consequently is a state of movement and performance.

'*Bossuet*: I think, Madame, I understand you. There is a distinction undoubtedly in the two classes of cases just mentioned; but as the term *passively active* will apply to both of them, I think it is to be preferred. You use this complex term, I suppose, because there are two distinct acts or operations to be expressed, namely the act of preparatory or *prevenient* grace on the part of God, and the co-operative act on the part of the creature; the soul being passive, or merely perceptive, in the former; and active, although always in accordance with the Divine leading, in the other.'

'Passively active', or 'actively passive', either will describe the mentality of the quietist type of the mystic. He is not generally conscious of his own active part in his religious experience, and may wish to ignore this part altogether on the ground of his religious philosophy. But, as I said before, there is no absolutely passive state of mind, for this would mean perfect emptiness, and to be passive means that there is something ready to receive. Even God cannot work where there is nothing to work on or with. Passivity is a relative term indicating a not fully analysed state of consciousness. In our religious life, passivity comes as the culmination of strenuous activity; passivity without this preliminary condition is sheer inanity, in which there will be no consciousness from the very first, even of any form of passivity.

'I live, yet not I but Christ liveth in me.' This is passivism as far as somebody else, and not the self has taken possession of that which liveth, but that which liveth stays there all

297

the time. 'Ye are dead, and your life is hid with Christ in God.' (Colos. III, 3.) Something in you is dead, which is to die sooner or later, but that which is to live keeps on living. This does not mean that you are altogether annihilated, but that you are living in the most lively sense of the word. Living is an activity, in fact the highest form of activity. Absolute passivity is death itself.[1]

## Passivity and Pure Land Buddhism

It is in the Pure Land school that the idea of passivity is most clearly traceable in Buddhism, though even in the Holy Path school it is not quite absent. Shinran, a great advocate of the *Tariki* ('other-power') doctrine, naturally upholds passivity in the religious life of his followers. His idea is manifest in such passages as this, in which he repudiates 'self-power' or 'self-will' (*hakarai*). 'By "self-power" is meant,' says he, 'the self-will of the [Holy Path] devotees, relying on which each of them, as he finds himself variously situated in the circumstances of life, recites the Buddha-names other [than Amida's], disciplines himself in good works other [than uttering the name of Amida]; he upholds his own will, by which he attempts to remedy all the disturbances arising from body, speech, and thought, and, thus making himself wholesome, he wishes to be reborn in the Land of Purity.

'The "other-power" devotees, on the other hand, put their whole-hearted faith in the original vow of Amida, as is expressed in the Eighteenth Vow in which he vows to receive all beings to his Land of Purity if they only recite his name and desire to be saved through him. In this, says the Holy One, there is no human scheme because there is here only the scheme of the Tathāgata's vow. By "human scheme" is meant "self-will", and "self-will" is self-power, which is a human scheme. As to "other-power", it is a whole-hearted belief in the original vow, and as the devotee

[1] Cf. pp. 46-7 *fn.*, where St. Francis' simile of a corpse is quoted.

is thus assured of his rebirth in Amida's land, there is no human scheme in the whole procedure. And, therefore, again he need not feel any anxiety in his mind as to whether he would be welcomed by the Tathāgata because of his sinfulness.

'Let him remain undisturbed, even with all his passions, because they belong by nature to him as an ignorant and sinful mortal, nor let him imagine himself that he should be reborn in Amida's land because of his good will and good conduct. For as long as he has the mind of relying on his "self-will", he has no chance for rebirth in the Pure Land.'[1]

Shinran's vocabulary is rich in such phrases as 'artless art', or 'meaningless meaning', 'no scheming whatever', 'naturalness', or 'suchness', or 'the natural course of things', 'the passages of absolute freedom' or 'unobstructed path', 'beyond the intelligence or contrivanace of the ignorant' as it is the will of the Buddha, 'an absolute trust in the Tathāgata's vow which is not tinged with human contrivance', 'the great believing heart is Buddhatā and Buddhatā is the Tathāgata', etc.

The ultimate meaning of all these phrases so common in the lexicon of Shin Buddhism, is the upholding of passivity in the psychology of its followers. Let Amida work out his original vow as he made it in the beginning of his religious career, which means, 'Let us believe in it whole-heartedly and it will find its way inevitably, naturally, spontaneously, and without any contrivance on our part, into our sinful hearts and take us up into his Land of Bliss and Purity, after our death.' While we are living here on earth as the result of our past Karma, bound by the laws of the flesh and driven by the instinctive and uncontrollable urge of life, we cannot escape its course, but so long as there is the original vow of Amida, which has proved efficient in his own attainment of supreme enlightenment, we need not worry about the sinful urge of our earthly life.

Absolute faith puts an end to our spiritual tribulations

[1] *The Mattōshō.*

299

which annoy us on account of our sins. Sins themselves as they are committed by us mortals may not be eradicated, for as long as we are relative existences, limited and governed by forces beyond our 'self-power' to control, we cannot rid ourselves completely of defiled passions and desires and impulses. In spite of this fact, we are not troubled about sin, because our sin no more affects our life after death; have we not already been saved by the original vow of Amida which we have unconditionally accepted? Was it not our worry about our after-death life, or immortality, as the Christians would put it, that made us feel concerned about this sinful state of affairs on earth? It is not that we keep on sinning, or that we take delight in sinning, as some antinomians do; indeed we feel seriously concerned about sinning, but this sinning no longer shakes our faith in Amida and our final enlightenment and emancipation. The soul is no more disturbed, and with all its sins and regrets and lamentations it retains its sincerity, its hope, and its transcendental joy.

Richard Rolle, the author of *The Amending of Life*, was a Christian mystic of the fourteenth century. His idea of sin and purity of heart has much to remind us of the view presented above. He writes (pp. 75–76):

'Who can truly say "I am free of sin?" No one in this life; for as Job says, "If I wash myself with snow water and make my hands never so clean, yet shalt thou plunge me in the ditch, and mine own clothes shall abhor me." "If I washed myself with snow water" meaning true penitence; "and make my hands never so clean" by works of innocence, "yet shalt thou plunge me in the ditch" of venial sins that cannot be avoided, "and mine own clothes shall abhor me," that is to say, my flesh makes me loathe myself, and sensuality that is so frail, slippery, and ready to love the beauty of this world, often makes me sin. The apostle said, "Let not sin reign in your mortal body," that is to say, "Sin must be in us, but it need not rule over us." . . . Though he sometimes commit a venial offence, yet henceforth, because his whole heart is turned to God, sin is

300

destroyed. The fire of love burns up in him all stain of sin, as a drop of water cast into a furnace is consumed.'

Here lies the teaching of 'other-power' Buddhism in a nutshell, and here also the signification of passivity in the psychology of Buddhism.

Ichiren-in (1788–1860) was a modern follower of the 'other-power' school; he used to teach in the following manner:[1] 'If you have yet something worrying you, however trivial it may be, your faith in Amida is not absolute. When you have a feeling of unrest, this is of course far from believing in Amida; but even when you are rejoicing as having at last found rest, this is not real rest either. To make strenuous effort because you have not yet gained a restful heart, is also not quite right. To put your belief to a test wishing to know if it is firmly resting on Amida, is again wrong.

'Why? Because all these are attempts to look into your own mind, you are turned away from Amida, you are wrongly oriented. Indeed, it is easy to say, "Abandon your self-power," but after all how difficult it is! I, therefore, repeat over and over again and say, "Don't look at your own mind, but look straight up to Amida himself." To rely on Amida means to turn towards the mirror of the original vow and see Amida face to face.'

## Passivity is Accepting Life As It Is

Passivity is not self-reflection or self-examination. It is an unqualified acceptance of Amida. So long as there is a trace of conscious contrivance (*hakarai*), you are not wholly possessed of Amida. You and the original vow are two separate items of thought, there is no unity, and this unity is to be attained by accepting and not by striving. In this case passivity is identifiable with accepting existence as it is.

To believe, then, is to be and not to become. Becoming implies a dissatisfaction with existence, a wishing to change;

[1] *Anjin Shōwa*, 'Talks on Spiritual Peace'.

301

that is, to work out 'my will' as against 'thy will', and whatever we may say about moral ideals of perfection, religion is after all the acceptance of things as they are, things evil together with things good. Religion wants first of all 'to be'. To believe, therefore, is to exist—this is the fundamental of all religions. When this is translated into terms of psychology, the religious mind turns on the axle of passivity. 'You are all right as you are', or 'to be well with God and the world', or 'don't think of the morrow'—this is the final word of all religion.

It was in this spirit that Rinzai (Lin-chi, died 867), the founder of the Rinzai branch of Zen Buddhism, said: 'The truly religious man has nothing to do but go on with his life as he finds it in the various circumstances of this worldly existence. He rises quietly in the morning, puts on his dress and goes out to his work. When he wants to walk, he walks; when he wants to sit, he sits. He has no hankering after Buddhahood, not the remotest thought of it. How is this possible? A wise man of old says, If you strive after Buddhahood by any conscious contrivances, your Buddha is indeed the source of eternal transmigration.'[1] To doubt is to commit suicide; to strive, which means to 'negate', is, according to Buddhist phraseology, eternally to transmigrate in the ocean of birth and death.

A man called Jōyemon, of Mino province, was much troubled about his soul. He had studied Buddhism but so far to no purpose. Finally, he went up to Kyoto where Ichiren-in, who was a great teacher of Shin Buddhism, at the time resided, and opened his heart to him, begging to be instructed in the teaching of Shinran Shōnin. Said Ichiren-in, 'You are as old as you are.' (Amida's salvation consists in accepting yourself as you are.) Jōyemon was not satisfied and made further remonstration, to which Ichiren repeated, 'You are saved as you are.'

The seeker after truth was not yet in a state of mind to accept the word of the teacher right off, he was not yet free

[1] Done after the sense, for a literal translation of Rinzai requires a great deal of comments.

from dependence on contrivances and strivings. He still pursued the teacher with some more postulations. The teacher, however, was not to be induced to deviate from his first course, for he repeated, 'You are saved as you are,' and quietly withdrew. It was fortunate that he was a 'tariki' teacher; for if he had been a Zen master, I feel sure that Jōyemon would have been handled in an altogether different manner.[1]

John Woolman (1720–1772), a Quaker, died of smallpox, and towards the end his throat was much affected and he could not speak. He asked for pen and ink and wrote with difficulty, 'I believe my being here is in the wisdom of Christ; I know not as to life or death.' This confession exactly tallies with that of Shinran when he says in *The Tannisho*: 'I say my Nembutsu as taught by my good teacher. As to my being reborn after death in the Land of Purity or in hell, I have no idea of it.'

Shinran quite frequently makes reference to the inconceivability of Buddha-wisdom. Our being here is entirely due to it, and it is not in our limited knowledge to probe into its mystery nor is it necessary to exercise our finite will about it; we just accept existence as it is, our trust is wholly placed in the infinite wisdom of Amida, and what we have to do is to get rested with this trust, this faith, this acceptance, and with this ignorance. And the wonderful thing is that this ignorance has such a wisdom in it as to give us entire satisfaction with this life and after.[2]

---

[1] Tê-shan Hsüan-chien, who used to be a great scholar of the *Vajracchedikā Prajñāpāramitā* before he was converted to Zen, appeared one evening in the pulpit and declared, 'I shall not allow any questioning tonight; questioners will get thirty blows.' A monk came forward, and when he was about to make bows, Tê-shan gave him a blow. Said the monk, 'When I am not even proposing a question, why should you strike me so?' The master asked, 'Where is your native place?' 'I come from Hsin-lo (=Korea).' 'You deserved,' insisted the master, 'thirty blows even before you got into the boat.' *The Transmission of the Lamp*, Vol. XV.

[2] There are two kinds of ignorance in Zen: the one has wisdom and trust in it, but the other is utter darkness.

Tung-shan came to see Hui-chao of Shu-shan, and the latter asked, 'You are already master of a monastery, and what do you want here?' 'I am distressed with a doubt and do not know what to do, hence my com-

The mystic knowledge or mystic ignorance and the satisfaction derived from it are also illustrated by the poem of thirty-one syllables composed by Ippen Shōnin (1229–1289). When he was studying Zen under Hōtō (1203–1298), the latter wanted to know how Ippen understood the meaning of the statement that 'As a thought is stirred there is an awakening.' Ippen's answer was in verse:

'When the Name is uttered
Neither the Buddha nor the Self
There is:
Na-mu-a-mi-da-bu-tsu—
The voice alone is heard.'

The Zen master, however, did not think Ippen rightly understood the point, whereby the latter uttered another verse:

'When the Name is uttered
Neither the Buddha nor the Self
There is:
Na-mu-a-mi-da-bu-tsu,
Na-mu-a-mi-da-bu-tsu!'[1]

ing here.' The master called out, 'O Liang-chieh!' which was Tung-shan's name, and Liang-chieh replied at once, 'Yes, sir.' 'What is that?' demanded the master. Chieh failed to answer, and Hui-chao gave this judgment, 'Fine Buddha no doubt, and what a pity he has no flames!' (*The Transmission*, IX.) As he has no flames, his 'ignorance' is not illuminating. When he becomes conscious of the fact, there is enlightenment.

Hui-lang asked Shih-t'ou, 'Who is the Buddha?' 'You have no Buddha nature.' 'How about these beings that go wriggling about?' 'They rather have the Buddha-nature,' 'How is it that I am devoid of it?' 'Because,' said the master, 'you do not acknowledge it yourself.' This is said to have awakened Hui-lang to his own 'ignorance' which now illuminates. (Op. cit. XIV.)

Yao-shan was sitting in meditation, and Shih-t'ou said, 'What are you doing here?' 'I am not doing anything.' 'If so, you are sitting idly.' 'Even an idle sitting is doing something,' retorted Yao-shan. 'If, as you say, you are not doing anything, what is it that is not doing anything?' Yao-shan said, 'Even the wise know it not.' (*Loc. cit.*) This 'ignorance' is of quite a different sort, is it not?

Chên-lang asked Shih-t'ou, 'What is the idea of the First Patriarch's coming from the West?' 'Ask the post over there.' 'I do not understand, sir.' 'I too fail to understand,' was Shih-t'ou's reply, which, however, lighted up Lang's 'ignorance', which in turn became illuminated. (*Loc. cit.*)

[1] *Sayings of Ippen.*

This met the master's approval. In Ippen's religion we find Zen and Shin harmonized in a most practical way. When this *sonomana* (*yathābhūtam*) idea is translated into human relations, we have the following in which self-will is de- nounced as hindering the work of the All-One, that is, Amida.

'When the rebellious will of your self-power is given up, you realize what is meant by putting trust in Amida. You desire to be saved and the Buddha is ever ready to save, and yet the fact of your rebirth in the Land of Purity does not seem to be so easily establishable.

'Why? Because your rebellious will still asserts itself. It is like contracting a marriage between a young man and a young woman. The parents on both sides want to see them united in marriage. The one party says, "There is no need of the bride's being provided with any sort of trous- seau." But the other thinks it necessary, seeing that the bridegroom belongs to a far richer family, and it would not do for the bride not to be supplied even with one wardrobe. Both are ready and yet the sense of pride is their barrier. If the bride's family took the proposal made by the other party in the same spirit as that made by the latter, the desired end would be accomplished without further fussing.

'Quite similar to this is the relationship between the Buddha and sentient beings. The Buddha says: "Come"; why not then go to him even as you are? But here the re- bellious will shakes its head and says, "With all his good will, I cannot go to him just as I am; I ought to do something to deserve the call." This is self-pride. This is more than what the Buddha requires of you, and anything extraneous coming out of your self-conceit and limited philosophy obstructs the passage of the Buddha's mercy into your hearts. For all that is asked of you is to put your hand for- ward, into which the Buddha is ready to drop the coin of salvation. The Buddha is beckoning to you, the boat is waiting to take you to the other shore of the stream, no fares are wanted, the only movement you are to make is to step right into the ferry. You cannot protest and say, "This is a difficult task." Why don't you then give yourself up entirely to the Buddha's vow of salvation and let his will prevail over yours?"[1]

Molinos writes to Petrucci: 'One of the fundamental rules which serve to keep my soul in constant inner peace is this: I may cherish no desire[2] for this or that separate good, but only for that good which is the highest of all, and I must be prepared for all which this highest good gives me and requires of me. These are few words but they contain much.'[3] If one asks a Shin teacher what are few words containing so much as productive of the highest good, he will at once say, 'Na-mu-a-mi-da-bu-tsu, Na-mu-a-mi-da-bu-tsu!' For this is indeed the magic sesame that carries you right to the other side of birth and death.

## Ignorance and Passivity

The significant fact about religious experience, which is to be noticed in this connection, is that it always insists on abandoning all knowledge and learnedness acquired by the seeker of God or truth. Whether it is Christian or Buddhist, whether it is the Pure Land or the Holy Path, the insistence is equally emphatic.

It is evident that religious experience stands diametrically opposed to intellectual knowledge, for learnedness and scholarship do not guarantee one to be a member of the kingdom of God, but 'being like a child' not only in humbleness of heart but in simpleness of thought. The stains of vanity, conceit, and self-love which are so-called human righteousnesses are indeed 'as a polluted garment' which is

---

[1] Condensed from VIII–XIII of *Sayings of Shūson*, one of the modern teachers of Shin Buddhism, 1788–1860. Compiled by Gessho Sasaki, 1907.

[2] That the Catholic monks avow absolute obedience to their superior is also an expression of passivism in our religious life. When a man can submit himself to a life of obedience, he feels a certain sense of relief from the oppressing burden of self-responsibility, which is akin to the genuine religious feeling of peace and rest.

[3] Kathleen Lyttleton's Introduction to Molinos' *Spiritual Guide*, p. 25.

to be cast off by every one of us, but why is the use of the intellect too to be avoided? The soul may long for solitude and silence, but why does the constant reading of religious books grow wearisome? Why was Jesus thankful for his Father's hiding 'these things' from the wise and prudent and revealing them unto babes, who are incapable of 'careful meditations and subtle reasoning'?

St. Bonaventura 'teaches us not to form a conception of anything, no, not even of God, because it is imperfection to be satisfied with representations, images, and definitions, however subtle and ingenious they may be, either of the will or of the goodness, trinity and unity; nay, of the divine essence itself'.[1]

St. Augustine soliloquizes: 'I, Lord, went wandering like a strayed sheep, seeking thee with anxious reasoning without whilst thou wast within me. I wearied myself much in looking for thee without, and yet thou hast thy habitation within me, if only I desire thee and pant after thee. I went round the streets and squares of the city of this world seeking thee; and I found thee not, because in vain I sought without for him, who was within myself.'[1]

The reason why intellection is in disfavour with religious teachers is this: it does not give us the thing itself, but its representations, images, explanations, and references; it always leads us away from ourselves, which means that we become lost in the jungle of endless speculation and imagination, giving us no inner peace and spiritual rest. The intellect always looks outwardly, forgetting that 'there is an inward sight which hath power to perceive the One True God'. So Gerson expresses himself,[2] 'Though I have spent forty years in reading and prayer, yet I could never find

---

[1] Quoted from *The Spiritual Guide*, pp. 76, 77. This strong personal note is what differentiates Christianity from Buddhism. Even where a personal relationship is deeply felt, for instance in the Shin sect which regards Amida as 'Oya-sama' (a parent), there is no such intensity of human feeling as is described here. In Zen one fails to find anything approaching this. Zen is singularly metaphysical if the term could be used here appropriately; it is remarkably impersonal.

[2] Molinos, p. 72.

any thing more efficacious, nor, for attaining to mystical theology, more direct than that the spirit should become like a little child and a beggar in the presence of God.'

Buddhism, however, is fundamentally a religion against and not for ignorance (*avidyā*), as shown in the foregoing quotations. The ignorant (*bāla*) and confused (*bhrānti*) and simple-minded (*prithagjana*) are very much condemned in all Buddhist sūtras as not being able to grasp the deepest truths of enlightenment.

It is true that Buddhism is more intellectual than Christianity and that the whole drift of Buddhist thought tends to encourage an intuitive grasp of the emptiness of existence instead of being embraced in the love of the highest being. But in spite of this fact there is a strong under-current in the Buddhist teaching to uphold the futility of all intellectual attempts in the experience of the Buddhist life which consists really in abandoning every self-centred striving and preconceived metaphysical standpoint. This is to keep the consciousness in utter purity or in a state of absolute neutrality or blankness; in other words, to make the mind as simple as that of the child, which is not at all stuffed with learning and pride.

Hōnen Shōnin's (1133–1212) 'One-Sheet Document' illustrates the Pure Land attitude towards ignorance and simple-heartedness:

'By Nembutsu I do not mean such practice of meditation on the Buddha as is referred to by the wise men of China and Japan, nor is it the recitation of the Buddha's name, which is practised as the result of study and understanding as to the meaning of Nembutsu. It is just to recite the name of Amida, without doubting that this will issue in the re-birth of the believer in the Pure Land. Just this, and no other considerations are needed. Mention is often made of the threefold heart and the four sorts of exercise, but these are all included in the belief that a rebirth in the Pure Land is most conclusively assured by the "Namu Amida Butsu". If one imagines something more than this, one will be excluded from the blessings of the two holy ones,

308

Amida and Śākyamuni, and left out of the original vow. Those who believe in the Nembutsu, however learned they may be in all the teachings of Śākyamuni, should behave themselves like an ignoramus who knows nothing, or like a simple-hearted woman-devotee; avoid pedantry, and recite the Buddha's name with singleness of heart.'

Shinran Shōnin (1173–1262) as disciple of Hōnen voices the same sentiment in his *Tannisho*:

'[Some say that] the salvation of those who do not read and study the sūtras and commentaries is doubtful. Such a view as this is to be regarded as very far from the truth. All the sacred books devoted to the explanation of the truth of the Other-power show that every one who, believing in the original vow recites the Nembutsu will become a Buddha. Excepting this, what learning is needed to be reborn in the Pure Land? Let those who have any doubt on this point learn hard and study in order to understand the meaning of the original vow. It is a great pity that there are some who in spite of a hard study of the sacred books are unable to understand the true meaning of the sacred doctrine. Since the Name is so formed as to be recited by any simple-hearted person who may have no understanding of even a single phrase in the sacred books, the practice is called easy.'

That Zen, representing the Holy Path wing of Buddhism, also avoids learning and sūtra-reading can be seen from the way the historians of Zen treat Hui-nêng, the sixth patriarch of Zen; for he is made an ignorant pedlar of kindling as compared with his rival Shên-hsiu, whose scholarship was the object of envy among the five hundred disciples of Hung-jên; and also from one of the chief mottoes adopted by Zen followers, 'Depend not on letters!', for it was indeed on this that the T'ien-tai advocates of the Sung concentrated their assaults on Zen.

Those who have at all studied Zen know well what attitude is assumed by Zen toward scholarship and intellection. Its literature is filled with such passages as these: 'I have not a word to give to you as the teaching of Zen';

'I have not uttered even a syllable these forty-nine years of my preaching'; 'That is your learning; let me have what you have discovered within yourself'; 'What are you going to do with your sūtra-reading, which does not at all belong to your inner self?'; 'With all your erudition, do you think you can cope with Death?'; 'All the sūtras and commentaries so reverently studied by you, are they not after all mere rubbish to wipe dirt?' and so on.

Of the reasons why ignorance or simple-mindedness is so exalted in religious experience, the most weighty one is perhaps to be found in the nature of the intellect itself. Being essentially dualistic, it requires a point of reference from which it starts to make a statement, or to advance an argument, or to give a judgment.

This mental habit of having a proposition definitely ascertained and holding fast to it goes against the religious frame of mind which principally consists in accepting existence as it is without asking questions, without making protests, without entertaining doubts. Religious experience depicts in plain, unqualified, and straightforward statements, refusing to have anything to do with quibblings and dialectics. Whether of the Zen or of the Shin kind of Buddhism, mystic intuition thrives best in a mind which has no predilection, especially nursed by learning. When the mirror of consciousness is thoroughly cleansed of intellectual muddle it reflects the glory and love of God, as the Christians would say. Hence ignorance and naïvety go hand in hand with passivity.

### Selflessness and Emptiness

When this doctrine of passivity is rendered into philosophical phraseology, it is the doctrine of Anātman or non-ego, which, when further developed, turns into that of Śūnyatā or emptiness. As I explained elsewhere, the doctrine of no self-substance is not so nihilistic as non-Buddhist scholars may imagine, for this denial of the ego is also constantly on the lips of the Christian mystics. When St. Bernard, quoting Isaiah x, 15, 'Shall the axe boast itself against him that heweth therewith? or shall the saw magnify itself against him that shaketh it? as if the rod should shake itself against them that lift it up, or if the staff should lift up itself, as if it were no wood,' concludes, 'In fact, the ability to glory in God comes from God alone'; cannot we draw another conclusion, saying, 'God is all in all, there is no ego-substance'?, or 'In him we live and move and have our being, and therefore all relative existences are as such empty (*śūnya*) and unborn (*anutpanna*)'? Logically speaking, Buddhist scholars are more frank and radical and self-consistent in developing this theme.

Says the author of *Theologia Germanica*, 'We must understand it as though God said: "He who willeth without me, or willeth not what I will, or otherwise than as I will, he willeth contrary to me, for my will is that no one should will otherwise than I, and that there should be no will without me, and without my will; even as without me there is neither substance, nor life, nor this, nor that, so also there should be no will apart from me, and without my will."' When this is translated into the language of Buddhist psychology, it is 'I am nowhere a somewhatness for any one, and nowhere for me is there a somewhatness of any one.'[1] Or, according to the *Visuddhimagga* (Chap. XVI):

> 'Misery only doth exist, none miserable,
> No doer is there; naught save the deed is found.
> Nirvāna is, but not the man who seeks it.
> The Path exists, but not the traveller on it.'

We must remember that the Buddha's teaching of Anātman or Anatta is not the outcome of psychological analysis but is a statement of religious intuition in which no discursive reasoning whatever is employed. The Buddhist experience found out by immediate knowledge that when one's heart was cleansed of the defilements of the

[1] Translated by H. C. Warren.

ordinary ego-centred impulses and desires, nothing was left there to claim itself as the ego-residuum. It was Buddhist philosophy that formed the theory, but that which supplied it with facts to substantiate it was Buddhist experience. We ought always to remember this truth, that religion first starts with experience and later philosophizes, and, therefore, the criticism of the philosophy must be based on facts and not on the philosophy itself as thus formulated.

The doctrine of Śūnyatā too is a statement of religious intuition, and not an abstract formulation of empty ideas. If this were not so, it could never be the fundamental concept of all the schools of Mahāyāna Buddhism, and have such an inspiring influence upon the religious consciousness of its followers. The subject was treated somewhat fully in my *Studies in the Laṅkāvatāra Sūtra*, and I would not repeat it here except that Śūnyatā, which is generally translated emptiness or vacuity, which is its literal meaning, is not to be interpreted in terms of relative knowledge and logical analysis; but it is the utterance of direct insight into the nature of existence. Whatever philosophy it has gathered about it is later addition and the work of Buddhist scholarship.


# IV

## *Passivity and Patience or Humility*

While the life of passivity on the one hand tends to libertinism, it shows on the other hand much aloofness from human concerns. There are, however, some practical moral virtues arising from the experience of passivity, or, stated conversely, where there are these virtues they issue from the experience. They are highly characteristic of the religious life irrespective of its theology, be it Buddhist or Christian.

In Buddhism the virtues thus realized are generally

estimated at six, called *Pāramitā*: *Dāna*, *Śīla*, *Kṣānti*, *Vīrya*, *Dhyāna*, and *Prajñā*.[1] The latter two, meditation (*dhyāna*) and intuitive knowledge (*prajñā*), may not be in any direct relationship to passivity, and here we will not touch upon them. The first four are important and we may say that the Mahāyānist life is summed up in them. Still, of these four, the first, the practice of charity, which in Buddhism also involves the giving up of one's life to the cause, and the second, the observance of the moral precepts, may not engage our attention here. For I wish to give especial consideration to one or two classical instances of *Kṣānti* and *Vīrya*, both of which I take to be closely connected with the life of passivity and the philosophy of Śūnyatā. We may think that *Kṣānti* (patience) may have something to do with passivity; but how about *Vīrya* (energy), which is apparently an opposite quality of meed suffering? How could energy be thought of as issuing from religious passivity and emptiness?

This is a significant point in the life of the Mahāyāna Buddhist and in the teaching of the *Prajñāpāramitā Sūtra*. For according to the latter, which is lived by the Bodhisattva, an inexhausible mine of energy obtains just because of the emptiness of things; if there were something determinable at the back of our existence, we could not put forward such an energy exhibited by the Bodhisattva Sadāprarudita. And, owing to this energy, patience or humility is again made possible. To be patient or to practise *Kṣānti* does not mean merely to submit oneself to sufferings of all kinds which are brought upon him from external sources, but it means to exert the virtue of energy (*vīrya*) in the life of emptiness, which is no less than what is known in all the Mahāyāna sūtras as the life of a Bodhisattva (*bodhisattvacaryā*). So we read in the *Diamond Sūtra*:

'O Subhūti, at the time when Kalirāja cut my flesh from every limb, I had no idea of a self, of a person, of a being,

───────────

[1] The six virtues of perfection are: 1. Charity, or giving; 2. Morality; 3. Patience, or humility; 4. Strenuousness; 5. Meditation; and 6. Intuitive Knowledge.

or of a living being; I had neither an idea nor no-idea. And why? Because, O Subhūti, if I at that time had had an idea of self, of a person, or a being, or of a living being, I should also have had an idea of malevolence. And why? Because, O Subhūti, I remember the past five hundred births when I was a Rishi Kṣāntivādin. At that time also I had no idea of a self, of a person, of a being, or of a living being. . . .'[1]

We can thus see that without a philosophical comprehension of emptiness there will be no real patience or passivity in the life of the Mahāyāna Buddhist, which, supported by energy, never grows weary of seeking for the highest good. *Sūnyatā*, *Kṣānti*, and *Vīrya* are inseparable. The story of the Bodhisattva Sadāprarudita is in this respect quite illuminating. The story runs as follows.[2]


## The Story of Sadāprarudita

The Buddha said to Subhūti: If thou shouldst really desire Prajñāpāramitā, thou shouldest behave like the Bodhisattva Sadāprarudita who is at present living the life of a Bodhisattva under the Tathāgata Bhīshma-gar-jita-nirghoshasvara. When he was intently bent upon realizing Prajñāpāramitā, there was a voice from the sky, saying, 'If thou goest eastward thou wilt have the chance of listening to Prajñāpāramitā. While proceeding there abandon all thy thoughts about growing tired, about sleep, eating and drinking, day and night, cold and heat; do not trouble thyself at all about such affairs, have no thought whatever about them; be done away with flattery; cherish no self-conceit, no arrogance; free thyself from the idea of a being, from the desire of making a name, of amassing wealth; free thyself from the five hindrances, from envy; assert no dualistic notions as to subject and object, inner and outer, etc.; while walking along, do not turn either side,

[1] S.B.E., XLIX, pp. 127–8.
[2] *The Aṣṭhasāhasrikā-prajñāpāramitā-sūtra.* Chapter on the Bodhisattva Sadāprarudita.

left or right; do not think of the points of the compass, front or behind, above or below; do not be disturbed with thy form (*rūpa*), sensation (*vedanā*), thought (*saṁjña*), conformation (*sanskāra*), and consciousness (*vijñāna*). Why? Because he who is disturbed in these walks into birth-and-death and not into the Buddhist life, and will never attain Prajñāpāramitā.'

When Sadāprarudita heard this voice from the sky, he said: 'I will behave indeed in the way I am instructed. For my wish is to become a light for all sentient beings by storing up all the truths of Buddhism.' The mysterious voice gives the Bodhisattva further advice regarding the Mahāyānistic view of the world, absolute confidence to be placed in the teacher of Prajñāpāramitā, the temptations of the Evil One which would appear in various forms to a serious seeker of truth, etc.

Sadāprarudita now following the advice starts on his eastern pilgrimage, but before he is very far off, he thinks again: 'Why did I not ask the voice how far east I have to go and of whom to hear about Prajñāpāramitā?' When he was seized with this thought, he felt so grieved over his stupidity that he did not know what to do but gave himself up to intense grief and self-reproach. But he was determined to stay on the spot, no matter how long, if he could only have another advice from the sky. He felt like a person who had lost his only child, there was no other thought in his mind than wishing to know about his further procedure, when lo! a form looking like the Tathāgata appeared before him and said:

'Well done, Sadāprarudita! All the Buddhas in the past have behaved like thee when they were intently bent upon realizing Prajñāpāramitā. Go eastward for a distance of 500 yojanas, where thou wilt come to a city known as Gandhavatī which is constructed of seven precious stones and most magnificently decorated in every way. In this city there is a high wide terrace on which stands a splendidly-built palace belonging to a Bodhisattva called Dharmodgata. A large assemblage of gods and men is gathered here, who are desirous of listening to the discourses given by this Bodhisattva on Prajñāpāramitā.

'Sadāprarudita, he is thy teacher and it is through him that thou comest to the understanding of Prajñāpāramitā. Go, therefore, on thy eastward journey until thou reachest the city. Conduct thyself as if thou wert pierced with a poisonous arrow, have no other thoughts than having it withdrawn from thy flesh at the earliest possible opportunity; have no rest until thou comest into the presence of thy teacher, the Bodhisattva Dharmodgata.'

When Sadāprarudita was listening to this voice, he entered upon a state of ecstasy whereby he could see more or less clearly into the spiritual conditions of all the Buddhas. When he came out of the Samādhi, all the Buddhas who were before him suddenly disappeared. He was now troubled with the new question: 'Whence are these Buddhas? Whither did they go?' He was grieved but at the same time more determined than ever to reach the palace of Dharmodgata.

He had, however, to think of the offerings[1] he had to make to his teacher. He was poor, and did not know how to get the necessary offerings. But he was not to be daunted, he decided to sell himself, thinking, 'I have gone through many a rebirth, but ever being haunted by selfish impulses

[1] Offerings are made by Buddhists to their object of devotion for their own spiritual development, which results from giving up all that is regarded as belonging to themselves. Offerings are therefore not meant to please the recipient, for what would the Buddhas do with all those material treasures, musical instruments, or celestial maidens? The practice of self-sacrifice is for the benefit of the donor himself. When this is done in the real spirit of selflessness, the Buddha accepts the offerings. A story is told of a noted Zen master who resided at Engakuji, Kamakura, early in the Tokugawa era, which illustrates the nature of Buddhist donation. When his temple required renovation, a wealthy merchant who was one of his admirers offered him a large sum of money for the work. The master received it nonchalantly, put it aside, and uttered not a word of thanks. The merchant was dissatisfied, and explained how deeply the donation cut into his capital and that it was quite a sacrifice on his part, which perhaps deserved just one word of acknowledgment from the master. The master quietly said, 'Why shall I have to thank you for the merit you are accumulating for yourself?' Offerings are thus self-sacrifice, part of the giving-up of selfhood.

I have never performed deeds of goodness and purity, which save me from the tortures of purgatories.'

When he came to a large town, he went up to the market calling out loudly for someone who would buy his person. The Evil One heard the cry and lost no time in keeping the inhabitants of the town away from him, for Mara was afraid of Sadāprarudita's attaining his object and later leading people to the realization of Prajñāpāramitā. There was, however, one maiden of a wealthy householder, whom Māra could not overshadow.

When there was no response, Sadāprarudita was exceedingly mortified. 'How heavy my sin is! Even when I am ready to sacrifice myself for the sake of supreme enlightenment, nobody is forthcoming to help me out!' Śakradevendra, god of the gods, however, hearing him, conceived the idea of testing the sincerity of this truth-seeker. The god assumed the form of a Brahman and appeared before Sadāprarudita. Finding out what was the reason of his excessive lamentation, the Brahman said: 'I do not want your person, but as I am going to conduct a certain religious ritual, I wish to have a human heart, human blood, and human marrow. Would you give them to me?' Sadāprarudita was overjoyed because of the opportunity of gaining some offerings for his teacher and thus enabling him to listen to his discourses on Prajñāpāramitā. He agreed at once to give up everything demanded by the Brahman for any price, he did not care how much it was.

The Brahman took out a sharp knife, and incising it into Sadāprarudita's right arm, he got enough blood needed for his purpose. When he was about to rip up the poor victim's right thigh in order to get the marrow, the maiden of a wealthy householder saw it from her apartment. She at once came down and interfered, 'O sir, what is all this for?' Sadāprarudita explained. The maiden was struck with his unselfish motives and promised him that she would see to whatever offerings he needed for his visit to Dharmodgata.

The Brahman, then resuming his proper form, said to

Sadāprarudita: 'Well done, indeed, son of a good family! I am now convinced of your devotion to the Dharma. Such was also the devotion of all the Buddhas of the past when they were still seeking after Prajñāpāramitā. My only wish with you was to see how earnest you were in this. How can I recompense you?'

Said Sadāprarudita, 'Give me supreme enlightenment.'

The god confessed his inability to give him this kind of gift, whereupon Sadāprarudita wished to have his mutilated body restored. This was accomplished at once and Śakradevendra disappeared. The maiden of a wealthy house-holder then took him into her house, where he was introduced to her parents. They were also greatly moved and even permitted their daughter to go along with him. Rich offerings of all sorts were prepared, and, accompanied by five hundred attendant-maidens, they proceeded further eastward to the city of Gandhavatī.

The city was finally reached, and they saw the Bodhi-sattva Dharmodgata discoursing on the Dharma. As the party of truth-seekers approached him, they were again accosted by Śakradevendra, who performed some miraculous deeds over a treasure-casket. The casket was explained to contain Prajñāpāramitā, but nobody was allowed to open it, as it was sealed seven times by Dharmodgata himself. Some offerings were made to it.

At the palace of Dharmodgata, Sadāprarudita, the maiden of a wealthy householder and five hundred maiden-attendants all paid him due respect; flowers, incense of various kinds, necklaces, banners, canopies, robes, gold, silver, precious stones, and other things were offered, accompanied by music. Sadāprarudita informed him of his mission and the experiences which he had had on his way to Gandhavatī; then he expressed his desire to know whence all those Buddhas came who appeared before him and whither they disappeared later, as he wished to be all the time in their presence. To this answered Dharmodgata:

'From nowhere the Buddhas come and to nowhere they go. Why? Because all things are of suchness and immovable, and this suchness is no less than the Tathāgata himself. In the Tathāgata there is no going, no coming, no birth, no death; for ultimate reality knows neither coming nor going, and this reality is the Tathāgata himself. Emptiness knows neither coming nor going, and this emptiness is the Tathāgata himself. The same can be said of suchness (*yathāvatta*), of detachment (*viragata*), of cessation (*nirodha*), and of space; and all these qualities also belong to the Tathāgata. O son of a good family, apart from all these dharmas, there is no Tathāgata. As they are of suchness, so is the Tathāgata; they are all of one suchness which is neither two nor three; it is above numbers and nowhere attainable.

'Towards the end of the spring, when it is warm, there appears a mirage on the fields, which is taken for a sheet of water by the ignorant. Son of a good family, whence thinkest thou this vapoury appearance comes? From the eastern sea? or from the western sea? or from the northern sea? or from the southern sea?'

Replied Sadāprarudita: 'In the mirage there is no real water, and how can one talk of its whence and whither? The ignorant take it for water where there is really none whatever.'

'And so,' continued Dharmodgata, 'it is with the Tathāgata. If a man gets attached to his body, form, and voice, and begins to think about his whence and whither, he is an ignoramus who, altogether destitute of intelligence, imagines the presence of real water in a mirage. Why? Because no Buddhas are to be regarded as having the material body, they are the Dharma-body, and the Dharma in its essence knows no whence, no whither.

'Son of a good family, it is again like those magic-created figures—elephants, horses, carriages, foot-soldiers; they come from nowhere, go nowhere. It is again like those Tathāgatas who appear to a man in a dream, one, two, ten, twenty, fifty, one hundred, or even over one hundred in number; when he awakes from the dream he sees not even one of them.

'All things are like a dream, they have no substantiality. But as the ignorant realize it not, they are attached to forms, names, physical bodies (*rūpakāya*), words, and phrases; they imagine various Buddhas to be coming into existence and going out of it. They comprehend not the true nature of things nor that of the Buddhas. Such will transmigrate through the six paths of existence, separated from Prajñā-pāramitā, separated from all the teachings of Buddhism. It is only those who understand the nature of ultimate reality (*dharmatā*) who would cherish no discrimination as regards the whence and whither of the Tathāgata. They live Prajñāpāramitā, they attain supreme enlightenment, they are true followers of the Buddha, they are worthy of being revered by others, they are indeed the fountain of blessings to the world.

'Son of a good family, it is like those treasures in the sea which have not come from the east, from the west, from the south, or from the north, or again from above or below. They grow in the sea owing to the good meritorious deeds of sentient beings. They are there not independent of the chain of causation, but when they disappear they do not go east or west or anywhere. When conditions are so combined they come into existence; when they are dissolved things disappear.

'Son of a good family, it is even so with the Tathāgata-body which is not a fixed existence. It does not come from any definite direction, nor does it exist outside the chain of causation, for it is the product of previous karma (*pūrva-karmavipāka*).

'Son of a good family, it is like the musical sound of a lute which issues from the combination of its frame, skin, strings, and stick as it is played by the human hand. The sound comes not from any one of these parts when they are disconnected. Their concordant action is needed to produce the sound. In a similar manner the Tathāgata is the out-come of numberless meritorious deeds of the past, apart from which his whence and whither cannot be conceived. From any one single cause nothing takes place, there must be several of them which when combined produce a result. When they discontinue to act conjointly the Tathāgata goes out of existence. This being the case the wise do not talk of his appearance and disappearance. Indeed, with all things, not only with the Tathāgata, there is no birth, no death, no coming, no going. This is the way to reach supreme enlightenment and also to realize Prajñāpāramitā.'

When this discourse was finished the whole universe trembled violently, including the abodes of the gods and those of the evil ones. All the plants at once burst out in full bloom, and Śakradevendra with his four guardian-kings showered a rain of flowers over the Bodhisattva Dharmodgata. It was explained that these miraculous phenomena took place owing to the fact that the discourse given by the Bodhisattva Dharmodgata on the whence and whither of the Tathāgata opened the spiritual eyes leading to supreme enlightenment of ever so many beings.

This pleased the Bodhisattva Sadāprarudita immensely, for he was now more than ever confirmed in his belief in Prajñāpāramitā and his destiny of attaining Buddhahood. More offerings were given to Dharmodgata who, first accepting them in order to complete the meritorious deeds of the Sadāprarudita, returned them to him. He then retired into his own palace not to come out of it again before seven years elapsed; for it was his habit to enter upon a profound Samādhi for that space of time. But Sadāprarudita was determined to wait, how long it did not matter, by the palace of Dharmodgata, since he wished to listen to his discourses again on Prajñāpāramitā and its skilful means (upāyakauśalya). He was so devoted to his teacher that all the while he never laid himself in bed, never tasted any delicious food, never gave himself to his own sensuous pleasure, but anxiously waited for the rise of Dharmodgata from his deep meditation.

Dharmodgata finally awoke from his meditation. Sadāprarudita prepared the ground for his teacher's discourse by shedding his own blood, for he was again frustrated by the Evil One in his attempt to obtain water. But Śakra-devendra came to his assistance once more, and all the due decorations and offerings were supplied. Dhar-modgata then gave a further discourse on the identity of all things, and, therefore, of Prajñāpāramitā, in which there is neither birth nor death, being free from all sorts of logical predicates.

While listening to this profound discourse on the tran-scendental nature of Prajñāpāramitā, Sadāprarudita realized 6,000,000 Samādhis and came into the presence of the Buddhas numbering even more than the sands of the River Gangā, who, surrounded by a large assemblage of great Bhikshus, were discoursing on Prajñāpāramitā. After this the wisdom and learning of the Bodhisattva Sadā-prarudita was beyond the conceivability of an ordinary mortal; it was like a boundless expanse of ocean, and wherever he went he was never separated from the Buddhas.

# V

## Prayer and Nembutsu

The Christian method of awakening the religious feeling of passivity is prayer. 'When thou prayest, enter into thy closet, and when thou hast shut thy door, pray to thy Father which is in secret; and thy Father which seeth in secret shall reward thee openly.'[1] This is the example shown by the founder of Christianity on how to bring about the state of religious consciousness in which 'thy will' and not 'my will' is to prevail. And the author of the *Imitation of Christ* simply follows this when he says: 'If thou desirest true condition of heart, enter into thy secret chamber and shut out the tumults of the world, as it is written, "Commune with your own heart and in your chamber, and be still." In

[1] Matthew iv, 6, *et seq.*

thy chamber thou shalt find what abroad thou shalt too often lose.' (Book I, Chapter XX, 5.)

To retire into solitude and devote oneself to praying, if one is a Christian, or to meditating if one is a Buddhist, is one of the necessary conditions for all religious souls to gain access to the ultimate reality with which it is always seeking to be in communion.

The following story of three monks is taken from the Introduction to Rolle's *Amending of Life*, by H. L. Hubbard, in which each of them 'seeks to exercise his vocation in a different direction. One chose the part of peace-making between men, the second to visit the sick, and the third to dwell in quietness in the desert. The first two finding it impossible to fulfil their self-chosen tasks, went and re-counted their failures to the third. The latter suggested that each of them should fill a vessel with water and pour it into a basin. Then he bade them look into the basin immediately and tell him what they saw. They replied that they saw nothing. After the water had ceased to move he told them to look again. Then they told him that they could see their faces clearly reflected in the water. "So is it with you and me," said the hermit; "you who live in the world can see nothing because of the activities of men. I who dwell alone in peace and quietness can see both God and men."'

Evidently God does not cast his image on a body of disturbed water. To use Buddhist terminology, as long as *jiriki* (self-power) is trying to realize itself there is no room in one's soul for the *tariki* (other-power) of God to get into it, however intellectually this concept may be interpreted. A Catholic Father Tissot writes in his *Interior Life* that 'God wishes himself to be the life of my life, the soul of my soul, the all of my being, he wishes to glorify himself in me and to beautify me in himself'.[1] To effect this state of spirituality, 'my' mind must be like a mirror, freshly polished and with no stain of 'self-dust' on it, in which God reflects himself and 'I' see him then 'face to face'.

[1] Quoted from *The Life of Prayer*, by W. A. Brown, p. 157.

As regards the spiritual training of the mind so that it may finally experience passivity in the communion with God, Catholics seem to have a fuller literature than the Protestants. It is natural, seeing that the latter emphasize faith in the scheme of salvation more than any form of mental training. Catholics may tend towards formalism and ritualism, but their 'spiritual exercises' are psychologically quite an effective means to induce the state they contrive to bring about, as long as they have no intellectual difficulties in taking in all they teach. The mystical experiences which they consider to be special gifts of God require, no doubt, some such preliminary steps for the devotee, which are variously designated by them as 'preparation', 'purgation', 'consideration', 'meditation', or 'contemplation'.

In Buddhism, the Shin, like Protestantism, emphasizes faith, and as the result its followers have no special psychological method with which they attempt to strengthen the subjective force of faith, except attending religious discourses given by the preacher and being interviewed by him on doubtful points. It is true, however, that it is in Shin more than in any other school of Buddhism that the *tariki* (other-power) or passivity side of experience is most persistently insisted on. As far as their teaching goes Shin tells us not to put forward anything savouring of 'self' but just to listen to the teacher and accept him; that is, his message as transmitted onward from Śākyamuni, who was the first historically to get us acquainted with the original vow of Amida. The Shin is really a consistent passivity-religion.

The Jōdo, however, from which the Shin branched off as a special sect of the Pure Land school of Buddhism, has a way to prepare the mind for the final experience of what is known in Buddhism as *anjin* (*an*=peace, *jin* or *shin*=mind), that is, a restful state of mind, or 'interior quiet'. This is saying the Nembutsu; that is, reciting the name of Amida, Namu Amida Butsu (in Sanskrit, *namo 'mitābhāya*), 'Adoration to the Buddha of Infinite Light'. The formula or phrase is to be repeated in its Chinese form (*na-mo-o-mi-to-fu*) or in the Japanese (*na-mu-a-mi-da-bu-tsu*), and not in the original Sanskrit nor in any other translation. Some earnest devotees are reported to have repeated the phrase ten hundred thousand times a day; for instance, T'an-luan (476–542), Hōnen (1132–1212), etc.

The conscious object, of course, is to be embraced in the grace of Amida by repeatedly pronouncing his name, but psychologically it is to prepare the mind in such a way as to suspend all the surface activities of consciousness and to wake from its unconscious sources a power greater than the empirical ego. Theologically or metaphysically it may mean many things, but from the psychological point of view the Nembutsu is like a certain kind of prayer,[1] an attempt to tap new life for the mind that has reached as it were the end of its rope. The Nembutsu is thus meant to exhaust the power of a finite mind which, when it comes to this pass or *impasse*, throws itself down at the feet of something it knows not exactly what, except that the something is an infinite reality.

[1] Prayer is divided, according to the author of *Des Grâces d'Oraison*, into two categories, ordinary and extraordinary or mystic. Ordinary prayer may be called natural against the mystic which is supernatural, for the Catholic theologians retain the word mystic for what they designate as supernatural states of prayer, which are absolutely impossible to be realized by the human will alone. Psychologically, no doubt the 'supernatural' is the continuation of the 'natural', but from the theological point of view the Catholics would naturally desire to reserve a special room for the 'supernatural'. Ordinary prayer is regarded as having four degrees: 1. Vocal prayer which is a recitation; 2. Meditation where there is a chain of distinct reflections or arguments; 3. Affective prayer in which affections are made predominant; and 4. The prayer of simplicity where intuition replaces reasoning, and affections are not varied and are expressed in few words. The Nembutsu is, to use Catholic terminology, sometimes vocal prayer, sometimes the prayer of simplicity, and sometimes even mystic prayer when the devotee is embraced in the original vow of Amida. The character of the Nembutsu varies according to the individuality of the devotee and also to his mental attitude at the time.

## The Practice of Zazen and Passivity

In Zen there is apparently no passivity traceable. As it claims, it is the strong 'self-power' wing of Eastern Mahāyāna Buddhism, and besides it is intellectual in the sense that it puts its whole stress on the intuitive apprehension of the truth. It is almost a kind of philosophy. But as far as psychology is concerned, the Zen consciousness cannot be different from other religious consciousnesses; the way it works in our empirical mind is the same as in other religious experiences. Whatever metaphysical interpretations and contents we may give to its experience, there is a certain feeling of passivity in it. To go beyond the realm of limited intellection is not to use the strength of the intellect itself; it comes from something more than that, and as long as there is something transcending the mind, and yet its working is manifested in and through the mind, the latter must play the role of passivism; there is no other choice for it.

The consciousness of 'self-power' (*jiriki*) may be too prominent in the Zen mind, but this cannot overrule the principle of the experience by which alone the mind is made to realize what is beyond itself. 'Passively active' or 'actively passive'—the choice of one term or the other depends upon the individual psychology more than upon the fact itself, for the fact always lends itself to alternative interpretations. To understand the position of Zen in this matter we must have the knowledge of its practice of Dhyāna[1] or Zazen,[2] as it is called in China and Japan. Zen does not exactly coincide with Indian Dhyāna, though *zen* is an abbreviation of *zenna*,[3] which is in turn the transliteration of

---

[1] *Dhyāna* is generally translated as meditation, but it is really the practice of mental concentration, in which the reasoning process of the intellect is cut short and consciousness is kept clean of all other ideas except the one which is given as the subject of meditation.

[2] *Tso ch'an.* For explanation see the First Series of *Zen Essays*, p. 318, footnote.

[3] *Ch'an na.*

the Sanskrit *dhyāna*; in practice, however, the same bodily posture is assumed. The following directions[1] given by a Zen master may throw light on what Zen proposes to do.

'The Bodhisattva who disciplines himself in Prajñā should first of all awaken a great compassionate heart, make great universal vows, and thoroughly be versed in all Samādhis, in order to deliver all beings; for the Bodhisattva does not seek emancipation for his own benefit. Let him renounce all external relations and put a stop to all worldly doings, so that his mind and body becoming one they can be kept, moving or sitting, in perfect harmony with each other. His food should be regulated, neither too much nor too little; and his sleep also should be moderate, neither too long nor too short.

'When he wishes to practise meditation, let him retire into a quiet room where he prepares a thick well-wadded cushion for his seat, with his dress and belt loosely adjusted about his body. He then assumes his proper formal posture. He will sit with his legs fully crossed, that is, place the right foot over the left thigh and the left foot over the right thigh. Sometimes the half-cross-legged posture is permitted, in which case simply let the left leg rest over the right thigh. Next, he will place the right hand over the left leg with its palm up and over this have the left hand, while the thumbs press against each other over the palm.

'He now raises the whole body slowly and quietly, moves it repeatedly to the left and to the right, backward and forward, until the proper seat and straight posture are obtained. He will take care not to lean too much to one side,

[1] The author of these 'Directions' is not known, but they are generally regarded as coming originally from the 'Regulations of the Meditation Hall' compiled by Pai-chang (720–814), the founder of the Zen monastery in China. The original 'Regulations' were lost with the downfall of the T'ang dynasty; they were compiled again by Tsung-I, 1103, in the Sung. The work now known as *Pai-chang Ching-kuei* is a modern compilation in the year 1265 under the auspices of the Emperor Tai-tsu of Yüan. The present 'Directions' are found in these works. The reference to Yüan-t'ung of Fa-yün in them shows that they contain some insertions of Tsung-I himself because Yüan-t'ung was his own master.

either left or right, forward or backward; his spinal column stands erect with the head, shoulders, back, and loins each properly supporting others like a chaitya. But he is cautious not to sit too upright or rigidly, for he will then feel uneasy before long. The main thing is to have the ears and shoulders, nose and navel stand to each other in one vertical plane, while the tongue rests against the upper palate and the lips and teeth are firmly closed. Let the eyes be slightly opened in order to avoid falling asleep.

'When meditation advances the wisdom of this practice will grow apparent. Great masters of meditation from of old have their eyes kept open. Yüan-t'ung, the Zen master of Fa-yün, has also had a strong opinion against the habit of closing the eyes, and called such practisers "dwellers of the skeleton cave in the dark valley". There is a deep sense in this, which is well understood by those who know. When the position is steadied and the breathing regular, the practiser will now assume a somewhat relaxed attitude. Let him not be concerned with ideas good or bad. When a thought is awakened there is awareness; when there is awareness, the point is missed. When the exercise is kept up steadily and for a sufficient length of time, disturbing thoughts will naturally cease and there will prevail a state of oneness. This is the technique of practising meditation.

'Meditation is the road leading to peace and happiness. The reason why there are so many people who grow ill is because they do not know how to prepare themselves duly for the exercise. If they well understand the directions as given above, they will without straining themselves too much acquire not only the lightness of the body but the briskness of spirit, which finally brings about the clarification of the consciousness. The understanding of the Dharma will nourish the spirit and make the practiser enjoy the pure bliss of tranquillity.

'If he has already a realization within himself, his practice of meditation will be like a dragon getting into water, or a tiger crouching against a hillside. In case he has yet nothing of self-realization, the practice will be like fanning up the fire with the wind; not much effort is needed [he will soon get enlightened]. Only let him not too easily be deceived as to what he may regard as self-realization.

'When there is an enhanced spiritual quality, there is much susceptibility to the Evil One's temptation, which comes in every possible form both agreeable and disagreeable. Therefore the practiser must have his consciousness rightly adjusted and well in balance; then nothing will prevent his advancement in meditation. Concerning various mental aberrations worked out by the Evil One, a detailed treatment is given in *The Lêng-yen Sûtra*,[1] the *T'ien-tai Chih Kwan*, and Keui-fêng's *Book on Practice and Realisation*. Those who wish to prepare themselves against untoward events, should be well informed of the matter.

'When the practiser wants to rise from meditation, let him slowly and gently shake his body and quietly rise from the seat; never let him attempt to rise suddenly. After the rising let him always contrive to retain whatever mental power he has gained by meditation, as if he were watching over a baby; for this will help him in maturing the power of concentration.

'[In the study of Buddhism], the practice of meditation comes foremost. When the mind is not sufficiently brought under control no tranquillity obtains in it, and the practiser will be at a loss how to cope with a critical moment that may arise. When looking for a gem the water must not be disturbed; the waves make it difficult to get hold of the gem. Let the waters of meditation be clear and undisturbed, and the spiritual gem will all by itself shine forth. Therefore we read in the *Sûtra of Perfect Enlightenment*[2] that "Prajñā pure and flawless is produced by means of meditation"; in the *Sûtra of the Lotus of the Good Law*[3] that "Retire into a solitary place and have your mind under full discipline, and let it be as steady and immovable as Mount Sumeru".

'We thus know that the sure way to realize saintliness

---

[1] (*Śūraṅgama*), fas. VIII.
[2] Fas. II.
[3] Fas. V, of Kumārajīva's version.

which goes beyond worldly trivialities is attained by means of a quiet life. It is all through the power of concentration, indeed, that some of the old masters have passed away into eternity even while sitting cross-legged or standing upright. There are many chances of interruption and failure even when one is devoting one's life [to the realization of the truth]; how much more if illness gains the hold of you! How can you resist the assault of Karma? So says an ancient teacher. "If you have not acquired the power of concentration strong enough to destroy the camp of Death, you will have to come back [to this world] with your eyes blindfolded and with nothing achieved. Your life will thus be utterly wasted."

'Good friends of Zen, be pleased to read these words repeatedly, and whatever benefit that accrues [from the practice of meditation] will be not only yours but others', too, for you will thus all finally attain enlightenment.'

## The Function of Koan in Zen

When it is said that Buddhism, Mahāyāna as well as Hīnayāna, is rich in the intellectual element, it does not mean that Buddhism lays its principal stress on logic or philosophy in the unfoldment of religious consciousness, but that it upholds an intuitive understanding of ultimate religious truth rather than a merely faithful acceptance of the teaching of its founder. And as the most efficient means to come to this intuitive understanding it teaches the practice of meditation known as Dhyāna or Zazen. The direction given above is thus followed by all Buddhists, Indian, Tibetan, Chinese, and Japanese, except the adherents of the Pure Land school of Buddhism. For they believe that the understanding grows by itself from within when the practice of Zazen is brought to perfection. As is stated, Prajñā reflects itself on the serene undisturbed water of Dhyāna.

When, however, in the history of Zen the system of koan

came to be in vogue, meditation so-called was pushed behind in order to bring the intuition more to the foreground. Tai-hui[1] boldly declares, 'Others give priority to Dhyāna rather than to intuition (*prajñā*) but I give priority to intuition rather than to Dhyāna.' He was one of the strong advocates of the koan exercise in China in opposition to his great contemporary Hung-chih.[2] As I have already explained in my previous Essay as well as in the First Series, the koan students of Zen are almost violently aggressive in their attitude towards the realization of the passivity phase of the religious experience:[3]

No signs of passivity seem to be noticeable in their exercise, but what is aimed at here is intellectual passivity and not the emotional one which comes out in view so much in Christian mystics and also in the followers of the Pure Land school of Buddhism. The method of the koan exercise, however, on the other hand, is to blot out by sheer force of the will all the discursive traces of intellection whereby students of Zen prepare their consciousness to be the proper ground for intuitive knowledge to burst out. They march through a forest of ideas thickly crowding up into their minds; and when, thoroughly exhausted in their struggles, they give themselves up, the state of consciousness, psychologically viewed, after which they have so earnestly but rather blindly been seeking, unexpectedly prevails.

This last giving-up is what I would term a state of passivity in our religious experience. Without this giving-up, whether intellectually or conatively or emotionally, or in whatever way we may designate this psychological process, there is generally no experience of a final reality. Let me give here some quotations from a book known as

[1] 1089–1163.

[2] 1091–1157.

[3] For example, Torei, one of the chief disciples of Hakuin, writes in his edition (1762) of the *Ch'an-kuan t'sê-chin*, 'The lion refuses to eat the meat left by the eagle, and the tiger will not feed upon dead animals,' referring to the Zen Yogin's proud spirit which would not subscribe to the mawkish femininity of the 'other-power' teaching.

*Zenkwan Sakushin*,[1] which may be freely translated 'The Breaking Through the Frontier Gate of Zen', and which is very much read by Zen students as a most energizing stimulant to their wearied nerves.

'Have the two characters "birth" and "death" pasted on your forehead until you get an understanding into their meaning; for the Lord of Death will surely demand of you a strict account of your life when you have to appear before him. Don't say then, "I have never been reminded of this!"

'When you apply yourself to the study of Zen, what is necessary is to examine yourself from moment to moment and to keep the subject (*koan*) always before your mental eye, so that you can see by yourself when you have gained strength and when not, and also where your concentration is needed more and where not.

'There are some who begin to doze as soon as they are on the cushion, or allow all kinds of rambling thoughts to disturb them if they are at all wakeful; and when they are down from the cushion their tongues are at once set loose. If they try to master Zen in this fashion they would never succeed even if they are alive unto the day of Maitreya. Therefore you should, exerting all your energy, take up your subject (*koan*) and endeavour to get settled with it; you should never relax yourself day and night. Then you are not merely sitting quietly or vacantly as if you were a corpse. If you find yourself in a maze of confusing thoughts and unable to extricate yourself in spite of your efforts, drop them lightly, and coming down from the seat, quickly run across the floor once, and then resume your position on the cushion. Have your eyes open, hold your hands clasped, and keeping your backbone straight up, apply yourself as before to the koan, when you will feel greatly refreshed. It will be like pouring one dipperful of cold water into a boiling cauldron. If you go on thus exercising yourself, you will surely reach the destination.'[2]

[1] *Ch'an-kuan t'sê-chin*, compiled by Chu-hung, 1531–1615.
[2] This is the admonition given by Fa-yen of Wu-tsu Shan to one of his disciples about to start on his Zen pilgrimage.

Another Zen master[1] advises thus: 'Some masters there are these days who in spite of their eyes not being clearly opened teach people to remain satisfied with mere empty-mindedness;[2] then there are others who teach people to accept things blindly as they are and contemplate on them as such; there are still others who advise people not to pay any attention to anything at all. These are all one-sided views of Zen, their course of exercise is altogether on the wrong track, it will never come to a definite termination. The main idea in the study of Zen is to concentrate your mind on one point; when this is done everybody will get it; that is, when thus the proper time comes and conditions are fully matured, realization will come by itself all of a sudden like a flash of lightning.

'Let your everyday worldly consciousness be directed towards Prajñā, and then you will avoid coming under the control of your past evil Karma at the moment of death even if you may not attain to realization while in this life. In your next birth you will surely be in the midst of Prajñā itself and enjoy its full realization; this is a certainty, you need not cherish any doubt about it.

'Only let your mind have a good hold of the koan without interruption. If any disturbing thoughts assail you, do not necessarily try to suppress them too vigorously; rather try to keep your attention on the koan itself. Whether walking or sitting, apply yourself surely and steadily on it, give no time to relaxation. When your application goes on thus constantly a period of indifference [literally, tasteless-ness] will set in. This is good, do not let go, but keep on and the mental flower will abruptly come to full bloom; the light illuminating the ten quarters will manifest the land

[1] From a letter of Tsung-kao Tai-hui.

[2] It may not be inopportune to call the reader's special attention to this repudiation by Tai-hui of 'mere emptiness'. Zen has been frequently criticized, not only by the outsiders but by some Buddhists, for teaching the doctrine of blank nothingness or a state of absolute passivity, which effaces all the traces of voluntarism in every possible form. That this is the 'spirit of inquiry' was discussed in connection with the 'Koan Exercise'. When this spirit is absent, a wrong form of passivity may be cherished by Yogins of Zen.

of the treasure-lord on the tip of a single hair; you will then be revolving the great wheel of the Dharma even when you are sitting in the midst of an atom.'

This Zen exercise, full of arduousness and strenuousness, with which the task of self-inspection is carried on, seems to be the very reverse of passivity. But we must remember that passivity never comes by itself, nor is it to be confounded with a mere apathetic, indolent state of mind, which is no less than vegetation. Passivity in its highest religious connotation means breaking up the hard crust of egotism or relativism and melting itself in the infinity of the Dharmadhātu. This melting is felt psychologically as a mood of receptivity, and, theologically interpreted, as the feeling of absolute dependence, which is what I have designated in this Essay as passivity.

With followers of Zen this is 'being wholly possessed by Prajñā', or 'realizing Prajñā'. The Mahāyāna sūtras are generally dedicated not only to the Buddhas and Bodhisattvas but to Prajñāpāramitā, which is remarkable. In all the Zen hymnals reference is always made to 'Mahāprajñāpāramitā' as if it were a personality like the Buddhas and Bodhisattvas of the past, present, and future. Further, Prajñā is compared to a great perfect mirror in which is reflected a world of multiplicities just as they are, *yathābhūtam*. This is the perfect mirror of passivity, to use the terminology adopted here. What follows, I hope, will make this point clearer.[1]

VI

*The Perfection of Passivity in Buddhist Life*

When the religious experience just described is matured, i.e. when it accompanies moral perfection, Buddhists will

---

[1] See also the Appendices to this Essay in which translations are given from a Zen master and a Jōdo teacher.

finally acquire what is technically known as *anābhogacaryā*,[1] and theirs will also be its wonderful achievements as most elaborately detailed in the *Daśabhūmika Sūtra* where they are said to take place in the life of a Bodhisattva, the ideal being of Mahāyāna Buddhism. We can say that the effortless life is the perfection of passivism.

According to the *Daśabhūmika Sūtra*, the effortless life is attained when a Bodhisattva passes from the seventh to the eighth stage of spiritual life by realizing what is known as the 'acceptance of all things as unborn' (*anutpattikadharmakṣānti*).[2] To quote the Sūtra:[3]

'The Bodhisattva Vajragarbha said, O son of the Buddha, when the Bodhisattva, while at the seventh stage, has thoroughly finished examining what is meant by cleansing the paths with transcendental wisdom and skilful means (*prajñopāya*), has accumulated all the preparatory material (*sambhāra*), has well equipped himself with the vows, and is sustained by the power of the Tathāgatas, procuring in himself the power produced from the stock of merit, attentively thinking of and in conformity with the powers, convictions, and unique characteristics of the Tathāgatas, thoroughly purified, sincere in heart, and thoughtful, elevated in virtue, knowledge and power, great in pity and compassion which leaves no sentient beings unnoticed, and in pursuit of the path of wisdom, that is beyond measurement; and, further, when he enters, truly as it is, upon the knowledge that all things are, in their nature, from the first, unborn (*anutpanna*), unproduced (*ajāta*), devoid of individualizing marks (*alakshaṇa*), have never been combined (*asambhūta*), are never dissolved (*avināśita*), nor extinguished (*anishṭhita*), nor changing (*apravṛitti*), nor

---

[1] For the explanation of this important idea, see my *Zen Essays*, I, pp. 78 *fn.*, 93; *Studies in the Laṅkāvatāra Sūtra*, pp. 43, 378; *The Laṅkāvatāra-Sūtra*, p. 78; etc.

[2] This is one of the Mahāyāna terms quite frequently misinterpreted by Buddhist scholars of the West. The point is that they fail to grasp the central conception of the Mahāyāna according to which all things (*sarvadharma*) are unborn (*anutpanna*), unattainable (*anupalabdha*), and therefore empty (*śūnya*).

[3] Edited by Radher, p. 63 *et seq.*

ceasing (*anabhinivṛitti*), and are lacking in self-substance (*abhāvasvabhāva*); when he enters upon the knowledge that all things remain the same in the beginning, in the middle, and in the end, are of suchness, non-discriminative, and entering into the knowledge of the all-knowing one; [and finally] when he thus enters upon the knowledge of all things as they really are; he is then completely emancipated from such individualizing ideas as are created by the mind (*citta*) and its agent (*manovijñāna*); he is then as detached as the sky, and descends upon all objects as if upon an empty space; he is then said to have attained to the acceptance of all things as unborn (*anutpattika-dharma-kṣānti*).

'O son of the Buddha, as soon as a Bodhisattva attains this acceptance, he enters upon the eighth stage called immovable (*acalā*). This is the inner abode of Bodhisattvahood, which is difficult to comprehend, which goes beyond discrimination, separated from all forms, all ideas, and all attachments; which transcends calculation and limitation, as it lies outside [the knowledge of] the Śrāvakas and Pratyekabuddhas and above all disturbances and ever in possession of tranquillity.

'As a Bhikshu, furnished with supernatural faculties and freedom of mind and gradually entering into the Samādhi of Cessation, has all his mental disturbances quieted and is free from discrimination, so the Bodhisattva now abides in the stage of immovability, that is, detached from all works of effort (*ābhoga*); he attained effortlessness, has put an end to strivings mental, verbal, and physical, and is beyond discrimination as he has put away all forms of vexation; he is now established in the Dharma itself which he enjoys as the fruit of his past work.

'It is like a man who, in a dream finding himself in a great river, attempts to go to the other side; he musters all his energy and strives hard with every possible means. And because of this effort and contrivance, he wakes from the dream, and being thus awakened all his strivings are set at rest. In like manner the Bodhisattva sees all beings drowning themselves in the four streams, and in his attempt to save them, exerts himself vigorously, unflinchingly; and because of his vigorous and unflinching exertion he attains the stage of immovability. Once in this stage, all his strivings are dropped, he is relieved of all activity that issues from the notion of duality or from an attachment to appearance.

'O son of the Buddha, as when one is born in the Brahman world, no tormenting passions present themselves in his mind; so when the Bodhisattva comes to abide in the stage of immovability, his mind is entirely relieved of all effortful activitities which grow out of a contriving consciousness. In the mind of this Bodhisattva there is indeed no conscious discrimination of a Bodhisattva, or a Buddha, or enlightenment, or Nirvāṇa; how much less the thought of things worldly.

'O son of the Buddha, on account of his original vows the Bodhisattva sees all the Buddhas, the Blessed ones personally presenting themselves before him in order to confer upon him the wisdom of Tathāgatahood whereby he is enabled to get into the stream of the Dharma. They would then declare: "Well done, well done, O son of a good family, this is the Kṣānti (acceptance) of the first order which is in accordance with the teaching of the Buddhas. But, O son of a good family, thou hast not yet acquired the ten powers, the fourfold fearlessness, and the eighteen special qualities possessed by all the Buddhas. Thou shouldst yet work for the acquirement of these qualities, and never let go thy hold of this Kṣānti.

' "O son of a good family, though thou art established in serenity and emancipation, there are ignorant beings who have not yet attained serenity, but are being harassed by evil passions and aggrieved by varieties of speculation. On such ones thou shouldst show thy compassion. O son of a good family, mindful of thy original vows, thou shouldst benefit all beings and have them all turn towards inconceivable wisdom.

' "O son of a good family, the ultimate essence of all things is eternally such as it is, whether or not Tathāgatas have come to appear; they are called Tathāgatas not because of their realization of this ultimate essence of things; for all the Śrāvakas and Pratyekabuddhas, too, have indeed realized this essence of non-discrimination. Again, O son of a good family, thou shouldst look up to our body, knowledge, Buddhaland, halo of illumination, skilful means, and voice of purity, each of which is beyond measurement; and with these mayest thou too be completely equipped.

' "Again, O son of a good family, thou hast now one light, it is the light that sees into the real nature of all things as unborn and beyond discrimination. But the light of truth possessed by the Tathāgatas is as regards its infinite mobility, activity, and manifestation, beyond all measurement, calculation, comparison, and proportion. Thou shouldst raise thy intention towards it in order to realize it.

' "O son of a good family, observing how boundlessly the lands extend, how numberless beings are, and how infinitely divided things are, thou shouldst know them all truthfully as they are."

'In this manner, O son of the Buddha, all Buddhas bestow upon the Bodhisattva who has come up to this stage of immovability infinitude of knowledge and make him turn towards knowledge of differentiation and work issuing therefrom, both of which are beyond measurement.

'O son of the Buddha, if the Buddhas did not awake in this Bodhisattva a desire for the knowledge of the all-knowing one, he would have passed into Parinirvāṇa abandoning all the work that will benefit beings. As he was, however, given by the Buddhas infinitude of knowledge and work issuing therefrom, his knowledge and work that is carried on even for a space of one moment surpasses all the achievements that have been accomplished since his first awakening of the desire for enlightenment till his attainment of the seventh stage; the latter is not comparable even to one-hundredth part of the former, nor indeed even to one immeasurably infinitesimal part of it; no comparision whatever is possible between the two. For what reason?

'Because, O son of the Buddha, the Bodhisattva who has now gained this eighth stage after starting first with his one body in his course of spiritual discipline, is now provided with infinite bodies, infinite voices, infinite knowledge, infinite birth, and infinite pure lands; and has also brought infinite beings into maturity, made offerings to infinite Buddhas, comprehended infinite teachings of the Buddhas; is furnished with infinite supernatural powers, attends infinite assemblages and sessions; and, by means of infinite bodies, speeches, thoughts, and deeds, acquires perfect understanding of everything concerning the life of the Bodhisattva, because of his attainment of immovability.

'O son of the Buddha, it is like a man going into the great ocean in a boat; before he gets into the high sea he labours hard, but as soon as his boat is pulled out to sea he can leave it to the wind, and no further efforts are required of him. When he is thus at sea, what he can accomplish in one day would easily surpass what is done even after one hundred years' exertion in the shallows.

'In like manner, O son of the Buddha, when the Bodhisattva, accumulating a great stock of meritorious deeds and riding in the Mahāyāna boat gets into the ocean of the life of a Bodhisattva, he enters in one moment and with effortless knowledge into the realm of knowledge gained by the omniscient. As long as he was dependent upon his previous achievements which were characterized with purposefulness (*sābhogakarma*), he could not expect to accomplish it even after the elapsing of innumerable kalpas. . . .'[1]

When the assertion is made that what has been described in the *Daśabhūmika Sūtra* somewhat diffusely is the Buddhist life of passivity, we may think it to be very different from

[1] Rather freely done, for a literal translation would be to most readers quite unintelligible. The text goes on still further into details of the life of the Bodhisattva at the eighth stage of immovability. But the above may be sufficient to show what the spirituality of the Bodhisattva is like when he realizes a life of effortless activities.

what is ordinarily, and especially in the Christian sense, understood to be passive or God-intoxicated or wholly resigned to 'thy will' or to Tariki, other-power. But the fact is that Buddhism is highly tinged with intellectualism as is seen in the so frequent use of the term 'knowledge' (*jñāna* or *prajñā*), though it does not mean knowledge in its relative sense but in its intuitive, supra-intellectual sense. Even in the Pure Land school of Buddhism, where the sentiment-aspect of the religious life is very much in evidence, the giving-up of the self to the unfathomable wisdom (*acintya-jñāna*) of the Tathāgata goes on hand in hand with the trust in the all-embracing love of Amitābha. Indeed, the final aim of the Shin followers is to attain supreme enlightenment as much as any other Buddhists, though the former's ambition is to do it in the Land of Purity presided over personally by Amitābha Buddha, and in order to be permitted to his Land they put themselves unconditionally under his loving guardianship.

As a matter of fact, the two sides of the religious experience, sentiment and intellect, are found commingled in the heart of the Shin devotee. The consciousness of sin is its sentimental aspect while the seeking after enlightenment is its intellectual aspect. While passivism is more strongly visible in the sentiment, it is not altogether missing in the Buddhist intellect either, as when the intellect is compelled to abandon its logical reasonings in order to experience the supreme enlightenment attained by the Buddha, or the life of the Bodhisattva which is purposeless, effortless, and above teleological strivings.

To show the difference between the Christian and the Buddhist point of view concerning the fundamental notion of passivism, whereby followers of the respective religions attempt to explain the experience, I quote a suggestive passage from *Theologia Germanica*,[1] which stands in close relation to the Buddhist sentiment and yet misses the central point of it.

'Dost thou say now: "Then there was a Wherefore in

[1] Translated by Susanna Winkworth, 1901, p. 96.

Christ"? I answer: "If you wert to ask the sun, Why shinest thou? he would say, 'I must shine and cannot do otherwise, for it is my nature and property, and the light I give is not of myself, and I do not call it mine.' So likewise is it with God and Christ and all who are godly and belong unto God. In them is no willing, nor working nor desiring but has for its end goodness as goodness, for the sake of goodness, and they have no other Wherefore than this." '

With this the Buddhists are in sympathy, no doubt, but 'goodness' is too Christian, and besides does not touch the ultimate ground of all things which is 'Emptiness'. Sings P'ang,[1] therefore, in the following rhythm:

'Old P'ang requires nothing in the world:
All is empty with him, even a seat he has not,
For absolute Emptiness reigns in his household;
How empty indeed it is with no treasures!
When the sun is risen, he walks through Emptiness,
When the sun sets, he sleeps in Emptiness;
Sitting in Emptiness he sings his empty songs,
And his empty songs reverberate through Emptiness:
Be not surprised at Emptiness so thoroughly empty,
For Emptiness is the seat of all the Buddhas;
And Emptiness is not understood by men of the world,
But Emptiness is the real treasure:
If you say there's no Emptiness,
You commit grave offence against the Buddhas.'

### Emptiness and the Zen Life

'Emptiness' (*śūnyatā*) is the gospel of the *Prajñāpāramitā-sūtra* and also the fountain-head of all the Mahāyāna philosophies and practical disciplines. It is indeed owing to this Emptiness as the ground of existence that this universe is at all possible with its logic, ethics, philosophy, and religion. Emptiness does not mean relativity as is sometimes interpreted by Buddhist scholars; it goes beyond

---

[1] Who flourished in the Yüan-ho period (806–821) and thereabout, and was a younger contemporary of Ma-tsu.

that, it is what makes relativity possible; Emptiness is an intuitive truth whereby we can describe existence as related and multifarious. And the Buddhist life of passivity grows out of this intuition which is called Prajñāpāramitā in the *Prajñāpāramitā-sūtra* and Pratyātmāryajñāna in the *Laṅkāvatāra-sūtra*. The intuition is enlightenment as the culmination of Buddhist discipline and as the beginning of the life of a Bodhisattva. Therefore, we read in the *Vimala-kīrtinirdeśa-sūtra* that all things are established in 'non-abiding', which is Emptiness, *apratishṭhiti=śūnyatā*, and in the *Vajracchedikā-sūtra* that *na kvacit pratishṭhitam cittam utpādayitavyam*, 'thoughts should be awakened without abiding anywhere.'

When a thing is established (*pratishṭhita*), there is something fixed, definitely settled, and this determination is the beginning at once of order and confusion. If God is the ultimate ground of all things, he must be Emptiness itself.[1] When he is at all determined in either way good or bad, straight or crooked, pure or impure, he submits himself to the principle of relativity; that is, he ceases to be God, but a

---

[1] To quote further from the *Theologia Germanica* (p. 184): 'For God is One and must be One, and God is All and must be All. And now what is, and is not One, is not God; and what is, and is not All and above All, is also not God, for God is One and above One, and All and above All. . . . And a man cannot find all satisfaction in God, unless all things are One to him, and One is All, and something and nothing are alike. But where it should be thus, there would be true satisfaction, and not else.' This is fine, indeed, but why stop short with God? If God is 'One and above One, All and above All', is this not Emptiness? God himself must be lodged in it. When we stop at God and refuse to go further, God himself loses his abode, he cannot stay even where he is placed. He is either to go with All or altogether part company with All, he cannot be 'All and above All' as the theologians would like to have him, for he thus murders him. To save God from this perplexity he must be placed in Emptiness where he can be 'All and above All'. If he is placed anywhere else, he is no more himself, and the 'true satisfaction' so fervently sought after by the Christians will no longer be obtainable. Inasmuch as Buddhist scholars fail to penetrate into the true signification of Śūnyatā and are contented with interpreting it as relativity or mere nothingness, they can never expect to understand the Mahāyāna. Again, it is only possible in Emptiness to see 'something and nothing alike'. 'Something' here is Buddhist *asti* and 'nothing' *nāsti*, and true Prajñā obtains only when the dualism of being and non-being is transcended. There is no doubt that in these respects Buddhist philosophy and experience go deeper.

god who is like ourselves mortal and suffers. 'To be established nowhere' thus means 'to be empty', 'to be un-
attached', 'to be perfectly passive', 'to be altogether given
up to other-power', etc.

This Buddhist or Zen life of Emptiness may be illustrated
in three ways, each of which has its own signification as it
depicts a particular aspect of the life.

1. When Subhūti was sitting quietly in a cave, the gods
praised him by showering celestial flowers. Said Subhūti,
'Who are you that shower flowers from the sky?'

'We are the gods whose chief is Śakradevendra.'

'What are you praising?'

'We praise your discourse on Prajñāpāramitā.'

'I have never uttered a word in the discourse of Prajñāpāramitā, and there is nothing for you to praise.'

But the gods asserted, 'You have not discoursed on anything, and we have not listened to anything; nothing discoursed, nothing heard indeed, and this is true Prajñāpāramitā.' So saying they shook the earth again and
showered more flowers.

To this Hsüeh-tou attaches his poem:

'The rain is over, the clouds are frozen, and day is about to
        break;
A few mountains, picture-like, make their appearance;
        how blue, how imposing!
Subhūti, knowing nothing, in the rock-cave quietly sits;
Lo, the heavenly flowers are pouring like rain with the earth
        shaking!'

This poem graphically depicts the inner life of Emptiness,
from which one can see readily that Emptiness is not
relativity, nor nothingness. In spite of, or rather because of,
Subhūti's 'knowing nothing', there is a shower of celestial
flowers, there tower the mountains huge and rugged, and
they are all like a painting beautiful to look at and enjoy-
able to all who understand.

2. While Vimalakīrti was discoursing with Mañjuśrī
and others, there was a heavenly maiden in the room who

was intently listening to all that was going on among them. She now assumed her original form as a goddess and showered heavenly flowers over all the saintly figures assembled there. The flowers that fell on the Bodhisattvas did not stick to them, but those on the Śrāvakas adhered and could not be shaken off though they tried to do so. The heavenly maiden asked Śāriputra, one of the foremost Śrāvakas in the group and well known for his dialectic ability:

'Why do you want to brush off the flowers?'

'They are not in accordance with the Dharma, hence my brushing,' replied Śāriputra.

'O Śāriputra,' said the maiden, 'think not that the flowers are not in accordance with the Dharma. Why? Because they do not discriminate and it is yourself that does the discriminating. Those who lead the ascetic life after the teaching of the Buddha commit an unlawful deed by giving themselves up to discrimination. Such must abandon discrimination whereby their life will be in accord with the Dharma.

'Look at those Bodhisattvas, no flowers touch them, for they are above all thoughts of discrimination. It is a timid person that affords a chance for an evil spirit to take hold of him. So with the Śrāvakas, as they dread the cycle of birth and death they fall a prey to the senses. Those who have gone beyond fears and worries, are not bound by the five desires. The flowers stick where there is yet no loosening of the knots, but they fall away when the loosening is complete.' (That is to say, when Emptiness is realized by us, nothing can take hold of us, neither the flower nor dirt has a point to which it can attach itself.)

The life of Emptiness, thus we can see, is that of non-discrimination, where the sun is allowed to rise on the evil and on the good, and rain is sent on the just and on the unjust. Discrimination is meant for a world of particulars where our relative individual lives are passed, but when we wish to abide beyond it, where real peace obtains, we have to shake off all the dust of relativity and discrimination, which has been clinging to us and tormented us so long.

Emptiness ought not to frighten us, as is repeatedly given warning in the *Prajñāpāramitā-sūtra*.

'When all is done and said,
  In the end thus shall you find:
  He most of all doth bathe in bliss
  That hath a quiet mind.'[1]

Where to find this quiet mind is the great religious problem, and the most decided Mahāyāna Buddhist answer is 'In Emptiness'.

3. According to the *Transmission of the Lamp* by Tao-yüan, it is recorded that before Fa-yung[2] interviewed Tao-hsin, the fourth patriarch of Zen in China, birds used to visit him in a rock-cave where he meditated and offered flowers. Though history remains silent, tradition developed later to the effect that Fa-yung after the interview no more received flower-offerings from his flying admirers of the air. Now a Zen master asks, 'Why were there flower-offerings to Fa-yung before his interview with the fourth patriarch? and why not after?' Fa-yung was a great student of the Prajñāpāramitā, that is, of the doctrine of Emptiness. Did the birds offer him flowers because he was holy, so empty-minded? But after the interview he lost his holiness for some reason, and did the birds cease to revere him? Is holiness or saintliness the same as Emptiness? Is there still anything to be called holy in Emptiness? When Emptiness is thoroughly realized, does not even holiness or godliness or anything else disappear? Is this not a state of shadowlessness (*anābhāsa*)?

Fa-yen of Wu-tsu Shan was asked this question, 'Why were there the flower-offerings to Fa-yung before the interview?'

'We all admire the rich and noble,' answered the master.

'Why did the offerings cease after the interview?'

'We all dislike the poor and humble.'

Does Wu-tsu mean that Fa-yung was rich before the

[1] Lord Vaux Thomas, 1510–1566.
[2] 594–657. This interview is told in the First Series of my *Zen Essays*, pp. 202–203. See also p. 226 of the present Series.

interview and therefore liked by all beings belonging to this world, but that, growing poor and empty after the interview, he was no more honoured by anything on earth?

Tao-ch'ien, who was a disciple of Wên-i,[1] however, gave one and the same answer to this double question.

'Why the flower-offerings to Fa-yung before the interview?'

'Niu-t'ou.'

'Why the cessation of the offering afterwards?'

'Niu-t'ou.'

Niu-t'ou is the name of the mountain where Fa-yung used to retire and meditate. Does this mean that Fa-yung is the same old hermit-monk no matter what experience he goes through? Does he mean that the ultimate ground of all things remains the same, remains empty for ever, whether or not diversity and multiplicity characterize its appearances? How Zen wants us to look for a life of passivity or that of Emptiness, as it is lived by the Buddhist, will be gleaned from the statements of Subhūti and the heavenly maiden and from the remarks on the flower-offering to Fa-yung.[2]

---

[1] 885–958.

[2] To give two or three more Zen remarks about the Fa-yung and Tao-hsin interview:

A monk asked Tê-shan Mi, 'What would you say about Niu-t'ou before he saw the fourth patriarch?'

'When the autumn comes, the leaves turn yellow and fall.'

'What about him after he saw.'

'When the spring comes, the meadows are green.'

T'ien-chu Shan to the first question, 'A lonely hamlet far away from human habitations; a remote mountain rarely frequented by friendly visitors.'

To the second, 'The autumn breeze is rustling through the pine groves along the mountain path; the full moon, bright and serene, shines all night long into the painted hall.'

Hsiang-t'ien Ch'ing to the first, 'Vinegar invites flies.'

To the second, 'The house is deserted, and there is not a shadow of a living being.'

Pao-fêng Ch'ing to the first, 'He is another plebeian.' (Literally, Ching-san and Pien-szŭ.)

To the second, 'His face and head are all covered with dirt and ashes.'

Those who wish to know what Mahāyāna Buddhism is or what is really meant by Emptiness (śūnyatā), would do well if they ponder these remarks given by the ancient masters regarding the purport of the Niu-t'ou and Tao-hsin interview.

# APPENDICES

## I

Tai-hui writes to one of his lay disciples, Ch'ên Ming-chung, in the following vein:[1]

The reason the Buddha teaches all kinds of doctrines is because there are all kinds of thoughts from which people are required to be liberated. If we are free from thoughts, there is no need of teaching any kind of doctrine. In truth, doctrines have no substantiality in them, nor have thoughts any fixed foundation from which they rise. Both doctrines and thoughts are by nature empty. To be thus empty is the character of reality.

Most Buddhists of these days, however, regard this Emptiness as a form of nothingness and are afraid of taking to it. Those who cherish this idea confound means with end and take disease for remedy. Pitying these unfortunate people, P'ang has this to say, 'Be not afraid of falling into Emptiness, for it is not after all a very bad thing.' Again, 'I pray you to hold all things empty which are thought real; never take them for realities, that are by nature empty.'

If you gain a penetrating insight into this truth you do away with all the evil karma and ignorance since the eternal past, and all the doubts you have entertained will melt away like a piece of ice. All the teachings of the Buddha preserved in the Tripitaka are no more than this truth [taught by P'ang in regard to Emptiness]. If you have enough faith definitely established, you will surely realize the great truth of liberation. Only let it be known that there is the moment of being aware when the upper hinge is loosened [which has kept you within the bounds of relativity].

[1] From his *Sayings* (*wu-lu*), Vol. XXIII.

347

This is the time you understand that between P'ang's utterance and the Buddha's teaching in the Tripitaka there is no distinction, no difference, no priority, no posteriority, no more-or-less-ness; further, you will see that there are no such things as doctrines, thoughts, etc. [whose reality you have been in the habit of believing].

[At this moment] all the worlds in the ten quarters are Emptiness itself, nor is there anyone who so regards them. If you think there is, this means that there is one who preaches Emptiness, that there is one who listens to the preaching, and further that there are all sorts of doctrines to which one may listen, and that there are all forms of thoughts which can be testified [as real]. If this be true, that is, if there is the listening and testifying, it comes to this:

There is, within, one who testifies; and, without, that which is testified. When this disease [of dualism] is not got rid of, the sūtras describe such a one as he who thinks that there is a real preacher of the Dharma, and who thereby commits the fault of blaspheming the Buddha, Dharma, and Sangha. Again, such blasphemers are stigmatized in the sūtras as those who, by holding up the reality of things, are attached to the notion of an ego, a person, a being, or a life-giver; or who, by holding up the non-reality of things, are equally attached to the notion of an ego, a person, a being, or a life-giver. This attachment in either sense takes place when the [dualistic] belief is asserted as I said before, that there is, within, one who testifies and, without, that which is testified. The warning of the sūtras is always against the dualism. . . .

As regards your view on the koan, I can assure you that you have already firmly grasped a general idea of the thing, but I am afraid that your eyes are not yet penetrating enough to see into the fundamental principle of Buddhism. This is usually the fault most liable to be committed by the beginners. When you really know what I mean here, put aside all that is characterized with onesidedness. Gathering up all the exquisite teachings of the Buddhas and Fathers, have them once for all covered up, and try to see into the working of things even prior to the rise of the Buddha Bhishma-svararāja.[1] Then you will be perfect master of all teachings. Says the Buddha, 'Those beings who praise the Buddha-vehicle fall into the evil paths of existence.' If you truly realize that such things really take place, you will be able to apply all that I say here [to your everyday practical life].

It is then possible for you to escape from the bondage of things, and also not to strive after liberation. 'To be so', or 'not to be so', or 'to be so and not to be so'—all will be well with you. All the teachings of Zen, all the experiences of life will become so readily intelligible to you as a stalwart man extends his arm without a help, or as an arrow shot from the fully-stretched bow. There is no artificial striving here, things go on in their natural order. When you come to this realization, you can truly declare that there is neither good nor evil, neither Buddha nor beings, etc.

Until then beware of making too much assertion, for you may perchance pass Yung-chia's warning unheeded, 'Take care not to invite a woeful state of existence upon yourselves by too boldly denying the law of causation; let not ignorance and licentiousness carry you away too far.' When the fundamentals are established, the rest will follow by themselves; the state of oneness will be realized without your being aware of it.

2

Ippen Shōnin (1239–1289), founder of the Ji-shu Branch of the Jōdo school, has been mentioned several times in the present work. Once he was a student of Zen, but his missionary activities consisted in the propagation of the Nembutsu, for which purpose his whole life was spent in peregrination from one end of the country to the other.

[1] That is, before the world evolved.

349

This habit of constant travelling later became the rule for all his successors, who thus follow the footsteps not only of their own Father but of Śākyamuni himself. When he was about to pass away, Ippen ordered all his books and writings to be burned, saying that what was worth leaving after him was only 'Namu Amida Butsu' and nothing else. The following is one of his comparatively few letters[1] saved after him:

'You ask me about the mental attitude you have to assume towards the Nembutsu. All that is required of the Nembutsu devotee is to say "Namu Amida Butsu", and there is no other instruction I can give you. By saying "Namu Amida Butsu" you get your spiritual peace.

'All the teachings that had been left by the learned and wise are so many pointers devised to save us from so many forms of delusion we cherish; they are after all provisional remedies. For the Nembutsu devotee such are not really needed. To say the Nembutsu in all circumstances—that is enough.

'When Kūya Shōnin was once asked, "How is the Nembutsu to be said?" he simply answered, "Abandon!"[2] There were no further remarks. This is recorded in Saigyo's poetical collection, and to my mind this is truly a golden saying. "Abandon!" is all that is required of the Nembutsu devotee. Let him abandon learning, wisdom, and ignorance as well; let him abandon all such notions as good and evil, rich and poor, noble and lowly, hell and paradise, together with all sorts of satori as cherished and taught by the various schools of Buddhism. Throwing up all these confusing notions and desires, give yourself entirely to saying "Namu Amida Butsu!" As this is in perfect accordance with Amida's transcendental vow, recite the Nembutsu over and over again with singleness of thought. The moment will then come to you when you realize that

---

[1] First compiled 1763.
[2] The following is Ippen's verse:
'When the mind that abandons the body is abandoned,
The world ceases to be distracting,
Where I live wrapped in the monk's black robe.'

while thus reciting "Namu Amida Butsu" there is neither Buddha nor self nor any reasoning to be advanced. In whatever environment you may find yourself, good or bad, it is all the Land of Purity to you; for you have here nothing to seek, nothing to shun. OSHO - JAIL ?

'Every living being together with mountains and rivers, grass and trees, the wind that blows and the waves that roll on—they are all in unison in saying the Nembutsu. It is not mankind alone that takes part in Amida's transcendental vow.

'If you find it difficult to comprehend what I tell you now, don't bother yourself about it, just leave it alone, abandon it with the rest, and without worrying, without scheming, give yourself up to the original vow and recite your Nembutsu. In whatever state of mind it is recited, whether contentedly or not, the saying "Namu Amida Butsu" does not go against the original vow issuing from Amida's transcendental wisdom, it is perfectly commensurable with the extent of his vow. Besides this, there is nothing to be concerned about. My only wish is that, regaining your original simplicity and innocence, you say the Nembutsu. "Namu Amida Butsu!" '


3


Kuei-tsung Chih-chih was the keeper of a humble hut on Lu-shan,[1] and composed the following verse when he first had an insight into Zen truth:

'If you have not yet been there, by all means be there for once;
 Once being there, however, I spy a smile on your face;
 The eyebrows are primarily a useless object,
 But without them how unshapely!'

He was also the author of the following, in which he

[1] *Hsü-chuan*, XVI.

aptly gives vent to his appreciation of Emptiness; the verse is not to be understood as merely describing his solitary hut where he lived in company with clouds.

> 'A lonely hut on the mountain-peak towering above a thou-
> sand others;
> One half is occupied by an old monk and the other by a cloud:
> Last night it was stormy and the cloud was blown away;
> After all a cloud could not equal the old man's quiet way.'

*INDEX*

355